FATAL CONFESSION

Landmark Cases in Canadian Law

Since Confederation, Canada's highest court – first the Judicial Committee of the Privy Council in England and then the Supreme Court of Canada – has issued a series of often contentious decisions that have fundamentally shaped the nation. Both cheered and jeered, these judgments have impacted every aspect of Canadian society, setting legal precedents and provoking social change. The issues in the judgments range from Aboriginal title, gender equality, and freedom of expression to Quebec secession and intellectual property. This series offers comprehensive, book-length examinations of high court cases that have had a major impact on Canadian law, politics, and society.

Other books in the series are:

Flawed Precedent: The St. Catherine's *Case and Aboriginal Title,* by Kent McNeil

Privacy in Peril: Hunter v Southam *and the Drift from Reasonable Search Protections,* by Richard Jochelson and David Ireland

The Tenth Justice: Judicial Appointments, Marc Nadon, and the Supreme Court Act *Reference,* by Carissima Mathen and Michael Plaxton

From Wardship to Rights: The Guerin *Case and Aboriginal Law,* by Jim Reynolds

Constitutional Pariah: Reference re Senate Reform *and the Future of Parliament,* by Emmett Macfarlane

No Legal Way Out: R v Ryan, *Domestic Abuse, and the Defence of Duress,* by Nadia Verelli and Lori Chambers

Debt and Federalism: Landmark Cases in Canadian Bankruptcy and Insolvency Law, 1894–1937, by Thomas G.W. Telfer and Virginia Torrie

Reckoning with Racism: Police, Judges, and the RDS *Case,* by Constance Backhouse

A Culture of Justification: Vavilov *and the Future of Administrative Law,* by Paul Daly

Judging Sex Work: Bedford *and the Attenuation of Rights,* by Colton Fehr

Deciding on Death: Rodriguez, Carter, *and Medically Assisted Dying in Canada,* by Kent McNeil and Wayne Sumner

For a list of other titles see www.ubcpress.ca/landmark-cases-in-canadian-law.

LANDMARK CASES
IN CANADIAN LAW

FATAL CONFESSION

A Girl's Murder, a Man's Execution, and the *Fitton* Case

Carolyn Strange

UBCPress · Vancouver

Printed in Canada on FSC-certified ancient-forest-free paper (100% post-consumer recycled) that is processed chlorine- and acid-free.

UBC Press is a Benetech Global Certified Accessible™ publisher. The epub version of this book meets stringent accessibility standards, ensuring it is available to people with diverse needs.

Library and Archives Canada Cataloguing in Publication

Title: Fatal confession : a girl's murder, a man's execution, and the Fitton case / Carolyn Strange.
Names: Strange, Carolyn, author
Series: Landmark cases in Canadian law.
Description: Series statement: Landmark cases in Canadian law | Includes bibliographical references and index.
Identifiers: Canadiana (print) 20250195682 | Canadiana (ebook) 20250195720 | ISBN 9780774872768 (softcover) | ISBN 9780774872775 (PDF) | ISBN 9780774872782 (EPUB)
Subjects: LCSH: Fitton, Robert – Trials, litigation, etc. | LCSH: Lampkin, Linda, 1942-1956. | LCSH: Trials (Murder) – Ontario – Toronto – Case studies. | LCSH: Trials (Rape) – Ontario – Toronto – Case studies. | LCSH: Sexual consent – Ontario – Toronto – Case studies. | LCSH: Confession (Law) – Ontario – Toronto – Case studies. | LCSH: Executions and executioners – Ontario – Toronto – Case studies. | LCGFT: Case studies.
Classification: LCC KE230.F58 S77 2025 | LCC KF225.F58 S77 2025 kfmod | DDC 345.71/0252309713541—dc23

Canada Council for the Arts | Conseil des arts du Canada
Canada
British Columbia Arts Council
British Columbia

UBC Press gratefully acknowledges the financial support for our publishing program of the Government of Canada, the Canada Council for the Arts, and the British Columbia Arts Council.

This book has been published with the help of a grant from the Canadian Federation for the Humanities and Social Sciences, through the Scholarly Book Awards, using funds provided by the Social Sciences and Humanities Research Council of Canada.

UBC Press is situated on the traditional, ancestral, and unceded territory of the xʷməθkʷəy̓əm (Musqueam) people. This land has always been a place of learning for the xʷməθkʷəy̓əm, who have passed on their culture, history, and traditions for millennia, from one generation to the next.

UBC Press
The University of British Columbia
www.ubcpress.ca

For Constance Backhouse

Contents

Illustrations

Acknowledgments

Numerous individuals and public institutions that bring books into being stand behind every author. Many people have assisted me from the moment of the book's conception to its final production. Kyle Mastarciyan was my Toronto-based research assistant whose work in archives and libraries was diligent, prompt, and reliable. My unpaid "assistants" include Mark "Marko" Strange, who applied his technical skills to create some of the images in the book and Shelley Hobbs, who alerted me to the significance of factums in appeals.

Librarians at the Law Society of Ontario's Great Library helped me unearth the factums in Fitton's case and staff at the Great Library also facilitated my analysis of the hearings held by the Royal Commission on the Criminal Law relating to Criminal Sexual Psychopaths. The Head of the Clara Thomas Archives and Special Collections, Anna St. Onge, proactively searched for a file on Linda Lampkin's murder and turned up an excellent image. Margaret McPhail, a co-founder of the Rise Up! digital archive of feminist activism, kindly provided permission to reproduce the image of a "Take Back the Night" button. Reference staff at the Marilyn & Charles Baillie Special Collections Centre were obliging when I needed to take photos from its historic newspaper collection. Paul Leatherdale, the Law Society's head archivist, was unfailingly generous and knowledgeable in answering my requests for information about former members of the bar associated with the Fitton case. The Osgoode Society's oral history collection was also invaluable, and fortunately it includes transcripts of interviews with the Crown and the defence in Fitton's trial, plus the Director of Public

Prosecutions who convinced the Supreme Court to restore the conviction after the Court of Appeal set it aside.

David M. Humphrey, the son of Fitton's defence lawyer, who represented him from his arrest to the last-ditch clemency appeal, graciously accepted my cold call and shared his recollections of his father's career.

I value the conversations and thoughtful interventions that improved the book through its iterations. I was fortunate to receive two press reader reports that identified infelicities and helped me make improvements. The School of History's book-writing group offered advice on an early draft and Lorna Weir was a convivial interlocutor in discussions over the latter rounds of revisions. My affiliation with the Faculty of Law at the University of Toronto was the ideal spot to spend my sabbatical. Professors Angela Fernandez, Kent Roach, Martha Shaffer, and Hamish Stewart offered expert advice (and friendly corrections) as did former justice Robert Sharpe. My longtime friend and legal history fellow traveller, Jim Phillips, offered astute commentary on the work-in-progress and he supported my visiting professorship. I also appreciate the friendly administrative staff who facilitated my visit.

The editor of the Landmark Cases series, Randy Schmidt, is a delight to work with. I appreciate his encouragement, support, and advice. Although the range of images I wished to include taxed the editorial team, I found I could count on Andrea Routley for prompt assistance and support. Ann Macklem and the production team worked at pace and with grace as the book neared publication.

This book is dedicated to the person who inspired it: Constance Backhouse. The idea to turn the Lampkin-Fitton case into a book arose after I heard her present her book, *Reckoning with Racism: Police, Judges and the* RDS *Case,* as a contribution to UBC Press's Landmark Cases series. More broadly, Professor Backhouse's feminist and anti-racist legal history trailblazing has cleared a path for my own and many others' scholarship and I am certain she will continue to do so for years to come.

Of Graves and Gallows

LINDA LAMPKIN WAS Broadway-bound, or maybe she'd get a break and make it in Hollywood. She sang in the school choir, her parents paid for dance lessons, and the studio portraits she had taken in 1955 might make those dreams come true. On January 18, 1956, she ate supper at home, then left Toronto's west end for her downtown class at Louise Burns's Studio of Dance. After she bid her fellow students goodbye, she made the return journey, stepping off the bus at her regular stop. But the thirteen-year-old didn't make it home. The next time Mr. Lampkin saw his daughter was in the city morgue, where he identified her.

For Torontonians, the news that broke the following morning – that a girl had been sexually assaulted and murdered – was shocking, though unsurprising. Over the winter of 1955–56, several young girls had suffered a similar fate in southern Ontario without an arrest being made.[1] A royal commission, prompted by widespread dissatisfaction with the recent sentencing provisions for criminal sexual psychopaths, was holding its hearings around the same time. Many Canadians had called for stiffer penalties for "sex maniacs," but demand for more scientific approaches to sexual deviance also mounted after the Second World War.[2] The country's foremost lobbyists for novel psychological and psychiatric treatment of sex offenders were concentrated in Toronto.[3] The city's leading daily newspaper, the Toronto *Star,* commended their efforts, and it demonstrated its support by announcing on January 20, 1956, that it would sponsor an expert-led Citizens' Forum on Sex Crime "to help bring the issue to the public in a constructive, logical manner."[4]

The death of Linda Lampkin set off a flurry of questions. Had a sex maniac murdered the girl? A criminal psychopath? The Toronto police provided a surprising answer when they announced they had arrested a suspect the day after the girl's body was discovered at the side of a road in the city's industrial waterfront. The headline, "Young Father Charged with Murder of Linda Lampkin after 11 Hours of Questioning," reassured the public the murderer was no longer on the loose.[5] Yet the man in custody likely puzzled readers. Could Robert Fitton, the youthful suspect pictured on the front pages of Toronto's dailies, have committed such a brutal crime? The prisoner didn't fit movie portrayals of crazed sex maniacs, and he wasn't a member of Canada's ethnic, racial, or religious minorities – those most often accused of threatening white Canadian womanhood.[6] Anglo-Celtic, working-class, a steady worker, and a family man, Fitton was as ordinary a fellow as Torontonians could have imagined in the mid-1950s. Despite this, the police were convinced they had the right man because they'd managed to "break"

Linda Lampkin's gravestone, Park Lawn Cemetery, Toronto. The inscription reads, "Safe in the arms of Jesus." The stone includes an inscription for Raymond Lampkin, her father.

him "after hours of grilling."[7] Fitton confessed, and detectives charged him with murder.

Although Fitton's admission to the police – that he had killed Linda Lampkin after a sexual encounter – sealed his fate, the steps that led from his arrest to his execution make his case unique in Canadian capital justice. Tried for murder in April 1956, Fitton appealed his conviction to the Ontario Court of Appeal. That court ruled the judge had erred in admitting the defendant's confession on the ground that it was not voluntary. Because one judge had dissented, however, the provincial attorney general had the right to lodge an appeal with the Supreme Court of Canada, and he exercised that right. The country's highest court ruled in favour of the appellant – only this time the decision restored the original verdict and with it the sentence of death, the mandatory punishment for murder. Although the federal Cabinet had the discretionary power to commute the sentence, it declined to do so despite the jury's and the trial judge's recommendation of mercy. Two days after this decision was announced, the door to the Don Jail's execution chamber clanged open, and Fitton was executed on November 21, 1956, shortly after midnight.

The prosecution of Linda Lampkin's killer is the only murder case in Canadian history that took this zigzag path from the police charge to the federal Cabinet. This executive body, acting as a privy council, reviewed all sentences of death to determine whether clemency might be warranted, based on case summaries prepared by officials in the Department of Justice's Remission Service. The minister responsible for presenting the case to his colleagues (from 1954, the solicitor general) opened the discussion of Fitton's sentence. The minutes of the meeting indicate the Cabinet required little time to agree that the "law be allowed to take its course."[8]

Like all capital cases, the outcome of *R v Fitton* was the product of macro trends and micro factors. No matter how predictable an execution might appear in retrospect, no hanging was inevitable. Consider the most infamous death penalty case in Canadian history – the execution of Louis Riel in 1885 for high treason.[9] At that time, central Canadian imperialism toward the North-West Territories was growing more assertive as the federal government flexed its muscular sovereignty over lands seized from Indigenous peoples. Eurocentric racism and anti-Catholicism made the Métis leader a poor candidate for clemency, as did prevailing understandings of mental illness. Yet smaller factors particular to Riel's case were equally significant to its outcome: the individuals who played critical legal roles, the court's territorial setting, the obscure statute under which he was prosecuted, Riel's defiance of the defence strategy, and the personal ambitions and prejudices of the prime minister. These ingredients congealed and interacted, leading to Riel's execution.[10] By contrast, the hanging of Robert Fitton for Linda Lampkin's murder has not been lodged in public memory, and his death was mourned by few beyond his circle of family and workmates.[11] No statues of him have been commissioned. No posthumous pardon appeals have been lodged.[12] However, Fitton's route to the gallows provides singular insight into the arbitrariness of capital justice.

A CASE OF SIGNIFICANCE

Linda Lampkin's murder and the legal repercussions that led ultimately to Robert Fitton's execution are events of deep significance to Canadian criminal justice history. Every arrest, indictment, prosecution, trial, and appeal defines certain acts as "criminal" and renders events into legal cases. At Fitton's arraignment, the judge instructed the jury of twelve "gentlemen" that it was their duty to "try this case."[13] In criminal trials and on appeal, lawyers reference reported cases, and in an adversarial system, they assert how the court should interpret decisions in ways favourable to their own cases. When the chief justice of the Ontario Court of Appeal delivered the majority decision – that Fitton's conviction be quashed and a second trial conducted – he agreed with the defence's argument that the trial judge had not explained "the full theory of the defence in this case."[14] The Supreme Court reversed that ruling in a majority decision that restored Fitton's conviction, and with it, the death sentence. Referring to Fitton's confession, the court concluded, "In the present case there was no evidence of inducement or coercion, no evidence of threat or promise of reward."[15] Yet historians of criminal justice are neither advocates nor judges: we must conjure our cases through sources beyond the legal residue of crimes and titrate matters of jurisprudence and criminal procedure in social, cultural, and political currents to extract the social, political, and cultural significance of cases.[16]

Context is king in historical case studies that aim to analyze the phenomena that shaped how contemporaries understood crimes and legal outcomes. Whereas jurists cite cases instrumentally, to draw out general principles that transcend the facts, historians endeavour to comprehend how cases unfolded in the time and place of their occurrence.[17] The murder of Linda Lampkin and the prosecution of Robert Fitton occurred in the mid-1950s, when the concept of the pickup was a mainstay of popular film and culture. In a variety of media, girls and women were depicted as bait for males – but females could also ensnare men.[18] The murder, the trial, and the execution all happened in the city of Toronto, which was more than just the drama's backdrop. By the 1950s, the city became the national centre for lobbyists who were campaigning for the police, the provincial government, and federal authorities to tackle the sex crime problem. And in 1956, the royal commission on the country's sexual psychopath laws held its hearings in Toronto just days after Fitton's arrest.[19] For the first time in Canadian history, the pleasures and dangers of heterosexual desire were hot-button issues in official circles, locally and nationally.

As Fitton's case made its way through the courts in 1956, another inquiry – the Special Joint Committee of the Senate and the House of Commons on Capital Punishment – reported its findings and recommended retaining the death penalty.[20] This was also the first point when government committees – including an inquiry into the Department of Justice's Remission Service and its role in administrating capital case files – publicly revealed the inner workings of clemency reviews.[21] The Crown attorneys, heads of the Service, and ministers of justice who testified before these inquiries insisted the trials and appeals were fair and that the granting of clemency was judicious and equitable, but prominent defence lawyers disagreed. The department's own record of capital cases, tabled in evidence, exposed glaring differences in outcomes over time and between types of offenders. As a convicted sex murderer, Fitton's fate was not unusual in the 1950s, but by that period, the execution of a defendant whom the jury and judge had recommended to mercy was extraordinary.[22]

When newspaper editors and writers of letters to the editor commented on this case, many found it difficult to regard Robert Fitton as a sexual predator and even harder to see Linda Lampkin as an innocent victim. Fitton's family and employer stood by the young man they considered a loyal son, a loving husband, a responsible father, and a reliable worker, and plenty of Torontonians agreed with them: here was a regular fellow, victimized by a flirtatious pickup. Despite the legal clarity of the verdict – guilty of murder – the judges who considered the case in appeal operated within the same milieu, in which heterosexual consent was readily assumed unless a girl was demure and homely.[23] The Criminal Code, revised and in force in 1955, set stiff penalties for rape and for intercourse with girls under the age of fourteen.[24] Yet their severity clashed with gender norms that readily excused men for assuming sexual consent, and they lent credibility to Fitton's claim, repeated up to the final clemency bids, that Linda Lampkin had eagerly engaged in intercourse. Ultimately, the evidence of grave trauma to her body persuaded the majority of judges and the Cabinet that the sex had been forcible and violent; even still, they were preoccupied with the victim's apparent sexual maturity. Linda Lampkin's appearance was legally irrelevant, but its social and cultural resonance was profound.

Describing any civil or criminal case as a landmark would be straightforward if the criteria were exclusively matters relevant to the law and lawyers. Legal scholarship conventionally refers to cases that have shaped law by setting a new course or direction as "landmarks."[25] By contrast, historians have applied the term in the sense of its commonest meaning – landmarks as orienting features.[26] Adopting that meaning, the Lampkin-Fitton case was a landmark in two significant respects: it put an end to the Cabinet's refusal to grant clemency after a recommendation to mercy; and Fitton's execution was the only one in Canadian history carried out despite split decisions in the provincial Court of Appeal and the Supreme Court, and the trial judge's endorsement of the jury's recommendation.[27] Like wayfarers who overlook landmarks (as unobservant hikers well know), legal observers did not register the significance of these facts in 1956. Criminal cases that may not appear noteworthy in their own time, especially decisions characterized by confused reasoning, can still be significant, Eric Rauchway argues, if they encapsulate "moral, social, and political conflict."[28] Legal cases that condense a range of concerns mark the landscape of law in ways that demonstrate, in retrospect, its embeddedness in those conflicts.[29]

Through a contextual reading of the Lampkin-Fitton case, we can see wider tensions at play in the spheres of criminal law, policing, jurisprudence, and the politics of the death penalty, as well as in gender and sexual norms. The decisions in Fitton's appeals were divided, and they did not establish a rule regarding the admission of confessions; nevertheless, the judges' conflicting interpretations illustrate the irresolution and inconsistency of rulings on suspects' rights against self-incrimination, which the Canadian Charter of Rights and Freedoms has not resolved.[30] Ambiguity over the age of consent and the credibility of victims, expressed in the 1950s through agitation over the problem of sexual predators, was transformed over the following two decades through feminist critiques of laws and trial procedures that exonerated perpetrators on the basis of the complainants' sexual reputations.[31] And despite the fact that Fitton's execution, authorized in secret by an unaccountable executive, did not put an end to capital punishment, it added fuel to the humming engine of abolitionism, which revved and sputtered until it reached the finishing line in 1976.[32]

CANADA'S DEATH PENALTY

The protocol that governed Canada's death penalty came into force shortly after Confederation, and owing to the preservation of capital case files, there is copious evidence that clemency was dispensed unevenly.[33] Periodic pronouncements on the management of capital justice invariably extolled the fair-mindedness of a system that ensured the review of death sentences imposed in Canadian criminal courts.[34] The Cabinet, exercising executive discretion, considered the sentence of every offender facing execution for possible commutation, no matter how poor they were, and irrespective of their representation by lawyers or petitioners.[35] In premodern times, these decisions were made by monarchs, who exercised the royal prerogative of mercy – the sovereign's authority over life and death. By 1867, when three of the British North American colonies federated, Queen Victoria was an ocean away, but a system of delegated "bureaucratic mercy" was already in place in England, and it was transplanted to post-Confederation Canada.[36] Orders in Council that determined whether clemency was to be granted or denied required the governor general's endorsement, but with few exceptions, he rubber-stamped the Cabinet's decisions.[37]

The records that made up case files currently sit in the holdings of Library and Archives Canada, and file CC 821 bears the name of Robert George Fitton.[38] The finding aid to the collection provides the bare bones of the case – Victim: Linda Lampkin. Method: Strangulation. Motive: rape. Recommendation to mercy: yes.[39] So why was Fitton hanged? Many clues appear in the official and unofficial records that found their way into his file. The *Criminal Procedure Act* obliged trial judges to provide a report to the Department of Justice on the trials of persons sentenced to death along with full trial transcripts.[40] In Fitton's case, the judge reported that he and the jury had recommended mercy. Since the defence appealed the conviction, the decision that quashed it appears in Fitton's file, along with the Supreme Court's decision to restore it. Like most prisoners under sentence of death in the postwar period, Fitton was examined by psychiatrists before the Cabinet reviewed his case. In their opinion the condemned man was neither mentally ill nor abnormal.

Unofficial correspondence in the form of petitioners' letters also appears in Fitton's file. His lawyer and his mother wrote last-minute pleas, but the boilerplate updates they received from the high-ranking clerks who managed capital case communications provided no comfort. Further form letters were issued after the Cabinet declined to commute Fitton's sentence: one informed Fitton's lawyer of the outcome, and another advised the sheriff of Toronto's Don Jail to prepare for the hanging on the prescribed date. Proof of the execution was recorded in a perfunctory coroner's inquest, which certified that Robert Fitton "came to his death from being hanged by the neck until he was dead in accordance with the sentence under which he lay in the said Gaol."[41]

Unfortunately, capital case files have little to say about victims, which is true of Fitton's file. When Alexander Smirle Lawson, Ontario's chief coroner, signed Fitton's death certificate on November 21, 1956, his mind must have turned back to the night eleven months earlier, when he ordered an autopsy on the body of a girl found at the side of a road, naked from the midriff down.[42] As soon as detectives established Linda Lampkin's identity, they looked into her home life, her schoolwork, and her social activities, as did reporters. Police confirmed the victim knew her assailant, and witnesses recalled she had chatted with Fitton, who picked up mail and delivered parcels in her neighbourhood. Vivid images of Linda Lampkin, used in evidence, appear in the case file. Some are studio portraits taken in life that depict a confident, vivacious teenager; others, the police photographs of her dead body, document the violent assault and the indignity she suffered. In their official roles, the lawyers, the jury, and the judges involved in Fitton's case were obliged to examine the postmortem pictures, but none of them appears in this book, with the exception of the police photo of a scuffed and sullied shoe – one of the pair Linda Lampkin had danced in just hours before she was murdered.

FRAMINGS OF A SEX MURDER

The public had no access to transcripts, official correspondence, reports, or certificates; instead, print media shaped readers' understanding of crime and punishment in the mid-1950s.[43] The case drew major attention through radio and television, but most Canadians still reached for the paper to catch up on the news.[44] When Robert Fitton faced trial in April 1956, two hundred spectators scrambled for seats in the small City Hall courtroom, but tens of thousands of Torontonians read about the case in one or more of the city's three major dailies.[45] Regional editors sent reporters to Toronto to cover the trial, and their stories were transmitted across the country and the United States through

Police photograph of Linda Lampkin's dancing shoe and makeup compact | LAC, RG 13-B-1, vol. 1755, "Fitton, Robert," vol. 2

wire services. News clippings about Lampkin and Fitton also appeared in the official case file, mailed to the government by individuals interested in the case and pasted in by Justice Department clerks to document public opinion. From the growing array of digitized newspapers, we can see how anxiety over sex crimes and the dangers women and children faced was channelled into coverage of the Lampkin-Fitton case. Yet the plots of film noir, true crime magazines, and comics can also be discerned in legal accounts of the murder that characterized Lampkin as a willing pickup.[46] Perhaps the "strangler-rapist" was really the victim of a precocious femme fatale?[47]

One might expect lawyers and jurists to have held more objective views of the principals in this murder case. These men certainly claimed to be dispassionate. Yet the politics of gender and sexuality that prevailed in mid-twentieth-century Canada saturate the trial transcript and the appellate court decisions. Every decision maker in the case against Robert Fitton was a man, from the truck driver who spotted Linda

Lampkin's body to the Cabinet ministers who allowed her killer's execution to proceed.[48] The range of emotions men expressed about the crime stretched from patriarchal rage against a brutal cad to sympathy and anguish over an ordinary fellow, hanged after a temptress inflamed his passions. The decisions rendered by the Ontario Court of Appeal and the Supreme Court also expressed a breadth of assumptions about culpability and blameworthiness. Judges in murder trials typically advised jurors to keep their emotions in check, and they always admonished spectators who expressed their feelings in courtrooms. Yet when lawyers and judges described accused killers and victims, especially in sex murder cases, they used emotionally expressive and normative terms.[49] Despite their book learning and claims of rationality and detachment, Canada's legal minds were inescapably men of their time.

From a legal viewpoint, the legacy of *R v Fitton,* cited in scores of decisions following the 1956 rulings, lies in the case's enduring relevance to the issue of confessions. The most compelling piece of Crown evidence against Fitton was his incriminating statement to police. But was it voluntary? His lawyer thought not, and he appealed against the conviction on this and several other grounds. In the Ontario Court of Appeal, all but one judge decided that the voluntariness of Fitton's confession had not been established at trial; in the Supreme Court of Canada, the majority ruled that it met the threshold of voluntariness. The Cabinet's decision did not, and could not, indulge in ambiguity; consequently, Fitton's confession proved to be fatal. However, the question of suspects' pretrial right to silence and the right to be protected from self-incrimination remains hazy. Canadian jurists still struggle to set a clear standard for the voluntariness of statements to police, and uncertainty lingers over the scope of the presumption of innocence. Since Parliament abolished the death penalty in 1976, the prospect of coerced or false confessions is no longer terminal, although it is far from inconsequential, as numerous inquiries into wrongful convictions in post-abolition Canada have confirmed.[50] And it is not beyond the realm of possibility that a future government may act on calls to restore the death penalty.[51]

THE MYSTERIES OF THE LAMPKIN-FITTON CASE

Some murders lend themselves to the narrative conventions of the mystery or the whodunit, in which the killer's identity is hidden until the final page. Other crimes, such as the rape-murder of Lynn Harper, for which Stephen Truscott was sentenced to death in 1959 and later exonerated, suit the journalistic and legal conventions of the wrongful conviction. If Truscott did not murder Harper, who did? Neither of these genres suits the Lampkin-Fitton case, since the police identified the killer immediately, and the defence acknowledged the victim died at their client's hands. Yet mysteries abound in this case. How did the fever-pitched concern about sex crimes and criminals and the spate of unsolved cases mould responses to Linda Lampkin's murder, and why did this framing alter after the press delved into her and her killer's backgrounds? Chapters 1 and 2 of this book reveal that lobbyists for progressive solutions to the sex crime problem were a vocal minority in a country where most citizens continued to support the death penalty. Similarly, a narrow notion of sexual victimhood prevailed, which flipped the suspect into the role of victim. How, then, can we explain Fitton's conviction? Chapters 3 and 4 confront that question by tracing the moves of the key legal players in the trial – the Crown, the defence, the judge, and the jury – as they grappled with the circumstantial evidence and the defendant's statements to police. A degree of mystery lingers over the verdict in any historical account of a criminal trial, but in this instance the prevailing rules of evidence persuaded the judge to admit Fitton's statement, and the Criminal Code's definition of constructive murder connected to sexual assault worked against the defence.

David Humphrey, as Fitton's legal counsel, was not required to appeal the verdict. Had he declined to do so, the mystery of Fitton's execution would have been easier to solve: condemned to death for murder, his client's sole hope of a commuted sentence would have sat with the federal Cabinet. Fitton's capital case file eventually came before the executive, which considered clemency, but only after the judges of the Ontario Court of Appeal and the Supreme Court had delivered their decisions. Chapters 5, 6, and 7 untangle the skein of the appellants' and respondents' arguments as well as the judges' reasoning about the admissibility of Fitton's confession. Initially pronounced involuntary, the final appeal decision found the opposite, based on a different reading of the same body of case law on the admissibility of statements. However, lawyers and judges are humans, not simply ciphers of law; they are motivated by individual convictions about justice, professional pride, and reputational concerns, which calls for attention to how the men's actions shaped the case's outcome. Just as the defence could have opted not to appeal, the Crown was under no legal compulsion to appeal to the Supreme Court, but neither party made its decision in a vacuum. In Fitton's case, the appeals were argued at a time when the administration of capital justice, including the role and scope of criminal appeals and the opaque operation of the royal prerogative of mercy, was subjected to unprecedented scrutiny.

Why did the executive decide to let the law take its course in Fitton's case? This is the deepest mystery. The recent opening of Cabinet records previously stamped "secret" provides clues, but no answers. Chapters 8 and 9 place the final months of Fitton's life in the context of debates about the death penalty and its administration, and they examine the testimony of its defenders against the record of capital case dispositions in the years leading up to this case. Justice officials and lawyers involved in capital trials knew it was highly unusual for the Cabinet to decide against mercy when the judge and jury had recommended it, but there was no public recognition at the time that the Fitton decision was unique: his execution was the only hanging in Canadian history that followed split decisions in the Court of Appeal and Supreme Court. Had the Cabinet recognized this, they might have commuted Fitton's sentence, but the record of their meeting suggests different concerns prevailed. Just as Linda Lampkin's mature looks contradicted the cultural stereotype of the victim, the defence's attempt to secure clemency by seeking affidavits from jurors – who stated they had understood their recommendation to mercy would save the defendant – touched a sensitive nerve of impropriety. Considering the government had just

Door to the Don Jail's execution chamber, opposite cells in the death corridor

accepted the parliamentary committee's recommendation to retain capital punishment, backed by a majority of Canadians, the Cabinet's decision appears less mysterious. However, Fitton and his family were mystified when they were informed the execution would proceed. Heartfelt testimonials about the young man's hard life and personal virtues, laced with poisonous insults against Linda Lampkin's character, were wired to Ottawa at the last minute, but the executive's decision held: Fitton was hanged.

The Lampkin-Fitton case lives on in citations to the decisions of the Court of Appeal and the Supreme Court, as Canadian jurists, police, prosecutors, and defence lawyers continue to spar over the rights of the accused against self-incrimination versus the imperative to investigate crime and attribute responsibility. Fitton's execution was one of the prompts for the decision to divide murder into two degrees, capital and noncapital, and the Cabinet's denial of clemency in this case occurred at a turning point in Canada's statutory retreat from capital punishment. In the decades that followed, feminists attacked the criminal justice system's handling of sexual assaults that subjected even the dead to victim blaming. The life of this young girl, full of zest until a vicious sexual attack and strangulation terminated it, and the death of this man, imposed by a state more committed to legal hairsplitting than tackling the inequities of capital justice, are parts of our history we should not forget.

1

The Problem of Sex Crime and Criminals

When Linda Lampkin was born in February 1942, Canadians were embroiled in a global war against external enemies. "Grim War Peril Faces Canada," the Toronto *Globe and Mail* declared.[1] The federal government also identified internal threats that imperilled the country – communists, fascists, and Japanese Canadians – whom it subjected to surveillance, deportation, and mass internment.[2] After the war, a new threat emerged that required a war-like footing to conquer. In 1947, journalist Sydney Katz alerted readers of *Maclean's Magazine* to the "growing problem of sex criminality." Worst in Canada's biggest cities, where police recorded a postwar rise in arrest rates for sex offences, this problem required new approaches. "The Truth about Sex Criminals," Katz asserted, was that existing laws and penalties did not protect society. To illustrate his point, he referred to a recent case of a thirteen-year-old girl, the victim of an attempted indecent assault. Although the youth charged with the offence was convicted and sentenced to two years' imprisonment, Katz doubted the penalty was likely to deter him or any other male. Even worse, he revealed, the rap sheets of minor offenders often ended with charges of rape and murder.[3]

In the decade leading up to Linda Lampkin's murder, the problem of sex crime and criminals became all-consuming; yet disagreement over the source and nature of the problem exposed deep social, cultural, legal, and political divisions among Canadians. This was the age of the expert, and plenty of psychiatrists and correctional penologists, supported by prominent politicians, were convinced that scientific analysis of sexual deviancy and the therapeutic treatment of offenders in separate programs and facilities were better responses than penal sentences.[4]

The federal government supported that conviction by introducing a law in 1948 to permit judges to sentence "criminal sexual psychopaths" to indefinite preventive detention. The amendment pleased Canadians concerned that existing laws had failed to protect women and children from sexual deviants. However, the rare enforcement of the law and lacklustre institutional support for the treatment of sexual offenders provoked widespread condemnation, which the government addressed in the mid-1950s.[5] By 1954, two royal commissions were underway: one to reassess the criminal law on sexual psychopathy and the other to study the defence of criminal insanity. A third inquiry examined the death penalty to consider the possible abolition of capital punishment. Yet, far from steering Canada toward a correctional approach to crime, these official inquiries reinforced the principle of criminal responsibility and the necessity of the ultimate penalty.

Nevertheless, postwar optimism over the promise of modern, scientific approaches to the sex crime problem lingered into the mid-1950s, particularly in Toronto. Ironically, the unsolved murders of two local girls by suspected sex killers, one in 1947 and the other in 1955, buoyed efforts to realize the promise of the 1948 amendment. Although Toronto was home to leading psychiatrists, clinics, and courts dedicated to the study and treatment of sex offenders, the city also became the launching pad for a grassroots lobby group called the Parents Action League (PAL). Together, they voiced the loudest calls for the provincial and federal governments to incorporate expert advice on the diagnosis and treatment of sexual deviancy. By late 1955, PAL and its nationwide allies had put governments on notice: the protection of women and children from sex offenders demanded a progressive new approach.

If there was any place in Canada in the mid-1950s in which the capture of a sex killer was likely to be interpreted through the lens of sexual psychopathy it was Toronto. However, the city was divided, like the country, between supporters of established notions of criminal responsibility and those who favoured the precept of diagnosable, treatable, and preventable deviancy. Both concepts hinged on the assumption that victims played no part in eliciting the attention of sexual offenders, an expectation that the two girls murdered in 1947 and 1955 met. The textual and visual depictions of predation and endangerment in those cases set up Robert Fitton and Linda Lampkin as unlikely cast members for the roles of "sex fiend" and victim.

CANADA IDENTIFIES ITS SEX CRIME PROBLEM

In Canada, where criminal law-making was a federal responsibility, Parliament took much longer than the state legislatures of the United States to draft legislation to fight sex crime. From the mid-1930s, the Federal Bureau of Investigation's director, J. Edgar Hoover, used national police data to warn that "perverts" were proliferating. In 1937, he launched the bureau's "War on the Sex Criminal," and the press granted him a mouthpiece to the nation. By 1939, five US states had introduced statutes that incorporated psychiatric evaluations and treatments, separate confinement, and preventive detention of sexual deviants.[6] At that juncture, the Dominion government was preoccupied with its royal commission on the penitentiary system, which canvassed the treatment of insane prisoners, the problem of habitual offenders, and the role of psychiatrists in determining the segregation of mentally deficient offenders. In 1938, the commission's final report made no reference to sexual offenders; a decade later, law reformers convinced Canadian legislators that the need for action against sex crime was urgent.[7]

Lobbying for change began outside the halls of Parliament. In 1947, the Crime and Delinquency Division of the Canadian Welfare Association (CWA) joined forces with the Canadian Penal Association (CPA) to examine the issue of sex crime and criminals. Working together, they formed an all-male contingent of leaders in the fields of law, corrections, psychiatry, welfare, and medicine and launched a joint investigatory committee. Although the lobbyists drew inspiration from south of the border, their emotional centre of gravity was squarely Canadian, which intensified every time a sex murder occurred locally. There were "very few parts of Canada which have not been shocked by a dramatic crime committed by a sex offender during the past year," the CWA observed as they set out in search of solutions.[8]

As the war drew to a close, the sex murder of nine-year-old John Benson in Montreal was likely the most shocking sex crime in the minds of many Canadians. The boy, out skiing on Mount Royal, was sodomized and bludgeoned to death in February 1945, and reports of his murder and the protracted police hunt riveted readers across the country for months.[9] The police faced immense pressure to capture Benson's killer, which subsided when they made an arrest two months later. Roland Chassé, the man in custody, had spent his life in and out of American penal and psychiatric institutions.[10] Despite that record, psychiatric evaluations prior to his trial determined he was sane, and the indictment stuck. After the jury found Chassé guilty of murder, his lawyer lodged several appeals that led to stays of execution, but the Cabinet allowed the law to take its course, and the "sadistic pervert" was hanged in Montreal's Bordeaux Jail on February 15, 1946.[11]

In the years leading up to the establishment of the CPA-CWA joint investigative committee, revulsion over homosexual perverts was rife, but the sexual murders of boys did not define the problem of sex crime in Canada, neither for the country's experts nor for the wider public.[12] Sex offences against girls were far more frequent, and reports of heterosexual crimes drove home the danger of sexual deviance. When police failed to make an arrest or when courts imposed light sentences, outrage increased. "Too many sex perverts are on the loose in Canada, either murdering or criminally assaulting their victims ... Why, then, are they at large?" the Toronto scandal sheet, *Justice Weekly,* demanded.[13] The committee members used more temperate language when they reported on their reviews of police, court, and penitentiary data. However, the sex murder of a thirteen-year-old girl, killed on her way home in central Toronto in November 1947 was both a tragedy and an opportunity for these law reformers to transform shock and outrage into political action.

CRIME OF A SADISTIC SEXUAL PSYCHOPATH

The same age as Linda Lampkin at her death, thirteen-year-old Arlene Anderson was as credible a victim as Benson, albeit for different reasons. Labelled a "cripple" by her parents and the press, she had cerebral palsy, and Toronto's public schools had barred the "handicapped" student from attending classes.[14] Due to her "limp" and her inability to speak clearly, she would have found it difficult to cry for help or to outrun the man who strangled her with her underpants, raped her, and left her body in a vacant lot in a residential zone of the inner city. The Andersons were working-class Torontonians who felt bitter and heartbroken since they had struggled to care for their child in ways not required for "normal" children. In a moment of despair, the victim's mother admitted she wished her daughter had died at birth since her life had "come to this terrible end." Mrs. Anderson believed the killer deserved no better: "I'd like to cut that man in half with my own hands."[15] The police likely shared the woman's sentiments about the unknown culprit. "Her slayer was 'somebody very powerful,'" an officer reckoned, "because of the way in which the underclothing was knotted about her neck so very tightly."[16]

Aware of growing calls for "more adequate institutional care for this type of offender," reporters for the *Globe and Mail* interviewed Torontonians about the "Crippled Girl's Murder." Just one person expressed the opinion that sex perversion could be detected or that "some authority" could determine a sex criminal's likelihood of killing his victim. Most of the interviewees felt more like Mrs. Anderson. "They should take [the killer] to the City Hall steps or some other public place and let the people at him," said an express company employee. A laundress from the city's east end agreed: "Present laws are 'too lenient.'" But she thought a surgical solution should be tried: any man who committed such a crime "should undergo a medical operation so he could never touch another girl again." Several interviewees repeated the laundress's veiled reference to castration or lobotomization, which some US states authorized. A parking lot attendant told the

LARGEST WANT AD AUDIENCE IN CANADA

TORONTO DAILY STAR

WANT AD SERVICE WAVERLEY 3636

SECOND SECTION

Schools 'Banned Arlene, Broken-Hearted Parents Say

GIRL MURDERS STIR PROVINCE ONE LIKE ARLENE YEARS AGO

Car Tosses Bear High Over Roof He Squats in Ditch, Ambles Away

1000 INEDUCABLES CALL FOR ACTION TRUSTEE SAYS

ADVERTISING DOLLARS

Arlene Anderson murder investigation | Toronto *Daily Star,* November 7, 1947

Globe there was no "cure for that kind of thing." Another interviewee, a sign painter, was more hopeful but out of patience: "Medical experts should have reached a decision by now as to the best methods of handling sex degenerates ... It's about time they ... drafted laws ... Known degenerates ... are a public menace."[17]

Five days after Anderson's murder made headlines, the CPA and the CWA received a boost from the Kiwanis Club, which offered to fund the committee's final report on sex criminals and any further research necessary before the committee approached Parliament.[18] Working in the club's tradition of serving community needs, its cash injection leveraged the committee's capacity to shape the response to the Anderson case in a cooler-headed fashion, drawing on the expertise of social workers, penologists, psychiatrists, and barristers. Yet J. Alex Edmison, king's counsel and chairman and president of the CPA, incautiously categorized the girl's murder as the "crime of a sadistic sexual psychopath." Another committee member, psychiatrist J.D.M. Griffin, agreed and predicted the culprit had likely committed lesser sexual offences before this crime. The issue, they stressed, was the lack of psychiatric treatment available to cure sexually aberrant offenders before they committed homicide. According to these experts, the sexual psychopath was "capable of rape, mutilation and murder," but the law as it existed had no capacity to detain deviants until cured, and prisons simply "turned loose onto society" sex offenders without treating them. "That is the tragedy."[19] Determined to promote reform, the CPA-CWA committee informed the public that its forthcoming report would include draft legislation to modernize Canada's approach to sex deviance and deviants.[20]

RAISED EXPECTATIONS AND DASHED HOPES

The Anderson case remained unsolved in 1948, but anticipation mounted that Canada would soon have its own legal and institutional means to address the problem of sex crime. According to a Montreal journalist, "a steadily increasing wave of sex offences from the relatively trivial ... to rape and murder," was a cause for alarm.[21] Yet his story – "We Can Do Something about Sex Crimes" – struck an upbeat tone since numerous branches of the federal government, including the Penitentiaries Branch and the Department of Health's Mental Health Division, were busy assessing Canadian and international data on sex offenders and their treatment.[22] The CPA-CWA committee also took a more public-facing approach, capped by a presentation of its preliminary results at a public event in central Toronto in May 1948. An advertisement announced that a "top-ranking roster of speakers" would present the committee's "eagerly-awaited, epoch-making Report on the Sex Offender."[23]

The committee's work was closely watched on Parliament Hill, as the Liberal government prepared a bill to amend the Criminal Code to deal specifically with the issue of sex crime. The most avid follower of the committee's work was opposition MP (and future prime minister) John G. Diefenbaker. A former defence lawyer and a student of American approaches to sexually deviant criminals, he thought Canada had taken too long to act, considering their offences were of a type that "creates fear in the minds of mothers and fathers." Urban parents had the most cause to fear, Diefenbaker surmised, since their children were "brought into close contact with strangers." Diefenbaker urged the government to "punish wrong-doers and protect the public at large" while also restoring "many of these wrongdoers after treatment."[24] In the debate over the bill's wording, he pressed James Ilsley, the minister of justice, to adopt a broader definition of sexual psychopathy and to widen the scope for psychiatrists to diagnose and treat sexual offenders. The minister disputed the notion that American state institutions had cured any sexual psychopaths: "Claims are made for certain methods of treatment and so on, and nothing can be proved."[25] Nevertheless, he grudgingly accepted the amendments to the wording, and the bill became law.

From November 1948, the Criminal Code included indeterminate sentencing provisions for the criminal sexual psychopath, whom it defined as any "person who, by a course of misconduct in sexual matters has evidenced a lack of power to control his sexual impulses and who as a result is likely to attack or otherwise inflict injury, loss, pain or other evil on any person."[26] The experts required to make such diagnoses were psychiatrists: if at least two reached the same diagnosis and prognosis, judges could exercise their discretion to sentence persons convicted of sexual offences to indefinite detention to allow for the prospect of a cure. Experts in criminal law objected, declaring the subjection of offenders to imprisonment for crimes they might commit in the future a serious violation of British justice, whereas hardliners complained that the provision of indeterminate "treatment" was too soft.[27] "I do not see why we should have compassion for these men who act like brutes, who attack young children and who kill them," a Quebec MP, Jean-François Pouliot, thundered: "These men are a menace to society ... They are monsters whom society cannot endure."[28] Yet, as evidence of the new criminal sexual psychopath law in action emerged, it became clear that neither group of naysayers had cause to fear: judges rarely sentenced sex offenders to indeterminate sentences, and specialized treatment was scarce.[29]

The late 1940s was also the period when the federal government decided to undertake a major revision of the Criminal Code, and it appointed a royal commission in 1948 to complete a draft bill to amend it. Although substantial changes were introduced in the revised code, including the removal of the death penalty for the offence of rape, the government decided the recent sexual psychopath amendment required a critical review.[30] It also set aside two other contentious matters for further study: capital punishment and the defence of criminal insanity.[31] The Liberal government assigned a Special Joint Committee of the Senate and the House of Commons to examine the death penalty (as well as corporal punishment), and it appointed a second royal commission to study the law and policies concerning criminal insanity and sexual psychopathy. The man the minister of justice, Stuart Garson, appointed to chair both royal commissions was Toronto's James C. McRuer, King's counsel, an experienced prosecutor and the chief justice of Ontario.[32] According to Garson, this judge was ideally suited because of his "long experience" prosecuting and punishing sex crimes. As chairman, McRuer was expected to seek advice from "a small body of really expert advisers," to probe this "extremely difficult matter."[33] What the minister of justice left out of his announcement was the mounting criticism the government faced over its lack of progress since the passage of the 1948 sexual psychopath law in the sentencing of sex offenders and the protection of the public from their crimes.

In March 1954, a Toronto *Globe and Mail* columnist revealed that across the entire country, a mere sixteen men were serving indefinite sentences after being declared sexual psychopaths. Presuming these "figures don't lie," he declared the government's own record showed it had made a "pretty casual ... drive against criminal sexual psychopaths."

The likelihood of these sixteen prisoners receiving psychiatric treatment was low, the columnist added, because resident psychiatrists were employed in just six of the country's eight penitentiaries. Consequently, untold numbers of sexual deviates were slipping through the cracks. "Why didn't the authorities make some effort to get them convicted of being sexual psychopaths?" he demanded. Since "law enforcement agencies have a strong law to enforce, they ought to enforce it." The announcement of a royal commission on the sexual psychopath law and expert involvement was positive, the writer conceded, but he insisted the government must remember that parents, more than any sector of society, "want strong action taken against sex perverts who prey on children."[34] Under this harsh light of public criticism, McRuer began in April 1954 to call for briefs from organizations and to hold hearings across the country to canvass opinion on whether the existing law "relating to criminal sexual psychopaths should be amended in any respect."[35]

PARENTS TAKE ACTION AND WOMEN TAKE CHARGE

In 1948, as Parliament was putting the final touches on the criminal sexual psychopath amendment, the Toronto *Star* declared, "Psychiatric Treatment for All Sex Criminals Is Planned by Ottawa."[36] Yet every reported sexual assault and brutal sex murder after 1948 was an alarming reminder that women and children were no safer. Politicians, police, lawyers, and medical experts had little to show after they pledged to fight sex crime apart from reports and statutes. However, alongside those largely ineffective professional and expert moves, numerous women's and parents' groups had been working unofficially on campaigns for better ways to prevent sexual violence and treat sexual deviance. In British Columbia, the Parent-Teacher Association passed a resolution in 1947 that recommended preventive detention and treatment legislation, and it further urged the provincial government to establish diagnostic and treatment clinics.[37] Local branches of the National Council of Women of Canada and the Federated Women's

Institute also worked on the issue from the late 1940s. In November 1949, when the Edmonton branch of the National Council of Women reflected on its work, it proudly declared it was "among the very first" to advocate the "enlightened and scientific view" that sex criminals required "special treatment." This idea had not come from experts: it "pretty well originated among the women of this city."[38]

In Ontario, clubwomen were active in these and other umbrella organizations, which took an interest in improving women's and children's safety in the postwar years. However, the abduction and murder of a girl in 1955 inspired a group of Toronto-based women to form the Parents Action League (PAL). Like other Torontonians, they were shocked by the banner headlines which announced that two girls, aged thirteen and eight, had vanished on February 25, 1955.[39] The thirteen-year-old had disappeared when her parents were out, and the eight-year-old had failed to return home from school. Although the elder girl turned up quickly, alive and well, "little Judy Carter" was not found until the spring. As the search dragged on, the city's dailies published scores of leads about strange men seen with young girls, men with physical deformities and men who accosted girls from cars. No matter what he looked like or how he had taken "little Judy," the police and the public were convinced her abductor was a sexual deviant.[40]

Several weeks after Judy disappeared from her inner-city neighbourhood, an editorial in the Toronto *Telegram* expressed the impatience many Canadians felt about Justice McRuer's royal commission

16 Pages of Color Comics

WEEKEND TELY

10¢

Combined With

THE TELEGRAM

The Pink Tely Night

Final Sports — Markets

Parents Frantic

TWO GIRLS 13, 8, VANISH

Threats to girls' safety sparked the formation of the Parents Action League in 1955. | Toronto *Telegram,* February 26, 1955

on the sexual psychopath law, still chugging along in hearings across the country. In the meantime, PAL charged ahead. By March 1955, its founders began to unite "various women's organizations" against "the problem of sex perverts."[41] Building on a long tradition of reformist activism, PAL's three founders made rapid headway as Torontonians followed daily reports on the search for Judy Carter. Although the local press dubbed the women "housewives" (sometimes "pretty young housewives"), Bertha Shvemar, Effie Hahn, and Evelyn Dorfman turned out to be well informed, media savvy, and politically astute.[42] Above all, they were committed to PAL's middle initial – action.

The Ontario government could not boast the same. Like the federal government, the province had promised to tackle sex crime through its constitutional responsibility to administer criminal justice and public health. From the early 1950s, provincial politicians had pledged to introduce a therapeutic approach to sexual deviants through Ontario's reformatories, hospitals, and clinics. In 1952, a riot at the province's Guelph Reformatory for male convicts had prompted a select committee inquiry into "Problems of Delinquent Individuals and Custodial Questions," and its members unanimously recommended that Ontario establish a separate institution for sexual deviants. However, experts disagreed over the proposal to segregate sexual deviants for special care and study, and the minister of reform institutions openly declared his doubt over the prospect of treating sexual psychopathy.[43] By the time Judy Carter became the victim of a suspected sexual psychopath in April 1955, women were prepared to work at all three levels of government – municipal, provincial, and federal – to ensure the rollout of the best possible means to diagnose and treat sexual deviancy.

The Toronto *Star*, one of many papers that commended PAL's founders, supported it by publicizing the next-to-nil progress on the sex crime problem. "That little has so far been done about it is due to both public and official prejudice, fear and ignorance."[44] PAL was different because it aimed to remove those blocks, as Effie Hahn explained: "We started our talking campaign by picking out 10 people each ... Then we asked each of them to talk to 10 more people." Soon, the campaign "spread like wildfire." In addition, they lined up "all kinds of community organizations" to support the changes they proposed to the Criminal Code, and they hoped a representative from each one would form an "action committee." The founders set five objectives: compulsory "medical treatment" for all "known criminal sexual psychopaths"; segregation of such prisoners; indefinite detention of incurable offenders; provision of "adequate medical personnel" (in schools) to "detect and treat abnormalities" in children; and the establishment of "mental health facilities of a general nature across the country." From Toronto's kitchens and living rooms, PAL hoped the organization would snowball into a national lobby group.[45]

Behind this female front stood two key male advocates: the publisher of the Toronto *Telegram,* John Bassett, and doctor Kenneth Gray, the chief of the Forensic Clinic at the Toronto Psychiatric Hospital. Basset was one of Canada's leading media barons, and he advised PAL on its promotional strategy, tossing in the services of one of his columnists to assist the group at its inception.[46] Gray became a powerful PAL ally and accepted the founders' request to serve as their medicolegal expert.[47] In the public eye from 1949, when he became head of the Forensic Clinic, he appeared frequently in the papers as an advocate of criminal law reform regarding insanity and as an expert witness in criminal trials. Gray was also a leader of the scientific planning council of the Canadian Mental Health Association, who advised all levels of government on medicolegal issues, including sex crime and psychopathy.[48] But if Gray or Basset anticipated the women were naive do-gooders, the leaders of PAL proved they were serious and committed.

As the mystery of Judy Carter's disappearance lingered without resolution, PAL made the most of the credibility its backers brought to the cause. Prominent women's affairs columnist Lotta Dempsey praised the women as successors to the pantheon of Canada's foremost female trailblazers – Emily Murphy, Nellie McClung, and Irene Parlby – who had shown how women can bring about reform: "Put your case clearly and be sure you are applying pressure in the right place." Evelyn Dorfman confirmed that PAL used the same tactics: "I realise that we must get all the information possible ... Already we have mapped a course of getting in touch with large clubs and organizations to sound them out. We are interviewing authorities in every phase of the matter, and would like to get in touch with all women who are interested." The column included the three leaders' phone numbers, and Dempsey described the telephone as their "potent weapon," wielded to reach other women who also felt like "shocked, terrified and largely helpless onlookers in the tragedy wrought by sex criminals."[49]

After an anxious six-week search for Judy Carter, the case ended as most had feared: "Little girl dead in Markham Creek."[50] The news was tragic, but it appeared to fit the theory of the police and the public – that a sex killer had abducted and murdered the girl to satisfy his perverted desires. The city's dailies published numerous articles that showed the victim's "grief-stricken" parents plus the usual image of detectives bent over the body. More unexpected news surfaced after the autopsy. Pathologist Chester Maclean's examination determined that the cause of the girl's death was asphyxiation caused by strangulation with her own scarf. The doctor surprised investigators by reporting he found no evidence that the deceased had suffered a sexual assault. The police had to admit they were wrong to have "worked on the theory that she had been picked up by a sex pervert." Now they had to "consider a new motive."[51]

Since the postmortem contradicted the theory that a sex maniac had murdered this eight-year-old girl, where did the pathologist's finding leave the organization that had built its support and membership on the same assumptions that oriented the police investigation? For several weeks, alternative theories swirled. Toronto's chief coroner, Smirle Lawson, was convinced Judy Carter's killer was someone she knew. When police started to look close to home, they made the girl's stepfather so uncomfortable he voluntarily travelled to Buffalo to take a lie detector test to establish his innocence. Although Canadian law did not recognize the technology (which gave him the all-clear), this lead and every subsequent one sputtered out.[52] Yet the cooling of the Carter case in the media and the absence of evidence of rape did not deter PAL and its allies. "It's amazing how much support we're getting ... Some of this reaction is due to the murder of Judy," one of the leaders commented after the girl's body was discovered.[53] Not only did PAL admit that this child murder had promoted their cause, but they also used the failure of the police to find the perpetrator to solicit further support for the preventive identification and treatment of sexual psychopaths, as they still believed the unknown assailant must surely have been.[54] Emboldened, the community-based campaigners pressed on for legal and medical reforms to fight sex crime.

PENAL AND THERAPEUTIC CROSS-CURRENTS

After the autopsy conducted on Judy Carter's body was completed, her family could finally lay their daughter to rest. The man they chose to conduct the funeral service was the minister of the Presbyterian church where the girl had attended Sunday school. Speaking before the flower-strewn "tiny white casket," he offered a comforting line from Dickens: "When death strikes down the young and innocent ... one hundred virtues rise in the shapes of charity, mercy and love." But he added that deaths of this nature could be prevented if citizens contacted police whenever they saw "even a hint of children being molested on the streets." Several officers of the Toronto police force attended the funeral, and they may have taken heart from the reverend's words, uttered as the casket was lowered into the ground: "No maudlin sentimentality must interfere with British justice if the perpetrator of this crime is caught."[55] For many who had followed the Judy case, the criminals who molested and killed the innocent were responsible for their crimes and must pay for them with their lives.

The Parents Action League and its local press supporters worked on civil society, hoping to enlighten the public. At the same time, provincial and federal government agencies and departments pursued a range of approaches to the problem of sex crime, including the strict application of penal law, which the reverend endorsed. The reputation of the municipal police took a beating. Had a pair of boys playing by a stream not found Judy Carter's body, the police might never have found her, but the case also revealed the challenges investigators faced in catching sex criminals. By 1955, the greater Toronto area had thirteen municipal forces that operated independently, and this led to "expensive duplication and delays," according to Toronto's chief constable, John J. Chisholm.[56] Fronting up before Toronto City Council in mid-April 1955, he stated the police were "handicapped" in the Carter case because each local force responded to reports of crimes committed on their own patches: "Criminals roam from one police jurisdiction to another," which the girl's abductor had evidently managed to do, taking her from Cabbagetown to Toronto's rural outskirts.[57] A better-organized force might have led to the swift arrest of the person who had taken this girl, but this did not mean he was a psychopath in need of treatment. Like other Canadian law enforcement agents in the mid-1950s, Toronto's police chief believed in prison and the ultimate penalty – death.[58]

The death penalty, and the question of its retention or abolition, was under scrutiny at the time of the Carter murder. Testifying before the special joint committee, most witnesses – particularly law enforcement agents, prison wardens, and all but a few clerics – strongly supported the death penalty. The Canadian Association of Chiefs of Police was one of many organizations that warned it was "too soon" to abolish capital punishment. Its president urged that until medical experts developed a "greater understanding of human nature," the safety and security of police and the public depended on the death penalty.[59] Although the royal commissions that McRuer chaired were not mandated to consider capital punishment, the matter was difficult to dodge in the course of deliberations over criminal insanity and psychopathy. McRuer's first inquiry was to consider whether "the criminal law of Canada relating to the defence of insanity should be amended in any respect and, if so, in what manner and to what extent?" Most of the expert witnesses who testified about criminal insanity warned against diluting the concept of criminal responsibility. In response to the government announcement of the insanity commission's establishment, Kenneth Gray set up a national committee of the Canadian Psychiatric Association in 1953 and prepared a brief on its behalf. Despite agreeing to head PAL's "scientific advisory committee," neither Gray nor the association believed the death penalty should be abolished. In fact, the association's brief warned against the expansion of the legal definition of insanity to encompass forms of mental illness that he considered "primarily due to emotional factors and without impairment of cognitive faculties." To do so would carry the "risk that the administration of justice would be weakened."[60] In the mid-1950s, the majority of Canadians agreed.[61]

The only change to Canada's death penalty occurred without significant debate in the amended Criminal Code of 1955, which removed the death penalty as a punishment for rape. Before 1955, judges had the discretion to sentence convicted rapists to death and to add whipping to noncapital sentences for rape or attempted rape.[62] Rapists had been sentenced to death, and judges had ordered that they be whipped in some cases, but no man was executed for rape after Confederation, and most convicted rapists were punished through imprisonment, some up to life. From 1948, judges could impose indefinite sentences on men convicted of rape if they were found to be criminal sexual psychopaths, but few served sentences under those terms.[63] Many psychiatrists – not just police, prosecutors, and judges – believed that long-established punitive responses were appropriate for rape unless sex offenders were found to be insane and therefore not criminally responsible. The psychiatrists who gave evidence before the commission disagreed over the meaning of "psychopathy," and some disputed the concept altogether. On the one hand, the men who committed violent and abusive sexual acts were "abnormal" or "diseased." Alastair MacLeod of McGill University's Department of Psychiatry described sexual psychopaths as "emotionally immature, impulsive and strikingly unable to control their desire for immediate satisfaction."[64] On the other hand, few accused sex criminals, including those who offended against children, were found not guilty by reason of insanity. Criminal court records from 1930 to 1955, reviewed by the commission on the criminal-insanity defence, confirmed that just 23 of 3,563 men convicted of rape, attempted rape, and carnal knowledge (sexual contact with girls under fourteen) had been found to be insane.[65] And as critics of the desultory application of indefinite detention laws continued to complain, judges had sentenced a scant number of sex offenders as psychopaths after the 1948 amendment.

Whatever definition the code used to describe the criminal sexual psychopath, psychiatrists had professional misgivings over the notion that irrepressible sexual urges constituted a mental disease. The most outspoken critic of the medicalization of sexual criminality was John M. Senn, a psychiatrist of three decades' standing and the superintendent of Hamilton's Ontario Hospital, a public institution for psychiatric treatment. Since the late 1940s, he told the commissioners, judges had routinely sent men charged with sexual offences to his hospital for pretrial observation. But Senn considered sexual deviants no less capable than other criminals of controlling their impulses – they simply chose to commit their crimes.[66] Another psychiatrist admitted what most of his fellow experts rarely acknowledged: the emperors of psychiatry wore no clothes when it came to diagnosing sexual psychopathy, let alone treating it. "I do not see how the greatest doctors in the world could look into a man's mind and say, this man could not control the impulse."[67] Even PAL's high-profile expert, Kenneth Gray, regarded most sexually deviant offenders as criminally responsible. In "a few cases," he found, they were "mentally ill or defective;" however, "the great majority are not."[68]

In the course of their duty to protect the public, Canada's police encountered sexual offenders on a regular basis, and they agreed with psychiatrists that deviant inclinations were difficult to detect. When Chief Constable Chisholm submitted a brief to Justice McRuer's commission on sexual psychopaths in January 1956, he added weight to the views of medical experts who considered sexual deviants criminally responsible. However, his job was to catch them, and this was "by no means an elementary task." According to Chisholm, a "great majority of them have all the outward appearance of ordinary citizens, many with no previous criminal record or contact with the Police ... [They] may be regularly employed and in other respects honest and industrious. Where are they found? ... Sometimes where least expected."[69]

Toronto's police chief was keenly aware of the public's expectation that the police do everything in their power to arrest and charge elusive sex offenders, but he asserted the community also had a role to play by reporting deviant behaviour. Although he shared PAL's frustrations

Toronto's chief constable, John C. Chisholm, 1946 | Toronto Star Photograph Archives, TSPA_0037664F

over the number of sex offenders who received light prison sentences, only to slide back into the soup of city life, he thought tougher judges and heavier sentences were the answer. And then there were men, as yet "unknown to medical or law enforcement authorities," whose first offence was "some very serious sex offence."[70] The police could but react.

AS SEX CRIME AND CRIMINALS pervaded the consciousness of Canadians, postwar legislators and experts endorsed a model of therapeutic and corrective justice to address the problem. But government inquiries had charted strong cross-currents by the mid-1950s. While many lobbyists and news editors were splenetic over the limp application of the criminal sexual psychopath sentencing provisions, legal authorities concerned about civil liberties condemned the imposition of indefinite detention based on the likelihood of reoffending, since many psychiatrists doubted their profession's capacity to make such predictions. Just weeks after Judy Carter's funeral was held, the Toronto and District Trades and Labour Council declined PAL's invitation for endorsement because it anticipated that police, looking for sex perverts, were most likely to harass working-class men.[71] Rather than risk arresting innocent normal men, critics of using legal means to prevent sex crimes complained that parents and teachers ought to warn children and youth about consorting with strangers. Arlene Anderson and Judy Carter were innocent victims, but would they have died had their parents properly warned them?

2

Pickup on Jane Street

IN THE LATE 1940S and early 1950s, film noir was a popular form of entertainment for Canadians no less than Americans. The femme fatale – deadly to men drawn to her sexual flame – was a stock character, and her image adorned garish paperbacks and movie posters.[1] The advertisement for the 1951 movie *Pickup* read: "You can 'pick up' this Girl ... but you won't if you know what's good for you!"[2] Dreams of stage and screen may have flooded thirteen-year-old Linda Lampkin's mind when she posed for studio portraits and signed up for dancing lessons. After her class on the evening of January 18, 1956, however, the plot of her imagined life turned when Robert Fitton, a mail truck driver, made his way down Jane Street on his regular route. Pulling into a side street near the girl's bus stop, the convergence of their routes led to a violent ending.

The discovery of Linda Lampkin's remains on a roadside in Toronto's industrial waterfront led police to determine that a man had strangled and raped the girl. The following morning, the local newspapers slotted her death into the problem of sex crime and sex criminals. The headlines, "GIRL, 13, SEX KILLER'S VICTIM" and "YOUNG GIRL BRUTALLY MURDERED BY SEX FIEND," would have reminded Torontonians of several recent unsolved murders of girls.[3] Since 1954, when the Royal Commission on the Criminal Law relating to Criminal Sexual Psychopaths was struck to address the law on sexual psychopathy, citizen lobby groups had also formed to find better ways to prevent sexual deviance, and politicians had pledged to devise better means to treat offenders.[4] Yet another girl had fallen victim to a sex killer. The Toronto *Star* had promised late in 1955 to hold a citizens' forum on sexual deviance led by experts on sexual psychopathy, and the event took place a week after this latest murder. Around the same time, clerks to the royal commission were cataloguing submissions from interested parties and finalizing the list of witnesses scheduled for its Toronto hearings in February 1956.

Reports of Robert Fitton's arrest for Linda Lampkin's murder came with the news that the victim knew her killer, and this revelation immediately frayed the murder's connection to the sex crime problem. Accounts of their relationship flushed out ambivalence about the girl's sexual morality and the perpetrator's criminal responsibility, which the defence would later exploit. Because the murdered girl and the driver had chatted on previous occasions, their familiarity led to speculation that she had been a willing pickup. The detectives who questioned Fitton obtained an incriminating statement and quickly collected damning circumstantial evidence, sufficient to support a charge of murder; however, press coverage of the case questioned whether a man who picked up a flirtatious girl could be considered a criminal. The *Star*'s forum experts thought not, and the lawyer who represented Fitton hoped the jury would share those doubts. At a time when most Canadians still believed that hanging was just punishment for murder and the only way to deter homicidal sexual deviants, contrasting the victim's dubious character against her accused killer's blameless background was the best strategy to prevent a capital conviction.

A FINE NORMAL GIRL

In the grey winter gloom of Toronto's industrial waterfront, late at night, a truck driver noticed a suspicious object by the roadside. Stepping out for a closer look, he was in for a shock – the object was the body of a girl, naked below the waist, her clothes torn, her throat abraded. He jumped back into his truck and flagged down a motorcycle

The coroner bends over Linda Lampkin's blanketed body as detectives look on, January 18, 1956.

patrol officer, who radioed for backup. Within minutes, detectives and the province's chief coroner, Smirle Lawson, appeared. "Why do they do it? Why a kid?" Lawson asked.[5] The coroner's remark suggests he may have been thinking back to Judy Carter's murder and the discovery of her body – washed up beside a creek, bearing signs of strangulation – the previous spring.[6] Lawson had also been involved in the unsolved "rape-murder" of a "new Canadian" woman in the fall of 1954.[7] Yet the investigation of this victim's death unfolded differently from those recent crimes, which remained unsolved: the police quickly connected the body's description to that of missing thirteen-year-old Linda Lampkin, and the following morning they questioned a suspect. By nightfall, they had charged him with murder.

Two of Toronto's afternoon dailies – the *Star* and the *Telegram* – were the chief sources of news for Torontonians, with over half a million subscribers combined. Movies about hard-bitten crime reporters on big city papers were also popular in the 1950s.[8] Locked in a war for readers, robberies and murders were the chief battlegrounds for reporters on the crime beat.[9] On January 19, both papers published large spreads that identified the girl found on Commissioners Street as Linda Lampkin, the first of Raymond and Barbara Lampkin's two girls.

Interviews with her parents revealed the family lived on Brookside Avenue in a modest semi-detached house in metropolitan Toronto's west end. Their home was a five-minute walk from the school Linda attended, Humbercrest Public. The local Anglican church, Saint Paul's Runnymede, was a short drive away, and Linda sang in its junior choir. She belonged to the Girl Guides, in which she had earned several badges, and she also participated in the 4-H club.[10] In addition to dancing, Linda enjoyed a range of physical activities – swimming and playing schoolyard games in the summer and skating in winter. After she turned thirteen in February 1955, her parents allowed her out to skating rinks close to home, and she attended the pictures on the odd Friday night with boys her parents had met. They permitted their daughter to stay out in summer until the streetlights came on, but in the winter months, she stayed in on school nights. The only exception was their daughter's weekly downtown dance classes, which she started late in 1955.[11]

To reach the Louise Burns Dance Studio, ten kilometres from home, Linda took public transit, which required that she set out before her father returned from his job as a supervisor at Maple Leaf Milling Company. After a short walk to the bus, which ran south on Jane Street, she transferred to the cross-town streetcar eastbound to Yonge, followed by a short subway ride to Wellesley Station, a few steps from the studio. After her class, she made the trip in reverse. By wearing her exercise clothes beneath her outerwear, she saved time, and the extra layers helped her keep warm when the weather was chilly (on January 18, Toronto's high was four degrees Celsius). Linda wore a brassiere and a pair of underpants, plus heavy cotton gym shorts, a slip, a brown tweed skirt, a blue wool sweater, a sweater coat, fur-lined gloves, white wool socks, flat black shoes, and a turquoise scarf.[12] In one of her coat pockets, she carried a wallet that contained a five-dollar bill to pay for the lesson; in the other, she kept a compact and a tube of lipstick.

Linda Lampkin's attire on the night of her death was plain and practical, unlike the outfit she wore in a set of professional headshots she'd had taken several weeks earlier. Posed like a starlet, she fit the beauty standards of the day – her thick dark hair swept into waves, her lips, brows and eyelashes prominently defined, and her shoulders bare. By contrast, her home life was unglamorous. She liked to knit and draw. In her bedroom, she kept a doll collection and she drew pictures of them in a sketchbook. Linda's bedtime was 10:00 p.m., but she could stay up a bit later when *The $64,000 Question* game show was on. When her mother and her great-grandmother needed shopping done, she performed that chore in local stores. To her family, Linda was a "fine, normal girl."[13]

While carrying out her shopping errands, Linda Lampkin walked along the commercial thoroughfares of Dundas and Jane Streets, both dotted with post boxes, which Royal Mail truck drivers emptied twice daily. Sometime in the summer of 1955, she noticed the man who regularly covered the mail route in her neighbourhood – Robert Fitton. She spoke with the twenty-one-year-old driver on numerous occasions, and he gave her a ride in the truck on at least one occasion, which violated a rule that prohibited drivers of mail trucks from taking passengers.[14] The girl likely kept the unauthorized ride a secret from her parents, but she later pointed out the driver to her mother and told her she knew him by name. Mrs. Lampkin subsequently stated she had considered her daughter's contact with Fitton "merely friendly." She also believed Linda knew how to handle advances by strange boys and men whenever they called out, "What's your name?" If this happened, her daughter told her, she replied, "Deborah Randall," to throw them off.[15] However, Robert Fitton knew her name, where she lived, and where he might find her.

DEADLY CROSSROAD

On her arrival at the Burns studio, Linda Lampkin peeled off her gym shorts and sweater and danced with her fellow students until 7:30 p.m. After she got dressed, she paid for her lesson, which left $3.75 in her wallet. Her parents expected her home at the usual time – no later than nine in the evening. She was on schedule when she reached the streetcar loop at Jane and Bloor Streets and transferred onto the northbound bus, travelling up Jane. One of the other passengers, a

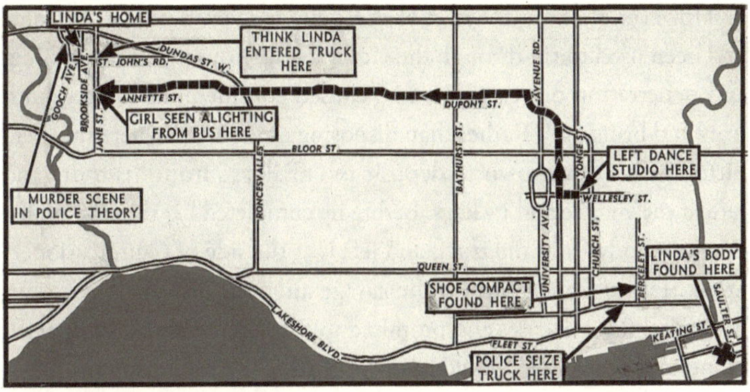

Map of Linda Lampkin's movements and the location of her body. | Toronto *Telegram,* January 20, 1956; courtesy York University Libraries, Clara Thomas Archives and Special Collections, Toronto Telegram fonds, ASC61980

neighbour of the Lampkins on Brookside, noticed her sitting near the front, and they both alighted at their stop at 8:37 p.m. Normally, they would have walked the same route home, but he saw her turn into a side street and then walk back to a mailbox at the corner of Jane Street. Around the same time, a Royal Mail truck was driving south on Jane. It turned into Saint John's Road to pick up the mail. Linda Lampkin crossed the street to the truck, placed one foot on the running board, and talked to the driver.[16] Already late for home, she went for another ride.

After waiting longer than usual for their daughter to return from her dance lesson, the Lampkins began to fret, and they called her friends in the hope she might have stopped by. When none of them had news of Linda's whereabouts, her father drove around the neighbourhood, anxiously searching for his girl. Finally, at 10:30 p.m., he reported their daughter missing, but unbeknownst to him, Linda was already dead, her bloodied and mud-splattered body lying exposed near the lake-front.[17] As they later learned, she had died less than a kilometre from her home, in a quiet spot where Fitton parked his truck, had intercourse with the girl, and then asphyxiated her with her scarf.[18] Somehow, possibly by falling when the truck had turned a corner, Linda also sustained a blow to her head.

However, that was the least of the wounds she suffered. Great force had been used to rip through the victim's numerous layers of clothing, and penetration of her vagina had caused considerable trauma, both tears and bruising.[19] Rather than disposing of her body where she died, Fitton drove downtown to deposit the mailbags from his route and return the vehicle and its keys. Before he completed his shift, he pulled the girl's body from the truck and left it at the side of Commissioners Street. Fitton's late return to the garage annoyed his supervisors, but he offered them excuses and promised to turn up for his morning shift. None of his coworkers would have dreamed of the real reason the driver was delayed.

The man who discovered Linda Lampkin's body was no forensic expert, but anyone could have seen the girl had died an unnatural death. In a gesture of decorum, he took a blanket from his truck to cover her body.[20] Shortly after 11 p.m., the police photographer arrived to take images of the victim and the surrounding area. His close-ups showed the skin on her neck was reddened and deeply cut under the scarf knotted around her neck.[21] The girl's clothing was ripped and shoved up above her waist. Blood oozed from her pubic area onto her inner thighs.[22] One of her dance shoes was on her foot, but the other was missing. Although several hemorrhages associated with asphyxiation were visible on her face, she was recognizable to the victim's father. Brought by police to the city morgue, Raymond Lampkin confirmed the body was that of his daughter.[23] But who was responsible for her death?

A DASTARDLY CRIME

Reporters on the scene had copy ready for the January 19 morning editions, and editors had familiar headlines at the ready: "SEX MURDER OF GIRL." The commissioner of the Ontario Provincial Police assigned an inspector from the Criminal Investigation Branch to assist the Metropolitan Toronto Police, and he notified every inspector and detachment to "check all known sex deviates in their areas."[24] The City of Toronto announced a reward of five thousand dollars for information leading to the arrest and conviction of the culprit, and the York Township reeve (the local mayor of the district where the Lampkins lived) and the provincial attorney general each tipped in one thousand dollars to help solve this "dastardly crime." Toronto's mayor, Nathan Phillips, urged all citizens to "report any sex deviates to police," emphasizing that the parents of Toronto should exercise more vigilance to prevent "young girls" from going out alone. The reeve vowed that

> the little girl's brutal slaying must be avenged. Her killer was a wild animal and must be put in a cage before he harms others: the time was long overdue when all sex offenders should be put in cages. If there isn't a law strong enough to put them away ... then we, as citizens, must fight for one. Sex killers are more dangerous than the most ferocious animals.[25]

The pressure on the police to find this latest "sex fiend" was intense, especially since another girl had died after a sexual assault in a nearby city two weeks before Lampkin's murder.

In London, Ontario, southwest of Toronto, a twenty-two-man police squad was deployed to work the case of Susan Cadieux, aged five, after her dead body was discovered on January 7, 1956. Playing after dinner with her brothers in a churchyard, she was abducted, sexually assaulted, and left to freeze in a warehouse.[26] News of the crime led the Parents Action League (PAL), the women-led lobby group seeking solutions to the sex crime problem, to request an emergency meeting with ministers from three Ontario government departments – health, reform institutions, and the Attorney General's office. One outcome of their January 13 meeting was the attorney general's pledge to urge magistrates to use their power to send individuals charged with sex offences to psychiatric hospitals, either before or after sentencing. Another was the establishment of a special committee to consider how to keep "sex deviates" in provincial prisons under psychiatric treatment until experts pronounced them cured.[27] Yet the police and magistrates could not meet the lobbyists' and politicians' calls for prompt action. The questioning of numerous sex deviates in and around London and the offer of a reward, which quickly topped three thousand dollars, failed to turn up a suspect. Just like the unsolved murder of Judy Carter in Toronto in 1955 and Arlene Anderson's back in 1947, the trail in the Cadieux case ran cold.[28]

There was every reason to anticipate that Linda Lampkin's killer would also elude capture since there were no witnesses to the violation of the girl's body, her strangulation, or the dumping of her remains miles from her home. Yet, in this case, timely assistance from observant citizens gave the Toronto police an edge. The editor of the Toronto *Star* commented that this latest "brutal murder of a young girl by a sex criminal" had "outraged the feelings of the whole city and raised new demands for some sort of action to stop those horrifying crimes," but all the dailies praised the police for catching and arresting a suspect within a day.[29] By following a string of leads that led them to the mail truck driver on duty in the west end the night the girl had disappeared, the police were confident they had solved the mystery of her death. When the afternoon editions of the papers hit Toronto's newsstands and landed on front porches on January 19, readers learned that detectives had Robert Fitton in custody and had charged him with murder.[30] This man's name had not appeared on their list of known deviates, however. A married man, aged twenty-one, Fitton lived with his wife, their two children, and his parents in Toronto's east end, and he was a steady worker with no criminal record of any sort. The man in custody for this crime looked nothing like the "fiends" and "wild animals" thought capable of rape and murder.

GRILLED FOR ELEVEN HOURS

The reward money offered for information leading to the arrest and conviction of Linda Lampkin's murderer was never paid because the police, aided by witnesses, did all the work that led them to charge Robert Fitton.[31] The truck he drove was distinctive – red with "Royal Mail" above the windshield and a large coat of arms on the side. Parked late at night where there were no post boxes, a mail truck stood out to

City of Toronto police photo of the mail truck driven by Robert Fitton, taken at 9 a.m. on January 19, 1956 | LAC, RG 13-B-1, vol. 1755, "Fitton, Robert," vol. 2, pt. 2

waterfront labourers familiar with the comings and goings of vehicles on the streets where much of the city's gas and petroleum was stored. A man walking to work on the night shift at a fuel company noticed a red truck parked on Commissioners Street with its lights on and its side door open. After a fellow employee told him a girl had been murdered, he thought he ought to ring the police.[32] By midnight, plans were underway to track down the drivers who had worked in Royal Mail trucks that evening.

At seven in the morning on the nineteenth, two of Toronto's most experienced detectives arrived at the garage that dispatched the city's mail trucks. A local cartage company, H.H. Bacon, held the contract to deliver and pick up mail and packages, and its supervisors assigned each driver his truck and ensured the return of vehicles and keys. Because Bacon's employees had to punch in and out, the management knew the time it took, on average, to complete each route.[33] When detectives asked for the records of drivers on the previous night's shift, the dispatcher told them Fitton had returned an hour later than usual to complete Route 27 in Toronto's west end. However, the driver had showed up on time for his morning shift on January 19, and he was working in the garage at the corner of Front and Bay Streets, loading empty bags into Truck 51. As soon as he saw the officers, Fitton broke into a sweat and slumped. While one detective kept him upright, the other searched the truck interior and found a bobby pin and a tube of lipstick plus a paper bag with a suspicious stain. These items, plus Fitton's unusual tardiness the night before, led the detectives to ask if they could "have a little talk with him, interview him."[34]

The grilling of suspects by hard-edged cops determined to solve crimes was a standard feature of true crime stories and crime dramas, but the use of mental coercion and physical abuse to extract confessions had come under increasing fire since the 1930s.[35] These practices were associated more with policing in the United States, but the conviction of a sex killer known as the Windsor "slasher" had brought the issue to Canada in 1946. Although the jury found the defendant, Ronald Sears, guilty, the verdict was quashed largely because the police had used coercive methods.[36] The Ontario Court of Appeal found detectives had subjected the eighteen-year-old suspect to the third degree – a prolonged interrogation in which he was deprived of food and water for many hours after his repeated claims of innocence. The chief justice condemned the "considerable force ... to arrest that boy at his home, the handcuffs used, his condition of collapse."[37] Under the circumstances, the appellate court ruled the trial judge should not have admitted Sears's statement.

Fitton was three years older than Sears, but the police admitted they "grilled" him for a longer period than the suspected slasher – eleven hours – before detectives could find enough evidence to charge him with murder. The nervous truck driver agreed to answer questions in the interrogation room at police headquarters where a detective

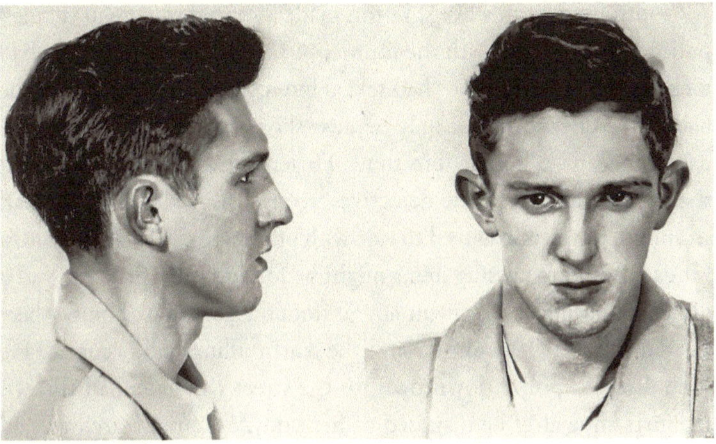

Police mugshot of Robert Fitton, taken shortly after his arrest on the evening of January 19, 1956 | LAC, RG 13-B-1, vol. 1755, "Fitton, Robert," vol. 2, pt. 1

informed him they were investigating the "death and the rape of a girl by the name of Linda Lampkin."[38] Although he admitted he knew her and said he had seen her two days earlier when he picked up mail on Jane Street, Fitton denied meeting the victim the night she died. Police recorded their suspect's statement, removed his clothes for the crime lab to examine, and then fanned across the city to collect evidence. One set of detectives inquired into Fitton's pickup stops on his mail route and searched for witnesses who might have seen him with the victim. Another visited all the depots and garages associated with his job to piece together the final moments of his journey the night before. A third searched the locations where the mail truck had been spotted, hoping to find two missing items: Linda Lampkin's right shoe and her wallet. As the search was underway, detectives gave Fitton clothes to wear and offered him food and drink while he sat without handcuffs in the detectives' office. However, the pressure on the suspect mounted when detectives returned to headquarters after their search: witnesses had seen Linda Lampkin at his truck on the night she died, and her mother told the police the lipstick they found in Truck 51 belonged to her daughter.[39]

Confronted by this news, Fitton made a second statement that led police to charge him with the murder of Linda Lampkin. Yes, he had picked up the girl and they had sexual intercourse in the truck. Yes, he had yanked her scarf, but only because she became annoying. No, he had not meant to stop her breathing. Fingerprinted and photographed, the accused agreed to the detectives' request for hair and fingernail scrapings. Fitton also agreed to ride with officers to the locations where Linda Lampkin's missing items might be found. Their first stop was a dimly lit housing development not far from the Lampkins' home, where he said the sexual encounter and the scarf pulling had occurred. He then directed police downtown, to the street where he had thrown the girl's shoe after he disposed of her body.[40] A brief search turned up the victim's shoe with her shattered compact stuffed inside. Even without the wallet, police had gathered, in less than a day, a confession and a substantial body of evidence to support the charge.

The Toronto police force's arrest of a suspect in "the city's most brutal sex slaying in many years" was a coup for the agency after its failed attempts to solve several sex murders.[41] The editor of the *Telegram* reminded readers that this "shocking murder and rape of a young girl in Toronto" was one in a "wave" of sexual crimes against girls and women, not just the Cadieux case but numerous others in the past few years. Yet just two culprits had been "brought to justice" for those crimes. By contrast, the "alert police work" that led detectives to charge Fitton "within 24 hours of the murder of Linda Lampkin" was bound to reassure the public.[42] Over a two-page spread, the Toronto *Star* published pictures of the six detectives whose work had stitched together the evidence that prompted Fitton's statement: "Police Say Suspect 'Breaks' after Hours of Grilling." The *Globe* also applauded the way the police had laid a charge of murder "after 11-hour Grilling." The story of the successful "manhunt" was sufficiently newsworthy that newspapers across Canada, the United States, and at least one English paper covered it.[43] Accounts of the arrest revealed that Fitton had led detectives to the site of the sexual relations and shown them where to find her belongings; however, they also published his claim that he did not intend to kill the girl.[44] Despite his admissions, he rejected the charge of murder: "I did not do it."[45]

PICKED UP?

On January 20, the Toronto *Star*'s front-page news – that the man charged with Linda Lampkin's murder was a "father of two" – came with an announcement above the headline: the paper's promised sex crime citizens' forum would take place in six days as scheduled. The public was invited to attend, free of charge, and to submit questions in advance. Two experts from the United States plus two from Ontario accepted the paper's invitation to respond to the biggest question: "What should be done about sex offenders?" The panellists, all psychiatrists, included Kenneth Gray of the Toronto Psychiatric Hospital. His qualifications included a law degree, but he specialized in forensic psychiatry, and he served PAL as the expert it chose to support its campaign for more effective means to prevent sex crimes. Since the murder of Judy Carter almost a year earlier, the women who founded the league had drawn many other allies to their cause, including lawyers. One of them, Toronto barrister David Humphrey, was chairman of the Criminal Justice Committee of the Canadian Bar Association, and he joined PAL's "scientific advisory committee" in April 1955.[46] Although Toronto had better-known lawyers with greater experience defending persons accused of murder, Humphrey, possibly at PAL's request, volunteered to represent Fitton the day after police charged him with the murder of Linda Lampkin.

David Humphrey had launched his law career in the York County Crown Attorney's office after his call to the bar in 1950. Four years later, he switched to criminal defence work in private practice. Prior to 1956, Humphrey appeared as a junior in several capital trials, but Fitton's was his first major case, which he took on at the age of thirty.[47] In Ontario, an ethos of unremunerated assistance for indigent persons was a tradition that many members of the legal profession treasured; however, concerns over inequity in the administration of justice grew after the Second World War, and reformers in favour of establishing a statutory legal aid system succeeded in 1951. Under that scheme, members willing to serve registered their names with the local sheriff, and lawyers who represented clients could draw disbursements from the small fund the province tipped in.[48] Humphrey was one of the registered members of the County of York Law Association (which covered metropolitan Toronto and its surroundings), and because he represented a capitally charged defendant, he was eligible to receive a special per diem payment for the days he spent at trial.[49] Nevertheless, the funding was meagre recompense for the time involved in preparing for trial, plus the legal expertise required to defend clients in court. Humphrey was one of the province's barristers who upheld the profession's "pauper's defence" tradition, and he did all in his power to defend Fitton.[50]

Aware of the onslaught of sensational, overwhelmingly condemnatory headlines about the brutal sex slaying his client was accused of committing, Humphrey set out to humanize Fitton before his trial. The city's press obliged. On January 20, the *Star* published Fitton's claim of innocence, which he'd penned on the back of Humphrey's church membership card. In the favourable spread, a blow-up of the card appeared alongside Fitton's wedding photo and a picture of him with his nineteen-year-old wife, Florence, holding one of their two sons. From a feared sex fiend, the illustrated story transformed Humphrey's client into a respectable "young father." Reporters who interviewed Fitton's family described him as a devoted son and a tender-hearted husband who "adored" his two babies and liked "children in general." Florence Fitton, who lived with her in-laws, said her husband "often stopped his truck to help small children across the street." Fitton's mother was convinced her son could not have committed the offence: "He couldn't even stand to see chicken killed."[51]

When Humphrey first appeared in court on January 20 to represent Fitton, he requested a further remand to prepare for the preliminary hearing. Much of his time had been consumed by neutralizing negative pretrial publicity. "I am sick and tired of all this talk in the press and the public at large of [Fitton] being a 'sex deviate,'" Humphrey vented.[52]

THE TELEGRAM

Night

Girl, 13, Strangled – $7,000 Reward

QUIZ FATHER OF TWO 10 HOURS IN SLAYING

A studio portrait of Linda Lampkin, taken several weeks before her death, aside a school photo, both given to the press by her parents. Each of Toronto's dailies published these portraits along with three other studio portraits. | Toronto *Telegram*, January 19, 1956

He insisted that the publicity was uniformly negative toward his client. The *Telegram*'s report of Fitton's court appearance on January 27 referred to him as the man police had charged with "picking up the Lampkin girl, strangling her with her silk scarf, assaulting her, and dumping her body." Yet the story also normalized Fitton by describing how he had turned to smile at his wife in court, brought her to tears, and then faced the magistrate with tears that "trickled down his cheeks."[53]

Unlike the defence, the Crown counsel played no part in managing the image of the deceased or her family, and they could but watch as public impressions of the Lampkins also transformed. The men assigned to prosecute criminal cases were appointed by the Crown Attorney's office since criminal offences were acts against the monarch, not victims or their loved ones. In advance of the preliminary hearing, the police went over the evidence with the Crown and the witnesses to be called. While that process was underway, a media makeover of the victim unfolded, turning a murdered schoolgirl into a "pretty brunette" who "dressed and looked older than her thirteen years."[54] Linda Lampkin's studio portraits, which her parents innocently offered the press, supported that impression. If they anticipated that outsiders would see their "normal" daughter as they did, they were wrong.

As the Lampkins prepared to lay their daughter to rest, a woman showed up at their minister's home to protest: "This girl shouldn't be given a church funeral." Anonymous callers harassed the Lampkins, criticizing them for letting their "boy crazy" daughter roam the streets at night.[55] In a period when the law defined precocious female sexual activity as juvenile delinquency, a girl such as Lampkin looked and acted nothing like Judy Carter or Susan Cadieux – unambiguous child victims.[56] For the Crown, preparing to prosecute Fitton for murder became more challenging than it initially appeared when news broke that a sex fiend had slain a thirteen-year-old schoolgirl.

BAD PARENTING AND NORMAL MALE SEXUAL DESIRE

On the night before Robert Fitton's first court appearance on January 27, the Toronto *Star*'s citizens' forum on sex deviates went ahead as planned at Massey Hall. The event drew a near-capacity crowd of over two thousand Torontonians, many of whom were "parents, outraged by Linda Lampkin's murder and wondering how to protect their own children."[57] But Kenneth Gray told the audience the threat posed by sexual deviates should not be exaggerated. Only sadists who inflicted "mental suffering or physical violence on another person as a source of sex pleasure" and those who sexually molested "young children" were truly dangerous. Frederick Van Nostrand, director of neurological services in Ontario's reform institutions, agreed and added that negligent parents were partly responsible for sex offences against their children.[58] He illustrated his point by telling a story about a seventeen-year-old girl who had been sexually assaulted after she was "picked up in a car ... at a nearby dance." "In this case," Van Nostrand stated, the charge of rape had been excessive since her parents had failed in their duty of care: "The girl really had no chance; it was her parents who were delinquent."[59] He did not refer to the Lampkins by name, but his listeners likely made the connection. Two weeks later, when Van Nostrand testified at the Toronto hearings of the royal commission on sexual psychopathy, he reiterated the point: the root cause of the sex crime problem was "the lack of integrity at the home level."[60]

Unaware of the condemnation they would face for their daughter's murder, Raymond and Barbara Lampkin welcomed reporters into their home, hoping that something good might come of their loss. As far as they were concerned, Linda's murder was a painful but necessary reminder that any child could suffer the same fate: "'COULD HAPPEN TO YOU, TOO' LINDA'S PARENTS' WARNING TO ALL," was the headline that summed up their message. A *Star* reporter described the couple as

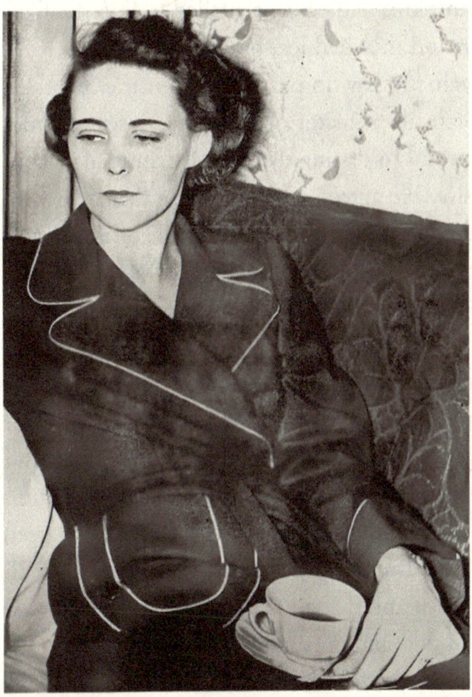

Mrs. Barbara Lampkin and her husband hoped their daughter's murder would serve as a warning to parents. | Toronto *Telegram*, 21 January 1956.

"distraught with anguish," but they were determined this horror might alert "other parents to keep their children from associating with strange men, and from accepting 'lifts' even from those they know."[61] Although the *Star*'s account of the "Horrible Tragedy They Suffered" was sympathetic, readers may have wondered why these parents had failed to heed their own advice.

Psychiatric experts agreed with the police and PAL that families had to do more than simply rely on law enforcement to protect children from sex criminals – parents must make children wary of anyone the family did not know and approve of. Shortly after Judy Carter's body was discovered in 1955, a *Telegram* reporter conducted an experiment to "show how girls should NOT react when approached by a stranger." He and a photographer cruised along Toronto's streets trying to pick up girls and their first target was a "pretty, flaxen-haired girl of 13 or 14." Fortunately, she took off "at a brisk trot," which proved to the reporters that "parents are winning the battle" to "protect children from perverts."[62] However, the Lampkins had evidently failed to join the fight to protect their daughter, and they had lost her as a result.

One of the other psychiatrists who participated in the *Star*'s sex deviates forum, Ralph Brancale, director of New Jersey's sex offender diagnostic centre, was careful to distinguish sexual criminality from normal heterosexual desire. He agreed with Dr. Gray that men who committed brutal sexual assaults against females were abnormal, but he disagreed with the criminalization of men charged with "statutory rape, simply because the girl involved is under 16, even though she may be co-operating with the man."[63] As an American, Brancale was unaware that the Canadian Criminal Code set fourteen as the age of consent for sexual intercourse with a girl. Regardless of whether the offender believed a girl under fourteen was that age or older, and whether she appeared desirous of sex, it was a crime, with a maximum penalty of life in prison and a whipping.[64] Nevertheless, Brancale agreed with his fellow experts that draconian penalties, calls to lock up all sexually aberrant individuals, and demands for castration and forced hormonal treatment could not, and must not, be considered solutions to the sex crime problem. Instead, he and his fellow male panellists

A pickup cartoon by artist Bert Grassick | Toronto *Telegram,* April 12, 1955

reassured attendees that most expressions of masculine heterosexual desire were perfectly normal.

North America's most famous expert on men's sexuality, Alfred Kinsey, did not appear at the *Star*'s forum, but his research was well known in Canada by the mid-1950s thanks to his landmark book, *Sexual Behaviour in the Human Male* (1948). Kinsey's disclosure that homosexual attraction and activities were common among men disturbed most Canadians. But his observation that behaviours ranging from men's wolf whistles to rough sex were so common as to be considered normal raised only a few eyebrows.[65] In 1953, the chairman of the Canadian Welfare Association's crime and delinquency division, Norman Borins, referred to Kinsey's research when he gave evidence on revisions to the Criminal Code. This book demonstrated the need for more "factual information" on the "question of sex behaviour," he believed.[66] Borins had clocked over a decade of service in Toronto's Crown Attorney office, where he had represented the Crown in rape cases under the code as it stood before 1955, setting death as the maximum penalty.[67] More recently, Kinsey's research had convinced Borins that the time had come for a more enlightened approach: "In most cases rape appears not to be primarily a sex crime but is rather an expression of normal sex impulses coupled with a lack of social inhibitions."[68] Thus, the clamour over the danger of sex offenders had reached such a volume by the mid-1950s that many male experts feared lobbyists, most of them female, had become overly emotional, even "hysterical."[69]

"I HOPE HE HANGS"

Despite implications and outright accusations that Linda Lampkin was promiscuous, her funeral, conducted at the church she had attended, was a sombre affair. Five days after her death, her body – dressed in a green jumper and yellow blouse, done up high to hide the gash around her neck – was placed inside a grey casket. Flowers from the family and neighbours encircled it, setting the focal point for the service. Aside from the Lampkin family, Linda's schoolteachers and classmates attended, as did local politicians. The minister who led the ceremony provided comforting words, which he followed with a call for government action: "We need and must demand some forceful legislation to prevent these unbearable crimes." He was unequivocal about the deceased's age and the cause of her death: "We find ourselves face to face with an inhuman crime ... Today we will commit the body of this child to the ground." As her choirmates sang, Linda was now "safe in the arms of Jesus." Four motorcycle policemen led the funeral cortège to Park Lawn Cemetery, where Linda Lampkin was buried on January 23, 1956.[70] On the same day, another breakthrough in the case against Fitton was reported: a detective had found Linda's wallet jammed into a sewer grate near Bacon's garage.[71] Emptied of money, it suggested the killer had robbed, raped, and murdered the victim. News of the discovery offered no comfort to the Lampkins, but it gave them further reason to anticipate that their daughter's killer would be convicted.

The penalty of death for murder was Canada's mandatory punishment for "inhuman crimes." In 1954, the federal government had assigned a special joint committee to examine capital punishment and to consider the prospect of abolition; however, in January 1956, the committee was still labouring over its report, and the government was not obliged to act on its advice were the committee to recommend abolition.[72] To most Canadians, hanging remained the only penalty appropriate for murder and the best means to deter others from offending, notwithstanding expert opinion to the contrary.[73] Some Torontonians were so enraged by the girl's murder that they called the Fittons's home, and their "hate attack" forced the family to change their phone number. Fitton's wife called the anonymous callers "terrible people" because they shouted: "I hope he hangs." Her mother-in-law complained that callers were "condemning the boy before he is proven guilty. They condemn me and the family. Do they not think we are suffering?"[74]

On the day after Linda Lampkin's funeral, the Toronto *Star* published a letter sent by a man who thought Fitton deserved to die and stressed the need to condemn this latest "sex pervert, who not only criminally assaulted but silenced by murder a young girl." The writer thought it was "ridiculous to assert that these men are driven by an uncontrollable urge. If they knew that their acts would cost them their lives, they would control themselves."[75] Whether this case involved a sudden loss of control or a planned attack, the convergence of Linda Lampkin's trip home and Fitton's mail route on the evening of January 18 left her dead and him facing a capital charge. However, Mrs. Fitton senior was correct to point out that her "boy" had yet to face trial for the girl's murder, and she insisted he was innocent, a claim his lawyer prepared to defend.

IN THE MID-1950S, Canadians were unevenly divided on the death penalty – a majority still favoured capital punishment, and similar divisions split public opinion on sexuality.[76] Explicit posters for films with sizzling plots of sex and danger, jokes and cartoons about strange men flirting with fast women, and tales of "lust-maddened fiends" pumped out for cheap novels and magazines were ubiquitous.[77] A chorus of concerned parents, educators, politicians, and religious figures decried these forms of entertainment and called for their suppression to fight the sex crime problem.[78] The sermon in the funeral service for Susan Cadieux excoriated sex deviates but it also condemned "those who opposed censorship of crime magazines and motion pictures."[79] However, there was no denying the appeal of titillating entertainment for a mass customer base, and tropes of masculine conquest and feminine flirtatiousness shaped public understandings of the Lampkin murder as details of the victim's and suspect's lives unspooled in the weeks after her death. Despite the brutality of the attack, neither Linda Lampkin nor Robert Fitton quite fit the narrative of the child victim and the sex killer that initially cast this murder's meaning.

The extraordinary police operation that led to Fitton's swift arrest boosted the force's public image after it had failed to find the men responsible for a troubling cluster of sex murders. The coincidence of Lampkin's murder, a public forum on the problem of sex crime, and the impending Toronto hearings of the royal commission into the sexual psychopath law produced saturation coverage of the case late in January.[80] Humphrey's request for the further remand extended Fitton's preliminary hearing date to the middle of March. Although the evidence of Fitton's involvement in Lampkin's death and the disposal of her body, revealed by the press, left little doubt the case would proceed to trial, journalists refrained from publishing the text of the accused's statements to police, as the law required. The question of whether the jury should allow that evidence was to become a matter for the trial judge to answer.

3

Let Justice Take Its Course

MARCH 15, THE DAY Robert Fitton's preliminary hearing opened in 1956, is also known as the Ides of March, a portent of doom in Shakespeare's *Julius Caesar*. Well-read followers of the case might have pondered the warning Caesar receives from a fortune teller who predicts his death. The mail truck driver charged with Linda Lampkin's murder was a reader of comic books, not Shakespeare, and he faced legal proceedings, not an assassination.[1] Nevertheless, the hearing was the first step in a path that led to the mandatory penalty of death if Fitton was convicted. Adjudicated by a magistrate, the hearing laid out the physical evidence and aired the testimony the Crown had to establish its case. Fitton's statements to police, which had prompted the murder charge, would also be considered as evidence if the case went to trial, and the defence was aware the Crown would seek to have them admitted. With these strikes against Fitton, his fortunes looked grim as he faced trial in April. But this defendant, a man of meagre means, had an advantage over most others of his station: a sharp lawyer, David Humphrey, who doggedly defended his client.[2]

The evidence that Fitton killed the victim was compelling, but the Crown's theory that Linda Lampkin had been raped and strangled hinged on the admissibility of the defendant's partially exculpatory confession – that the girl had stopped breathing when he tugged on her scarf after they had intercourse. According to the Crown, medical evidence of bodily trauma plus indications she was strangled during intercourse contradicted Fitton's statement. The prosecution also hinged on proving the defendant was guilty of "constructive murder."[3] Defined in the Criminal Code as "culpable homicide ... while committing or attempting to commit" certain offences – including rape – it did not require proving the victim's death was intended; however, in this case, it called on the Crown to convince the jury that Linda Lampkin had not consented to sex with Fitton. This made the prosecution dependent on medical evidence from a government pathologist, who insisted the victim had been sexually assaulted and strangled over several minutes. Without a medical expert of his own, Humphrey attacked the characterization of the intercourse as rape.

Fitton's trial unfolded over five days in April 1956, over which time the defence presented no witnesses; instead, Humphrey chipped away at the Crown's case in *voir dire* and his cross-examinations. He was adamant that "inflammatory" close-up images of Linda Lampkin's body be excluded, and he also objected to the Crown's request for the judge to admit Fitton's confession into evidence. Humphrey won the first point with the judge, Justice Russell W. Treleaven, but the Crown attorney, Arthur O. Klein, won on the admission of the defendant's statements to police. This was not fatal to the defence, since Humphrey could tap its exculpatory elements to contest the charge. But how to make Fitton's claim, that Linda Lampkin was eager for intercourse, persuasive? Conscious that he was speaking before an all-male jury, Humphrey composed a picture of Linda Lampkin as a deceptive, boy-crazy girl by skilfully putting questions and suggestions to Crown witnesses; by contrast, his questioning of Fitton's work associates and the police elicited a favourable impression of a law-abiding youth, a trustworthy worker, a family man.

The defence presented its portraits of the victim and the defendant at a time when most people – women as well as men, psychiatrists as well as nonexperts – believed that strict parenting ensured the chastity of young teenaged girls and that normal men could be excused for losing control if tempted by females whose dress or behaviour was sexually provocative.[4] Although Humphrey failed to shake Mrs. Lampkin's certainty that her daughter was an innocent "kid" savagely slain, the defence knew that Fitton's male peers, not the victim's mother, would decide whether the Crown had proved its case.

SUITING UP FOR BATTLE

At the time of Fitton's trial, the Queen Street exterior of Toronto's City Hall was considerably grander than its interior courtrooms. Opened in 1889 and built in the Romanesque revival style, it housed the civic offices and courtrooms where Toronto's magistrates and judges of the County of York and the judges of the provincial supreme court presided. Most defendants who appeared in the magistrate's court were charged with minor offences – infringements of bylaws, thefts, traffic violations, assaults – and the majority elected summary justice over trial by jury. Persons charged with murder were different because trials under indictment had to be held in superior courts of criminal jurisdiction.[5] In advance, a preliminary hearing, conducted by a magistrate, was held to determine whether the Crown had evidence sufficient to go to trial. Magistrates were bound to protect the accused's right to a fair trial, but in Fitton's case a blizzard of pretrial publicity left the public with little doubt he was responsible for Linda Lampkin's death. Although reporters had detailed where the sex and the victim's death allegedly took place, Fitton's statements to police about his involvement had not been published, and the magistrate, Frederick C. Gullen, was careful to keep it that way.

Frederick Gullen carried almost two decades' experience into court when he took the magistrate's bench in Fitton's hearing. A philosophy graduate of the University of Toronto, his 1910 yearbook described him as "possessed of a brilliant mind, a genial nature and a desire to be of service to mankind."[6] After he obtained his law degree, he practised until 1938, when he was appointed magistrate. One of the Crown attorneys who welcomed Gullen on his first day on the job was Arthur Klein, the lawyer later assigned to prosecute Fitton.[7] As a Toronto magistrate, Gullen worked regularly with Klein and the York County's

Frederick C. Gullen, sitting on the bench in one of Toronto City Hall's courtrooms | Still from *Problem Clinic* (1955), courtesy of National Film Board

Crown Attorney's office, also housed in City Hall, and Klein dealt with members of the Toronto police force daily. But there was nothing routine about a sex murder case in the magistrate's court, where the hearing brought the Lampkins and the Fittons together for the first time in grief and anxiety.

Arthur Klein worked his way up to the rank of senior assistant Crown attorney in the city's pack of prosecutors. When he took up law in 1930, he built on his family's impressive legal pedigree, as his father and uncle were prominent lawyers, both elevated to the bench.[8] Unlike his father, Otto, who worked in private practice for forty-four years before he was appointed a county court judge of the provincial court, Klein joined the Crown Attorney's office shortly after his call to the bar in 1933. In his days as an articling student, he prepared cases on "murder, rape, and manslaughter," and he learned how to prosecute capital cases.[9] Klein's status as a Crown attorney rose in 1952 through his prosecution of the "Boyd gang," regarded then as Canada's most notorious robbers and jailbreakers. In December of that year, two members of the gang, found guilty of the murder of a Toronto police sergeant, were hanged.[10] Since then, the Don Jail's execution chamber had not been used, but the hearing into the murder of Linda Lampkin, with Klein representing the Crown, raised the prospect that Fitton might be the next to step on the trap door.

David Humphrey dedicated himself to setting up a different outcome for the man accused of murdering Linda Lampkin. Despite his limited experience in capital cases, he had top-notch training, having articled with future chief justice of Ontario Charles L. Dubin, who enlisted his junior in criminal defence work.[11] In 1949, Humphrey assisted Dubin in the defence of a twenty-one-year-old worker charged with

Lawyer David Humphrey – shown here with Robert Fitton's mother, Pearl, and his wife, Florence – offered to represent Fitton as soon as he was arrested. | Toronto *Telegram*, January 21, 1956

murder after he bludgeoned a man who had allegedly made an "indecent attack."[12] The trial ended in their client's conviction for manslaughter, not murder, which the Toronto bar considered "a big win" for the defence.[13] After Humphrey was called to the bar in 1950, however, he joined the Crown Attorney's office (on Arthur Klein's recommendation) and collaborated in the prosecution of the Boyd gang.[14] Had Humphrey remained a Crown attorney, he could well have been assigned to prosecute Fitton; instead, he opted for a more lucrative career in private practice in 1954, concentrating on criminal defence work. But money was not Humphrey's sole motive, since he left his name on the Don Jail's "free list," which prisoners could consult to be defended "for nothing."[15] Fitton's family was fortunate that a lawyer of Humphrey's calibre upheld the principle that every person charged with a criminal offence, no matter how impoverished, deserved a robust defence.

THE BURDEN OF PROOF

In a courtroom where magistrates disposed of most accused offenders in a matter of minutes, a four-day hearing was a major event, and the murder of Linda Lampkin still commanded headlines two months after the crime. Since January 18, 1956, the police had tracked down scores of witnesses to support the charge. The Crown called the detectives who had built their case against Fitton, and Klein also found numerous witnesses who said they had seen the pair on numerous occasions. However, Humphrey's questions to Crown witnesses introduced the theory that Linda Lampkin had planned the pickup on the night she died. No matter how the encounter started, the Crown's medical expert focused on how it ended in her violent death.

Chester R. McLean, the thirty-eight-year-old pathologist-in-chief at Toronto Western Hospital, was unequivocal in the preliminary hearing that the victim had been raped and throttled. Ontario's chief coroner, Smirle Lawson, called on McLean frequently to perform autopsies, and both experts had taken part in determining the cause of Judy Carter's death in April 1955. In that case, McLean found that the scarf the girl had worn had been tied tightly around her throat, "strangling the little girl," and he concluded she had died from suffocation. Since he detected no further wounds on her body, and because she was fully clothed, McLean was the expert who had ruled out the theory that Judy Carter had been the victim of a "sex attack."[16] Nine months later, when he answered the coroner's call to conduct a postmortem on Linda Lampkin's body, McLean examined the body of another girl strangled with her own scarf. Only this victim, he declared, had definitely been raped.

In January 1956, shortly after the discovery of Linda Lampkin's body, newspapers had reported Dr. McLean's appraisal, but Fitton's hearing in March 1956 was the first time the doctor faced cross-examination. When he was asked to identify the victim's cause of death, McLean testified that Lampkin's breath had been stopped by the tightening of her scarf as a ligature. "Marks on the girl's throat" (an abrasion approximately one-quarter inch deep) as well as hemorrhages on her face led him to that conclusion.[17] When McLean examined the victim's genital region and vagina, he found tears in the introitus, blood, and seminal fluid, which the provincial laboratory confirmed. Together, this evidence indicated "forcible intercourse" had occurred prior to the victim's murder, the pathologist testified.[18] He also referred to the disarrangement of the girl's outer clothing and the fact that her undergarments had been ripped apart. Humphrey accused McLean of drifting from strictly medical evidence, and he objected to the expert witness expressing his opinion. Yet he knew that every newspaper had used the headlines "Sex Slaying" and "Rape-Murder" to describe the crime since it was first reported.

Although Robert Fitton was charged with murder, not rape, the cross-examination of McLean and other Crown witnesses at the preliminary hearing followed a strategy, common in the rape defence playbook, of victim blaming. Defending Fitton depended in large part on suggesting that Linda Lampkin had been an eager and willing sexual partner. Even the pathologist appeared ambivalent about the victim's sexual maturity. On the one hand, McLean confirmed the girl was a virgin; on the other, he described her as a young woman. "She was only a girl of prepubertal age but she was well developed and

Defence counsel John P. Nelligen (*standing*) and Crown counsel Henry C. Bull (*seated*) with court reporters in the foreground and members of the public behind the rail. The documentary *Problem Clinic* (1955) used real legal figures in its depiction of legal aid in Toronto. | Courtesy of National Film Board

appeared much older than 13," McLean commented.[19] Humphrey's cross-examinations of Crown witnesses drew out similar impressions but for different purposes. When the Crown called a school chum of Linda and a former schoolteacher as witnesses to Fitton's prior contact with the victim, Humphrey sought their views about Linda's eagerness to see the man, the frequency of their contact, and her numerous dates with boys and reports that her parents allowed her out at night.

Perhaps the most crucial Crown witness at the hearing was Linda Lampkin's mother. She was distraught over her girl's murder, yet she was also the person whom jurors might consider partly to blame for the girl's death through lax parenting. Barbara Lampkin had identified her daughter's personal items found by the police – her wallet, a compact and mirror, a tube of lipstick – and she identified them again in the hearing as evidence against Fitton. To her, these articles were the same as any girl of thirteen might carry, and experimenting with makeup was not unusual at that age. However, Mrs. Lampkin faced barbed accusations of bad parenting under cross-examination. Humphrey asked her why she had allowed her daughter out at night. Why hadn't she stopped her from associating with an older man? Neither of these questions contradicted the mother's evidence, but they undermined the contention that Linda Lampkin was a victim of forcible sex.

By the hearing's end, it would have been a shock if Magistrate Gullen had refused to send the case for trial. "I find there is sufficient evidence to put the accused on trial for the charge as laid," he announced. Crown witnesses had placed Linda Lampkin standing by Fitton's Royal Mail truck on January 18. The police described Fitton's collapse when detectives came to his workplace the morning after he returned late from his night shift. The deceased girl's lipstick was discovered in Fitton's vehicle. This evidence made it plausible that "a jury might find the accused guilty."[20] The decision left Humphrey clear-eyed about the challenge ahead, but the hearing also gave the Crown a taste of how to prepare for the defence's approach. Prosecuting Fitton for murder would depend on persuading the judge to admit Fitton's partly inculpatory confession into evidence. It would also depend on convincing a jury that an apparently sexually precocious girl had been raped and intentionally asphyxiated.

R v FITTON

Ontario was one of the jurisdictions that incorporated a further preliminary stage before a trial could be held, and this was performed by a grand jury, thirteen citizens of York County in Fitton's case.[21] If a majority agreed the Crown had a *prima facie* case, they were to return a true bill of indictment. The province's director of public prosecutions, William B. Common, venerated the ancient tradition of the grand jury as a "forum in which to dispose of frivolous or weak prosecutions, and [as a] shield to an accused person to ensure that his liberty and freedom is not lightly dealt with."[22] In the April 1956 Spring Assizes of the Supreme Court of Ontario, the grand jury handed down two true bills for murder: one, against a man charged with the stabbing murder of his wife, and the other against Robert Fitton. If convicted as charged, nothing could shield either man from the mandatory sentence of death.

Before the Assizes opened, sheriffs were also obliged to find a pool of eligible "petit" jurors. In April 1956, twenty-eight people appeared on the list from which counsel could choose. David Humphrey rejected sixteen potential jurors, some of whom might have been women.[23] Despite legislation introduced in 1951 to enable women to serve on juries in Ontario, few appeared in criminal trials prior to the 1960s.[24] News reports noted that an "all-male" jury had been selected in Fitton's trial, and the judge and counsel addressed them as "gentlemen." One of them – a racetrack director named John Cole – turned out to be a man of Charles Dubin's acquaintance, and the jury elected him as foreman.[25] More remarkably, Fitton's father had previously worked for Cole's boss, a wealthy racetrack owner, before he was struck ill early in 1955. These connections seemed like a stroke of luck that favoured the defence. When Dubin entered the courtroom after the jury selection, he shook Humphrey's hand, and they exchanged a knowing smile.[26] As Klein later reflected, the defence probably thought, "Boy, this is great."[27]

Neither the Crown nor the defence had any say over the justices assigned to preside in Supreme Court of Ontario trials. The man who sat on the bench in *R v Fitton,* Russell William Treleaven, was the son of a Methodist preacher who remained active in church work his entire life. Called to the bar in 1914, he established a practice with his brother in Hamilton, and they became active in civic affairs.[28] In 1937, Russell Treleaven was created a King's counsel, and eight years later he was appointed justice of the High Court at the age of fifty-eight. In that role, he presided over several murder trials, mainly robbery homicides and intimate partner killings but no "sex slayings." As a civic-minded Hamiltonian and churchman, however, Treleaven likely found the "despicable wave of heinous crimes" over the winter of 1955–56, including five "brutal rapes" in and around Hamilton, of grave concern. In Parliament, the federal member for Hamilton South possibly spoke for Justice Treleaven, a fellow Liberal, when he asked on January 20, 1956, why sex deviates were not put away before they committed such serious crimes. The MP also asked, "What will happen to the sadistic rapist who spirited away Linda Lampkin?"[29] If the Crown convinced the jury that Fitton was guilty of murder, Treleaven knew the answer: the Criminal Code required him to pronounce the sentence of death.

"Not guilty," was Fitton's reply when asked for his plea, and these were the only words he uttered in court before his sentencing four days later. The trial transcript does not describe the impression the accused made in court, but the press did. Reporters found his demeanour and voice noteworthy: "His head hunched forward, his shoulders rounded," the defendant had a "high, boyish voice." According to the *Star,* the married father of two, twenty-one years of age, "looked more like a 17-year-old." Fitton was clean-shaven and "well dressed" in a suit and tie, probably the first time he had donned such garments since his wedding. Despite his courtroom costume, the mail truck driver looked "much younger than his years," the *Telegram* commented.[30] The judge warned the jury not to read the papers or to listen to or watch news coverage of the trial, but the defence was happy to exploit these depictions of Fitton's youth and meekness and to reinforce them at every opportunity.

To substantiate the charge against Fitton, the Crown had to convince the jury that the defendant was criminally responsible for committing murder and to counter the defence's theory, Klein endeavoured to construct the victim as an innocent girl who was brutally assaulted and suffocated. Arthur Klein had a reputation for his "small-town, down-to-earth charm" in court, and he opened for the Crown with blunt language.[31] Linda Lampkin was a "schoolgirl" who had lived at home with her family until the events of the evening of January 18 led to her death. When he described the state of her body ("her private parts were badly injured and she had been strangled ... which left quite a mark on her neck"), he presented the Crown's theory of constructive murder – that "Linda Lampkin had been raped and strangled and the act of strangulation was done in furtherance of the act of rape," an assessment the pathologist's medical evidence would substantiate.[32] The Crown also informed the court he had forty-three witnesses and sixty-five exhibits to support the charge. Two of those exhibits were the statements

Fitton made to police, which Klein's opening did not mention, since it was up to the judge to determine their admissibility.

The Crown's first three witnesses detailed the state of the victim's body and explained the cause of her death, but because the defence had no expert witnesses of their own, Humphrey relied on questioning the admissibility of visual evidence and challenging the authority of the experts, foremost among them McLean. The police photographer, the first Crown witness, had taken a total of eighteen pictures, first at the roadside where Linda Lampkin's body was dumped and later in the city morgue. The Crown tendered every picture as exhibits, but Humphrey came out swinging. Primed to neutralize and disarm any evidence that might inspire outrage or anger toward his client, he challenged the admission of several pictures that showed "the injuries visible upon the deceased." This triggered a pause in the trial, and the jury retired while counsel argued the matter in voir dire. Humphrey contended these images were "unnecessary to identify the victim," and he asserted they were of a "prejudicial and inflammatory nature," a claim he backed with reference to *Lizotte v R* (1951). That decision established that technically admissible evidence of "little real value and yet indirectly so prejudicial to the prisoner" should be excluded.[33] Furthermore, Humphrey asserted, the pathologist and coroner could, "with some exactitude," describe the victim's injuries verbally.[34]

Justice Treleaven allowed counsel to argue for fifteen minutes, as they made opposing points on the probative versus inflammatory nature of the postmortem photos. Klein insisted each image of the deceased was necessary to prove the Crown's theory of intentional strangulation. Although the judge agreed to admit three of the morgue shots, he shared the defence's misgivings about the fourth – a brightly lit close-up of Linda Lampkin's face and neck, which showed deeply abraded flesh. Worried this stark image would have a "harrowing effect" on the jury, Justice Treleaven came up with a judgment of Solomon: the close-up could be admitted into evidence so long as the photographer cut out the deceased's facial features to leave just the abrasion visible.[35] Humphrey and Klein were content for the jury to see this image of the victim reduced to a piece of flesh.[36]

The Crown's contention that the defendant had raped Linda Lampkin was crafted to meet the definition of constructive murder. The first medical witness, the veteran coroner, Smirle Lawson, was circumspect. He testified that the victim had been "throttled" with her scarf. Each of the three pairs of pants she had worn that night was "torn at the crotch," and her brassiere was "split in two." Although Lawson observed fresh blood oozing from the girl's vagina when he conducted an initial examination, he did not describe her injuries as indicative of rape. But McLean, the medical expert who had already crossed swords with Humphrey in the preliminary hearing, was determined to stick to his assessment that Linda Lampkin had been raped.

Under questioning by Klein, McLean told the court the victim's face was dark and congested with blood above the scarf. When he examined her neck, he found the knot was tied so tightly that he had to cut the scarf to remove it. Froth exuded from the deceased's mouth and nostrils. His examination of the girl's bloodied genital region indicated she was alive when the tears to the perineum had occurred. Because the girl's hymen was torn and bleeding, McLean stated that "Miss Lampkin was a virgin" and concluded she had suffered "a forcible assault."[37] Klein followed this by asking McLean to describe how the girl would have felt under this "sexual attack":

> Her age was 13 years. ... She was not an adult person sexually and could not accommodate an adult organ of ordinary size. In other words, by some mechanism, which I will not attempt to define, a substantial tear in her lower vagina in addition to her hymen occurred. And that would be a most painful event.[38]

McLean ventured further, however. He had no doubt a "man had had intercourse with the deceased," and the tearing of the victim's flesh and the presence of spermatozoa indicated "forcible intercourse" had occurred. Linda Lampkin was "alive at the time she was raped."[39]

The defence immediately objected, complaining that the Crown's witness had veered well outside his "compass" of medical expertise. How could this pathologist determine the difference between consensual intercourse and rape, a criminal offence? Justice Treleaven decided the term had accidently "slipped out," so he asked the Crown to rephrase his question. This time, when Klein asked his expert witness if he based his understanding of rape on his "medical knowledge and experience," McLean gave a sarcastic answer: the only way he could have reached a different conclusion would have required that he "ignore all the evidence which would lead me to say that force had been used."[40]

When Humphrey cross-examined McLean, he hammered him for misrepresenting the victim's genital injuries. The defence insisted the autopsy showed that a "male penis" had "penetrated [the victim's] vagina, ruptured her hymen and caused the tearing" – nothing beyond that. This doctor was an expert in medicine, not law. McLean disagreed. Trying to prove he knew something about the Criminal Code, he referred to what he called "the statutory definition of rape. This is a thirteen year old girl."[41] Yet this was irrelevant in Fitton's trial: he was not charged with "sexual intercourse with a female person ... under the age of fourteen years," and Humphrey insisted on shutting down any such implication from a Crown witness.[42]

Attacking McLean's determination of strangulation as the cause of Linda Lampkin's death was a more technical way for the defence to raise the possibility that the victim had died suddenly and after intercourse. In the absence of the defence's own forensic expert, Humphrey referred to a text by an authoritative British pathologist who detailed the phenomenon of "sudden cardiac inhibition." To raise doubt about McLean's interpretation – that Fitton had used the scarf as a ligature – Humphrey read out a passage that described how death could occur in as few as twenty seconds if pressure was placed on particular nerves and blood vessels.[43] Surely this made it plausible that Fitton had accidently stopped the girl's breath by a quick tug on her scarf after a consensual sexual encounter. McLean acknowledged the possibility, but he insisted the evidence in this case indicated it would have taken three to five minutes of tight restraint before the victim stopped breathing. Despite Humphrey's digs (Did McLean fail to consider that shouting or laughing could hasten death?), the Crown's pathologist stuck to his interpretation.

The doctor's determination of prolonged strangulation as the cause of Linda Lampkin's death posed a major challenge for the defence because it suggested that Fitton had throttled and killed the victim in the course of committing rape.[44] Because the definition of constructive murder applied regardless of whether death was intended, many critics considered it unjust.[45] The Crown's opening statement and McLean's autopsy report connected the strangulation to the rape as Fitton's attempt to facilitate and cover up the crime. Aware that his client faced the death sentence if convicted under section 202, Humphrey repeatedly minimized the injury on the deceased's neck (calling it a superficial "brush burn") just as he suggested the injuries to the victim's genitals were normal for a virgin.[46] After all, every married man on the jury knew that initial intercourse with females usually produced bleeding. The defence's anodyne constructions arose from Humphrey's attempt to set up a verdict of manslaughter, not murder, but they were difficult to square with the redacted photo of the victim's deeply abraded neck and the postmortem evidence of her profound injuries and ruptures.

SHE DIDN'T BREATHE NO MORE

The Crown presented numerous witnesses who affirmed that Fitton was no stranger to Linda Lampkin, and several said they saw her at his truck, talking to him on the evening of January 18. Fitton's employers confirmed he arrived back late after completing his shift that night. And the pathologist stated she had been raped and strangled. But the prosecution for murder also depended on the judge's acceptance that the defendant had confessed to killing the victim and that his police statement had been voluntary. When first questioned, Fitton denied he had clapped eyes on the victim the night she died, and the police typed up his account in "a form of a statement" without recording any questions or answers. Detectives also issued "no caution of any kind" before they set out and found evidence that contradicted their suspect's claims. When they confronted Fitton and accused him of lying, he changed his story and gave them a second recorded statement. He confessed he had picked up Linda Lampkin on the evening of January 18 and had

'I KILLED LINDA'
FITTON STATEMENT
THE TELEGRAM
Night
Final Sports – Markets

Fitton's confession, Toronto *Telegram,* April 25, 1956. Justice Treleaven's admission of Robert Fitton's statement to police into evidence was a coup for the Crown but also a lifeline for the defence.

"intercourse" with the girl in his truck. But when she started "kibbitzing around," he "lost his head" and grabbed her by her scarf. Suddenly, she "went limp. She didn't breathe no more."[47]

Argument and counterargument over the admissibility of these statements consumed a two-hour voir dire, during which detectives told the court how they had obtained Fitton's confession. They claimed they pulled out a caution sheet and read out the formal charge of murder immediately after Fitton said the victim died at his hands. After his second statement, the detectives posed several follow-up questions, and they asked him to confirm the document's accuracy, which he did with his signature. The Crown wanted the statement in; the defence wanted it out. Yet the confession was not entirely damning, since Fitton stated the girl had asked to go for a ride – she was a willing pickup. He also claimed she had "started necking" and pestered him for more sex. The voir dire ended with the judge's decision that Fitton's confession was "admissible as a voluntary statement within the rules or the regulations covering admissibility of evidence of this kind."[48] But this did not sink the defence's boat. By referring selectively to his client's statement, Humphrey could keep floating his client's exculpatory claims – that the killing had been accidental and the intercourse a consensual act.

Humphrey did not object to the way detectives had obtained Fitton's second statement, but he was adamant that the judge exclude Fitton's conversations with the police after his initial court appearance. The defence asserted that detectives had improperly questioned the accused about the disposal of Linda Lampkin's wallet when they drove him from City Hall to the Don Jail. In a repetition of his objection to the morgue pictures, Humphrey referenced *Lizotte* to contend that the accused's responses to police after his remand had no probative value.[49] In fact, the only thing Fitton had said to police when they asked why he didn't reveal the wallet's location was, "I got my reasons."[50] In any event, it was sharp-minded police work, not the defendant's disclosures, that led a constable to discover the wallet, wedged into a sewer grate near Fitton's truck garage and emptied of money. Consequently, the defence stated it would be "very, very prejudicial" for the jury to learn what Fitton had said because they might conclude that robbery was the motive.[51]

On this matter, Justice Treleaven ruled in favour of the defence: nothing Fitton told police after he'd been arrested, fingerprinted, and photographed was admissible, aside from his directions to police to indicate where each event had occurred on the night Linda Lampkin had died. Furthermore, the offence of robbery should not be "dragged into this at all," since theft was not a part of the Crown's theory.[52] Arthur Klein did not contest the decision, since the wallet, discovered so close to Fitton's workplace, tied the defendant to the disposal of the victim's body. But Klein's "learned friend" had other uses in mind for Linda Lampkin's wallet, which contained photographs and notes he could use to piece together a picture of a sexually promiscuous and dishonest teenager.

CHARACTER ON TRIAL

Once the admissibility of key Crown evidence was sorted, the jury was recalled and a parade of police officers stepped in and out of the witness box, explaining how they had solved the crime and charged the culprit. Klein had the easier job. He took each police witness through the part he had played, and he carefully established, for the benefit of the jury, that no threats or inducements had been made to obtain Fitton's confession. When Humphrey cross-examined members of the force, he was respectful, almost conversational, in contrast to his caustic questioning of the Crown's pathologist. This friendly style diverted the police from the evidence against the defendant and led them to articulate his positive qualities.

The first detective cross-examined was the man who had turned up at Fitton's garage to inform him the police were investigating Linda Lampkin's murder. Although Fitton gave them what turned out to be a false account, a serious mark against his credibility, Humphrey asked the detective if he knew that Fitton lived with his wife in his parents' home and had two "baby boys." He followed by asking if his client had mentioned "his father had been in hospital and had been near death a couple of times." The officer confirmed these points, but Humphrey went further, asking how Fitton had "impressed" him. Surprisingly, the officer said he thought the young man had told the truth once he confessed. Humphrey kept feeding the witness positive lines: "Certainly not the type of person you would ever expect to be involved in anything like this? ... A quiet, mild type of fellow?" The cross-examination, more a man-to-man conversation than close questioning, ended with the officer's confirmation that the accused had no prior criminal record and "was just twenty-one."[53]

Linking the defendant's youth, family responsibilities, and good reputation as a worker was central to the defence's strategy, but so was Fitton's lack of sophistication and education. Detective Simmonds, one of the force's senior officers who handled the city's most serious crimes, including rapes and murders, was the authority figure who had confronted Fitton with evidence that contradicted his story. Simmonds was also the witness whom Klein asked to read out Fitton's second statement in court, and he testified about the discovery of the victim's shoe, compact, lipstick, and wallet. Again, Humphrey's cross-examination nudged the detective away from the crime and toward mitigating aspects of Fitton's behaviour. Perhaps the man's immaturity was the cause of his self-incrimination? "If you didn't know that his actual chronological age was twenty-one," Humphrey asked Simmonds, "what would he guess?" The detective couldn't say, but he did agree Fitton "didn't seem a mature type."[54]

Humphrey capitalized on the fact that Fitton had no criminal record, and he called on police witnesses to compare his client with the type of criminals they typically encountered. Was Fitton brash or cocky? Was he "bright or cunning" or "quick witted"? "No," Detective Simmonds replied. Finally, Humphrey asked the detective if he commended Fitton's willingness to assist police to solve the case and piece together the events of January 18. Did he not do "the best he could to accurately relate the events that had taken place?" Humphrey asked. The detective declined to go that far, but he did think Fitton "was endeavouring to co-operate in his own way."[55]

Thus, the police officers who had charged the defendant with murder agreed with the defence theory that Fitton was neither a sex maniac nor a crafty criminal – just an immature but reliable worker and father from a "decent, proper family."[56] Humphrey masterfully established Fitton's good character without taking the risk of putting his client, his wife, or his parents on the stand, which would have allowed the Crown to challenge the defence's portrayal of Fitton as a paragon of solid working-class masculine respectability. Instead, his employer and the police who had charged him with murder – key Crown witnesses – endorsed the defendant's virtues.

When it came to his cross-examination of Linda Lampkin's mother, Humphrey's questions bordered on cruel. He left her father, Raymond Lampkin, out of his sights. After Klein asked the bereaved man about his efforts to find his daughter on the night of the murder and the distress he and his wife felt when their girl did not return home, he had no more questions. Earlier in the trial, numerous witnesses, mainly girls and women, had made disparaging remarks about the victim, but Mrs. Lampkin was called as the last witness, whom the Crown asked again to identify the personal items on exhibit as her daughter's. To see the Crown attorney holding up her girl's torn and bloodied undergarments and other intimate items, one by one, was hard enough. However, her appearance at the trial also subjected Mrs. Lampkin to a lengthy cross-examination that built on other witnesses' statements about her daughter's character, which tarred both mother and daughter as responsible parties in the events that led to Linda's death.

Barbara Lampkin found herself having to defend her parenting and her daughter's behaviour when the defence referred to vilifying witness statements. One of Linda's playmates testified that her parents had forbidden her from playing with the victim because "Linda could go around with boys" and could stay out late. A former teacher of Linda's stated that the victim "definitely acted older" than her age. The woman said she'd been shocked to see Linda in Fitton's truck several weeks before the murder and had given the girl a "rather disapproving" nod after recognizing her. When Humphrey asked the teacher to estimate Linda's age based on her looks and "personality," she replied she would judge her to be seventeen or eighteen but no younger than fifteen years of age.[57] The victim's mother countered that her daughter was just thirteen, and the Crown had entered the girl's birth certificate in evidence to prove it. Mrs. Lampkin stated that she and her husband allowed their daughter out at night only on weekends. Her girl had gone on dates with boys but only ones they knew. The lipstick police found in Fitton's truck was easy to identify because it was an old tube she had given her daughter. "Like all kids, they like make-up when you are going to throw it out," she commented. And as for the compact, her daughter had a small scar on her face and "used that make-up to cover it." To the woman who knew her best, Linda Lampkin was an ordinary girl of thirteen, her chronological age.

Cross-examining the mother of a girl who had been raped, strangled, and dumped half-naked like curbside garbage could easily have derailed the defence. In a 1955 text on legal etiquette, a provincial magistrate advised against cross-examining women because they were too emotional and fainted at the "psychologically correct moment."[58] When Barbara Lampkin was called to testify, she faltered and was offered a chair to steady her nerves, but she withstood a barrage of questions from the defence. At the preliminary hearing, she told a reporter she'd lost thirteen pounds since her daughter was murdered. Dark rings circled her eyes, and her hair was "going grey quite fast." She admitted she was under a doctor's care: "I thought I could never go through with it ... I couldn't hear it all being brought back to me again."[59] Yet here she was testifying for a second time, forced to answer questions from a lawyer trying to keep his client from the noose. When Humphrey asked her if she knew Linda had an interest in Fitton, she batted away his inference by saying, "Her interest was merely friendly." The girl's other interests were the targets of Humphrey's next questions: Had the police not warned Linda "not to get in cars"? Had she ever gone missing? Mrs. Lampkin asserted the police had warned a different girl, and that she and her husband had reported Linda missing just one time, when she was late to return home. The second time was the night she was murdered.

In Humphrey's hands, the personal items in Linda Lampkin's wallet substantiated other witnesses' tales of her immorality and deviousness. Pulling out one of the snapshots of Linda, he asked Mrs. Lampkin why it was signed "Deborah Randall." Was that "connected with boys at all?" Humphrey asked. Her daughter had written "Randall's" age as fifteen on the back of the picture, so the defence confronted Mrs. Lampkin: "That wouldn't be correct, would it?" Now, it seemed, the victim was a liar with a false identity. Yet Barbara Lampkin did not faint at the challenge. Linda simply "thought it was a nice name," she replied, and "all children" tried on different names from time to time – "That is a kid's trick." Humphrey had no further questions for the witness, but he had posed enough to insinuate that a proper mother – one who taught her child to be virtuous, obedient, and truthful – would have reined in a girl prone to promiscuity. "The defence elects to call no witnesses," Humphrey informed Justice Treleaven, and the trial moved to the final stage leading up to the jury's deliberation.

THE PRELIMINARY HEARING'S revelations paved the way for Robert Fitton to face trial for Linda Lampkin's murder. The press had informed the public about the case, but this was the first time that all the players were assembled in court. The Crown had no eyewitnesses to the crime, and forensic analysis of the suspect had not positively identified him as the killer; however, circumstantial and medical evidence connected

Fitton to the girl's death. The main difference between the hearing and the trial was the Crown's use of the statements the defendant made to police. Although the trial judge ruled them admissible, the defence deftly appropriated Fitton's confession to support its theory of consensual sex, followed by an unintended killing.

In murder trials, it was common for the defence to proceed with no witnesses, especially when clients could not afford lawyers' fees. In the 1950s, when Ontario still had a rudimentary legal aid program, expert witnesses for the defence rarely appeared because they were too expensive to hire on paltry allowances. It would have cost Humphrey nothing to call members of Fitton's family, his workmates, or the pastor from the church his family attended as witnesses for the defence. He could also have called the defendant himself, but he was not so foolhardy as to allow a "dim" defendant to testify. Instead, the defence took the safest course by raising doubt and attempting to undermine the credibility of the medical evidence. Through a combination of convivial and confrontational questioning, Humphrey drew out his client's positive traits and insinuated that the victim had tempted Fitton into a sexual encounter that ended in accidental strangulation, folding the case against his client into gender norms that assigned responsibility for sexual restraint on women and girls.

In his opening address for the Crown, Klein sounded a clarion call: the defendant had "raped and strangled" a "schoolgirl."[60] When Humphrey argued that showing a full image of Linda Lampkin's face would prejudice the jury against Fitton, Klein gave ground without a strong challenge. He also agreed to exclude evidence of the police questioning the suspect about how he had disposed of the girl's wallet. To prepare for his closing statement, he would draw on his long service as a Crown attorney, summon up his experience in capital trials, and tap into his command of the Criminal Code's definition of constructive murder. However, the defence's strong performance in the hearing and the trial indicated that Klein had yet to face his toughest challenge – persuading the jury to see Linda Lampkin as a victim of rape and to find the defendant guilty of murder.

4

Condemned to Death

TWENTY-FOUR HOURS WAS ALL the time it took police to arrest and charge a man with Linda Lampkin's murder, but a further four months passed before a jury delivered its verdict. As the trial got underway, speculation over the outcome captivated the public. Outside the courtroom, over a hundred Torontonians jammed the corridor, clamouring to see the drama in person. A reporter heard a man in the crowd say he gave Fitton eight-to-five odds of a conviction.[1] But for which offence? Any canny wagerer who had followed the murder trial would have put their money on manslaughter, and the accused's lead counsel, David Humphrey, urged the jury to reach that decision. As the jury retired to deliberate on the fourth day of the trial, the Toronto *Star* declared: "VERDICT OF MANSLAUGHTER POSSIBLE IN LINDA CASE – JUDGE."[2] The next day, the headlines blared that the jury had found Fitton guilty as charged with a recommendation to mercy.

The verdict surprised everyone, including the Crown attorney, who was convinced the judge's instructions to the jury on the law concerning constructive murder and rape were inadequate and unclear. During the trial, Arthur Klein maintained a restrained and respectful approach to the bench and the defence, but his objections to Justice Treleaven's charge were vehement. Klein also thought the judge should have stated the Criminal Code's definition of "wilfully stop[ping], by any means, the breath" as a form of constructive murder if it occurred for the purpose of rape.[3] When Justice Treleaven refused the Crown's request to recall the jury, Klein protested that his decision undercut the prosecution's theory of the crime. When one juror requested a clearer definition of manslaughter from the judge, the Crown had further reason to anticipate they were leaning toward that decision.[4]

The defence's closing address confirmed that David Humphrey was also counting on the "all male" jury to decide that his client had killed the girl unintentionally and that, in consequence, he was not guilty of murder. Fitton, a married man and father, was "just a dull boy," not a homicidal sex fiend, and he had caused the girl's death accidentally in a moment of shared passion.[5] Thrown by the unexpected verdict, the defence had three courses of action. Humphrey could cut his ties with Fitton and hope that the jury's recommendation would give the convicted man a good chance at a commuted sentence. That was what the Toronto *Star* predicted: "The odds are the execution will never be carried out."[6] He could lead a clemency campaign or urge others to mount one. Or he could appeal against his client's conviction, a course of action that was becoming more common after capital convictions.[7] Following the wishes of Fitton's parents, who lacked the means to pay their son's lawyer, Humphrey prepared to suit up for a second battle to overturn the verdict.

CLOSING STATEMENTS

Over the course of the trial, Klein took several days to lead witnesses through their evidence, much of it dry and tedious. The pathologist's description of Linda Lampkin's injuries and Detective Simmonds's recitation of the defendant's second statement about the night he killed the girl were more riveting for the two hundred onlookers who squeezed into the courtroom. When Klein rose to deliver his closing remarks, he brought drama and emotional weight to his delivery. Almost a generation older than David Humphrey, he had a more paternal bearing in the courtroom, and he used it to remind the men, many of them fathers, of the terror and pain the virginal girl must have felt as she sustained the injuries that led to her death.[8]

Arthur O. Klein, 1964, the year he was appointed commissioner of the Toronto Police | Toronto Star Photograph Archives, TSPA_0060175F

Dr. McLean's assessment of the length of time – three to five minutes – it would have taken to stop her breathing was important for the jury to bear in mind, and he asked them to imagine how "it must have been an eternity for that girl." Without referring to the Criminal Code's section on stopping the breath, he paraphrased it, informing the jury that suffocation in the furtherance of sexual assault was murder, even if the perpetrator did not plan to kill. "Why do you think he strangled that girl?" Klein asked the jury. If they weren't sure, the Crown attorney had the answer: "He strangled her in order to satisfy his lust. That, gentlemen, is murder." According to courtroom reporters, Fitton sat "looking pale and thin [and] stared ahead" as Klein described the defendant's bestial motive. The "act speaks for itself," he insisted. Even though Fitton might not fit their image of a sex killer, Klein reminded them they must concentrate on the evidence, which revealed "what kind of man he is to have committed a crime like this."[9]

When Klein referred to the defendant's statement in his closing, he focused on its inculpatory weight, and he made light of Fitton's minimization of his responsibility for Linda Lampkin's death, defining it as cowardly. This admission did not convey the defendant's attempt to be truthful; rather, he told the jury, the statement was "just an attempt to excuse himself." The police had treated Fitton fairly, and he spoke voluntarily, without coercion or mistreatment. Although the defendant had stated that "he was the man," his tale of "how the girl met her death" did not stack up against the evidence: the victim's ripped clothes, the gashes to her private parts, and the ragged groove sliced into her throat. When Klein referred to Fitton's claim that he had "grabbed Linda by the scarf when she started 'kibbitzing around'" (implying the term meant asking for more sex), he lapsed into ribaldry: "Gentlemen: how many men of 21 do you know who would object to a girl kibbitzing around?"[10] Having ventured into locker room banter, Klein quickly wound back with a sober reminder: no matter what Linda Lampkin had anticipated might happen when she stepped into Fitton's truck, her injuries proved "she was in no condition to kibbitz around." And "whatever he did, he did intentionally," Klein insisted. "It couldn't have happened the way he says it did. Certainly he raped her."[11]

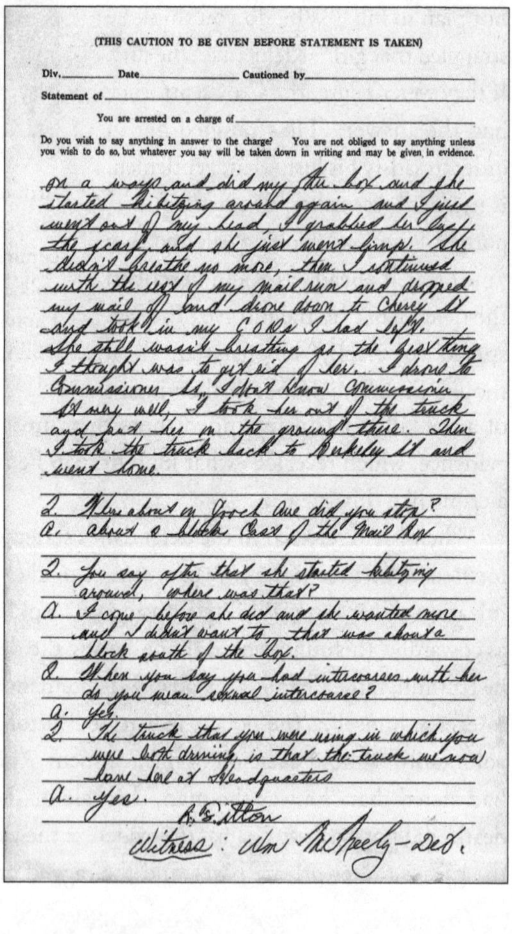

(THIS CAUTION TO BE GIVEN BEFORE STATEMENT IS TAKEN)

Div.______ Date__________ Cautioned by__________

Statement of__________

You are arrested on a charge of__________

Do you wish to say anything in answer to the charge? You are not obliged to say anything unless you wish to do so, but whatever you say will be taken down in writing and may be given in evidence.

on a ways and did my the box and she started kibitzing around again and I just went out of my head, I grabbed her by the scarf and she just went limp. She didn't breathe no more, then I continued with the rest of my mail run and dropped my mail off and drove down to Cherry St and took in my C.O.D.s I had left. She still wasn't breathing so the first thing I thought was to get rid of her. I drove to Commissioner St, I don't know Commissioner St very well, I took her out of the truck and put her on the ground there. Then I took the truck back to Berkeley St and went home.

Q. Where about on Gooch Ave did you stop?
A. about a block East of the Mail Box

Q. You say after that she started kibitzing around, where was that?
A. I came, before she did and she wanted more and I didn't want to, that was about a block south of the box.
Q. When you say you had intercourse with her do you mean sexual intercourse?
A. Yes.
Q. The truck that you were using in which you were both driving is that the truck we now have here at Headquarters
A. Yes.

R. Fitton

Witness: Wm McSpeely – Det.

Fitton's signature on his statement that he accidentally suffocated Linda Lampkin after she "kibbitzed" for more sex | LAC, RG 13-B-1, vol. 1755, "Fitton, Robert," vol. 1, pt. 1, January 19, 1956

In most trials, the Crown's closing remarks follow those of the defence, but because the defence had called no witnesses, focusing on cross-examinations of Crown witnesses, Humphrey was the last to address the jury before the judge's charge. By contrast to Klein's authoritative, fatherly bearing, Humphrey approached his closing as an opportunity to make his client's account of a pickup gone wrong more compelling. This was the theme he had threaded through his questions to witnesses for the prosecution, and he pulled it out in an address that portrayed Fitton as hapless, not homicidal, and certainly not psychopathic. Although he did not mention this in his closing, Humphrey had asked forensic psychiatrist Kenneth Gray, fellow consultant to the Parents Action League, to examine Fitton, and the doctor had diagnosed him as perfectly normal.[12] In the courtroom, the presence of the defendant's wife, mother, and father sitting behind the accused reinforced the image of normality that Humphrey underscored. As he addressed the jury, he described the Fittons's loved one as they wished him to be seen. "Look at the accused. He is 21 but looks much younger. He is of slight build, thin, mild. His fellow workers have testified they were shocked and surprised when he was arrested." At a young age, Fitton had accepted responsibility for the support of dependents, and he had taken on extra shifts, working from dawn to late at night, six days a week while his father was hospitalized. Humphrey could take it for granted that a Toronto-born, Anglo-Celtic working-class fellow, heterosexual and married with children, would appear normal to the jury, nothing like what they imagined a sex murderer to be. "He is not the kind who would ever intend to kill Linda Lampkin," Humphrey insisted, careful to avoid reference to constructive murder.[13]

The defence hinted that considering Linda Lampkin's looks and her sexual interest in Fitton, any man could have found himself in his client's position. In Humphrey's closing remarks, he spent more time raking over the victim's reputation – her eagerness to attract the accused and her sexual self-presentation – than he did shoring up Fitton's. "I do not want to blacken the girl's character," Humphrey declared as he proceeded to sully it. This girl, who looked "more like 17 than 13, made advances to Fitton," and several Crown witnesses told the court she often waited for him at mailboxes along his route. This is what Linda Lampkin did on January 18, Humphrey reminded the jury: she stayed out late after her dance lesson; she paced at the corner of Jane Street; she asked Fitton for a ride; she willingly stepped inside his truck. The defence inferred the accused hadn't just planned to meet Fitton – she wanted to be picked up. Having ridden in Fitton's truck on an earlier occasion, which her former teacher witnessed, the deceased had been the sexual instigator, according to Humphrey. He also told the jury to think back to the pictures in the victim's wallet, on which the girl had written a false age (fifteen) and name. This made it likely she lied to the accused about her age. "Let's face it," Humphrey confided, "Linda was infatuated with Fitton."[14]

The defence's closing remarks steered clear of the pathologist's evidence, and Humphrey was also the last person likely to remind them of McLean's inexpert definition of fourteen as the age of sexual consent. Likewise, it was not in the defence's interest to review the evidence of the girl's neck and genital injuries or her torn clothing. Instead, Humphrey asked the jury to consider the possibility the deceased "perhaps reluctantly consented to what happened." All he needed was one juror – maybe the foreman, who knew Fitton's father through the racetrack business – to take Fitton at his word when he told police the girl was so eager for intercourse that she had "kibbitzed" for more.[15] Humphrey even suggested the "h" in the 4-H insignia Linda had sewn onto a jacket stood for "hustler." According to Klein, such tactics showed the defence was "grasp[ing] at straws," implying the victim was "a girl of loose morals."[16] Yet the defence was under no obligation to prove anything in a criminal trial. Simply inferring the victim was a temptress who had entrapped his client was enough, Humphrey hoped, to raise doubt that Fitton was guilty of her rape and murder.

NOW, WHAT REMAINS, GENTLEMEN

Immediately after the opposing counsels' closing remarks, Justice Treleaven charged the jury, carrying out his duty to instruct them on the law as it applied in this case. He opened, as usual, by thanking the men for their patience. They had listened to forty-three witnesses and spent several periods sequestered while the lawyers argued before the judge over the admissibility of Crown evidence. The judge also commended Humphrey and Klein for their professionalism: "I don't think I've ever presided over a trial where counsel have been so fair and so co-operative and have complied in every way with the best traditions of their profession."[17] He singled out Humphrey for representing a working man of limited means charged with a capital offence. The defence had ably presented its theory that Fitton had not "wilfully, intentionally and by design" brought about Linda Lampkin's death.[18] By contrast, the Crown had presented evidence that supported the theory that Fitton's acts amounted to murder. To reach their verdict on these opposing versions of the homicide, the jury required an understanding of the law to "come to conclusions on questions of fact."[19]

The judge's reference to "fact" was not just *pro forma* since he knew Linda Lampkin's murder had generated a great deal of publicity about the problem of sex crime. Although Treleaven urged the jurors to consider their verdict solely in relation to the trial evidence, he acknowledged, "You must have read about it or heard about it, as practically everybody did." By "it" he meant the girl's murder and Fitton's arrest. "It is so easy to form prejudices or to have one's sympathy aroused," so, in view of this, he asked the jury to purge their presuppositions.[20] Public anxiety over the number and seriousness of sex crimes was at a fever pitch. Jurors might have felt sympathetic toward the victim and her family, but they might also have sympathized with the accused murderer and his hard-luck family. Treleaven himself reminded the jury that Fitton's fellow employees and employers – all witnesses for the Crown – had given "him a good name and reputation." The accused was not just law-abiding but an "industrious worker, apparently supporting his wife and children." Nevertheless, this man was on trial for Linda Lampkin's murder. It was essential that they remember that "a good man can commit a crime and his previous goodness cannot excuse the crime."[21]

Since the nature of the sexual encounter and the cause of the victim's asphyxiation were the principal points on which the Crown and the defence differed, the judge laid out the definition of culpable homicide in the Criminal Code, and he quoted passages from section 202 on constructive murder. In Justice Treleaven's opinion, this was "the crux of this case." If Robert Fitton had meant to kill Linda Lampkin by strangling her, "either before or after the sexual intercourse," the offence was murder. Paraphrasing the statute, the judge told the jury it was murder if Fitton choked her to stupefy her "that he might have his way" and she subsequently died.[22] Treleaven asked for the jurors' close attention as he spelled out the meaning of constructive murder in further detail. If a man tried to commit rape or indecent assault and committed a fatal act to perpetrate the offence, or to facilitate his flight after committing it, the offence was murder, irrespective of the intent to kill. This was the Crown's theory. If the jury decided the accused did none of those things but caused Linda Lampkin's death, which was the theory of the defence, he was guilty of manslaughter. In their deliberations, the jury had to apply this law to the facts as they understood them.

Despite the common law doctrine that the judge and jury had distinct powers – the jurors were triers of fact – judges had both an obligation and the discretion to direct the jury to evidence "material to the main issues raised in the case" and to highlight "any discrepancies in the evidence as to matters of fact which are important."[23] Justice Treleaven's charge reviewed the evidence that supported the Crown's case – that Fitton forced intercourse on Linda Lampkin – but he refrained from using the term "rape." There was no question that McLean's postmortem report was crucial, even though he had admonished the pathologist for "drawing conclusions" about the victim's genital injuries as evidence of rape. Although the judge referred both to the defence's and the Crown's contrasting interpretations of the medical evidence, he found the defence's implausible. "If the sexual intercourse in that truck was voluntary on the part of Linda – or even of her seeking, I think is suggested" (the judge nodded to the defence's theory), he told the jury, he found it "very difficult to reconcile" with the evidence – the victim's torn hymen and perineum, plus her ripped clothing. It would have been difficult for the jurors to forget the opening day of the trial, when Klein had presented article after article of the victim's garments, holding up her torn brassiere and panties while her parents and everyone else in the courtroom looked on. "She had been a virgin," Justice Treleaven quoted the pathologist, without defining the nature of the act that took her virginity.[24]

The judge's charge was the first time the jury heard about the rulings he had made to admit Fitton's confession, and Justice Treleaven explained how they should treat the defendant's statements. First of all, the defence accepted the Crown's contention that the police had acted "in fairness to the accused." As soon as Fitton "blurted out" that Linda Lampkin had died after he grabbed her scarf, the detectives had acted according to the law: they stopped him from speaking further and issued "the usual warning," telling him he was not obliged to say anything further. Aware that he was charged with murder, Fitton made a second full statement, which he signed. This was the critical one, the judge said. It was an expression of the defendant's "honest" attempt to "tell the truth," according to the defence and the police. Justice Treleaven saw it differently – as a "comparatively innocent way" to explain the victim's injuries. Yet he told the jury they could accept the accused's version since all defendants were entitled to the benefit of the doubt: if they believed Fitton's statement, they must find him guilty of manslaughter, not murder. But the jury also had to take McLean's testimony into account. The scarf had been tightened as a ligature, and it had been so tight that he needed to cut it to remove it. How else could a groove have been torn into the victim's neck unless Fitton had twisted the ligature tight for several minutes, not seconds? In the judge's view, the medical and circumstantial evidence indicated that parts of Fitton's statement "simply cannot be true." The jurors were directed to decide for themselves by "bringing to bear the very best judgement, and honest judgement" they had to offer.[25]

Just as the judge had complimented Humphrey and Klein for their fairness, he asked the same of the jury – fairness to the law and to society. In capital trials, judges frequently told jurors not to hesitate in finding defendants guilty as charged. Critics of the death penalty had long argued that jurors preferred to find persons tried for murder guilty of manslaughter out of squeamishness over capital punishment, thereby undermining the administration of justice. Russell Treleaven differed. In a 1952 speech for the Optimist Club, of which he was a long-serving member, he told the audience he believed Canadian juries were prepared to "bring in a guilty verdict" in murder trials whenever they "honestly believe[d]" the accused was guilty. He also claimed he found their verdicts "to be generally correct," and this gave him great respect for juries.[26] Treleaven expressed that belief as he instructed the jury to fulfill their duty to the sovereign and to the public. Although Fitton, he continued, was charged with the murder of a girl, his crime was an offence against society: "Linda Lampkin was a member of that society. She had a right to live. She had a right to live her life in a normal way, and for the normal span of years until that life was terminated by natural causes. That right to live is gone and gone forever." The judge's moving words connected the victim to the community and defined her loss beyond her family's tragedy. If the jury believed this defendant had murdered this girl, they would be "derelict in [their] duty" were they to find Fitton guilty of manslaughter or return a not guilty verdict.

In Justice Treleaven's Optimist speech about jury behaviour in capital cases, he also mentioned that jurors often found the legal distinction between murder and manslaughter confusing. "The fine difference between the legal definitions is often not clear to the layman," he observed.[27] Yet his instructions in Fitton's trial were far from clear. Despite his obligation to explain "how character evidence can be used, and the only way in which it can be used," the judge advised the jury to factor Crown witnesses' remarks about Fitton's positive qualities, elicited through Humphrey's cross-examination questions, into their verdict. If they were torn between murder and manslaughter, they could resolve their dilemma by reference to the accused's reputation: "Just so that even the least little thing would tip the scale, then a man's good character may be used to tip the scales in his favour."[28] The Criminal Code set out culpable homicides committed in "the heat of passion," or in response to insult or sudden provocation, as manslaughter, not murder, but there was no statutory or common law defence of previous good character.[29] Any law student, let alone one of the most experienced Crown attorneys in the country, could have seen Treleaven's charge as

Justice R.W. Treleaven (*centre*) on the occasion of his speech to the Optimist Club of Windsor | Windsor *Daily Star,* May 9, 1952

a prime example of the reason why so many laypeople found it difficult to apply the law to culpable homicides.[30]

Another distinction between murder and manslaughter, which the judge omitted, was the difference in the penalties for the crimes. Because this was customary practice, it was not out of keeping for Treleaven to instruct the jury to reach their verdict without stating the mandatory penalty of death applied if they found him guilty of murder, whereas the maximum penalty for manslaughter was life in prison.[31] Few judges referred to penalties when they charged jurors, whose sole sworn duty was to uphold the law faithfully and to fearlessly deliver their verdict. Nevertheless, in capital trials, judges occasionally informed jurors of their right to recommend mercy.[32] Because these were customary practices, not rules, many defence lawyers thought judges ought to be obliged to inform juries of their right to make such a recommendation for two reasons: jurors uncomfortable about the death penalty might be less hesitant to find accused murderers guilty, and every defendant found guilty of murder could benefit from an equal chance to receive a mercy recommendation. However, some abolitionists feared that a reform of that nature might encourage murder convictions and deter jurors from verdicts of manslaughter.[33] Although Justice Treleaven left out capital punishment and the possibility of adding a mercy recommendation, his references to Robert Fitton's good reputation hinted that the jury might bear that in mind if they decided he was guilty of an offence that carried the mandatory penalty of death.

But first, the jury had to reach a verdict. According to the defence, Fitton had lost his head after his sexual encounter with Linda Lampkin, whose death was inadvertent. Under cross-examination, almost every Crown witness described the victim in ways that made her consent to sexual intercourse plausible, if not her strangulation. At least one juror found it difficult to understand what evidence the law set to prove murder since he asked the judge for clearer instructions: "You read to the jury quotations from the Criminal Code relevant to the case which covered murder. Are there quotations that you could give us covering manslaughter?" the juror requested. Justice Treleaven's reply to the juror was technically correct but patronizing: "There is no specific definition of manslaughter. But I do not think that will trouble you." All the jury needed to know was that culpable homicide was "either murder or manslaughter," and they must follow the Criminal Code's definition of murder.[34]

ARE THERE ANY OBJECTIONS TO THE CHARGE?

After the jury was dismissed to deliberate, counsel had the opportunity to raise objections, and the tenor of Klein's and Humphrey's responses differed from their demeanour during the trial. Despite the judge's lack of explicit reference to the fact that the Crown needed to prove that Linda Lampkin had not consented to intercourse in order for her death to meet the definition of constructive murder, the defence raised no objection to the judge's instructions on manslaughter. By contrast, the Crown forcefully objected to the charge on several grounds. Because Klein thought it favoured the defence's theory, he asked the judge to recall the jury, since they had retired with insufficient instruction. In particular, the judge should have read out the entirety of section 202 on constructive murder, including the subsection that referred to "stopping the breath" of the victim for the purpose of rape. Klein also complained that the judge had not referred the jury to section 135, which defined intercourse with the victim's consent as rape if her consent had been "extorted by threats or fear of bodily harm." Treleaven rejected the Crown attorney's objection, but Klein persisted. The judge's failure to draw the jury's attention to section 135 gave undue support to the defence's theory that Linda Lampkin "did consent to some advance on his part in the first place and only withdrew her consent or objected after the act was underway and she found it was causing her some pain or injury."[35] Furthermore, the judge should have informed the jury of section 230, which referred to any form of assault "without the consent of another person or with consent" where it was obtained by any "threat, gesture or the application of force." At this point, the judge grew prickly and knocked Klein down a notch: "Do you think I didn't make it plain?" That admonition made it clear that the Crown attorney had come up empty with his shopping list of statutes.

Having observed the judge sweep aside the Crown's objections, the defence ventured more diffidently to suggest the charge should have put the defence's theory more forcefully. In Humphrey's "humble view," his client not only had no intention to kill Linda Lampkin, but her death had occurred *after* "sexual relations" took place, which he claimed the postmortem report indicated. The defence contended this sequence conflicted with the definition of constructive murder in section 202. Humphrey also objected to Treleaven's review of the pathologist's evidence because he thought the judge had endorsed McLean's opinion that those "relations" had been forced. But Treleaven also stopped Humphrey short. He had deliberately not used the word "rape" in his charge, and the jury had heard Humphrey's strong objections to the doctor's interpretation of Linda Lampkin's genital injuries. The seasoned judge also offered the defence some advice about charging juries: "The more technical you become, the more, I think you get away from the real issue."[36]

Although the defence was content with the judge's decision not to recall the jury, the Crown attorney was still aggrieved over the judge's sketchy instructions on constructive murder. As he saw it, Treleaven should have rejected the defence's suggestion that the defendant's lack of "intent to cause death" ruled out finding Fitton guilty of murder, and Klein kept hammering that point to the judge. Again, Treleaven refused to recall the jury, because recharging them on the clause that referred to "stopping the breath" would "stick out to the prejudice of the accused." Yet again, Klein counterpunched: to refer to that section would simply state the law, which was critical because "the whole theory of the Crown rests on that point." Although the judge conceded he had planned to read that section in his charge, he concluded that it "wouldn't make a particle of difference" to the jury. Klein was exasperated with the judge's decision since he anticipated the jury would find Fitton guilty of manslaughter due to their ignorance of the law. "That would be the end of any theory of murder," the Crown attorney complained sourly. But Justice Treleaven's word was final: the jury would deliberate under his instructions.[37]

SENTENCED TO HANG

The legal technicalities debated on the morning of April 27 were followed by the announcement that the jury had reached their verdict. "The courtroom was hushed and tense as the jury filed in," a *Star* reporter commented.[38] The man chosen as foreman averted his eyes from the accused and his counsel. When he stood to deliver the jury's verdict, the foreman seemed rattled and uncertain: "Charged as murder with a recommendation of mercy."[39] Justice Treleaven was confused. Did he mean to say the jury found Fitton guilty as charged? The foreman's slip was understandable, considering the emotional intensity of the moment. Yet it was another hint that the jury had struggled to distinguish between the charge – murder – and manslaughter, the defence's theory. David Humphrey exercised his right to request a poll to flush out any possible disagreement, but a scene at the front of the courtroom erupted. Despite the judge's usual warning – that members of the public must restrain themselves when the verdict was announced – Fitton's wife, Florence, shrieked, burst into tears, and stumbled out of the courtroom, her sobbing still audible from the anteroom.[40] While this scene unfolded, her husband stood stiff and upright, clenching his fists, as each juror stated "guilty" to the charge of murder.[41]

In an enactment of a centuries-old ceremony, Justice Treleaven donned a black cap and intoned the sentence of death. He prefaced his solemn words ("that you be hanged by the neck until you are dead") by saying he had "no choice in a matter of this kind." That matter, as he delicately put it, was the mandatory sentence of death. The judge closed by offering Fitton the conventional wish, that "God have mercy on your soul." The jury had articulated their own wish that earthly powers grant mercy to the man by commuting his death sentence. However they had come to their decision in the jury room, their deliberations were private, and observers could only speculate. The judge agreed with their verdict and added, "I don't see how, on the evidence you could have arrived at any other verdict." The jury had dutifully performed their role, Treleaven thought, and he thanked them for "what must have been an unpleasant task."[42] The next task the law set for the judge was the submission of his trial report "forthwith" to the minister of justice, whose administrators assembled capital case files.[43] As he set the execution date six weeks hence, on July 10, the judge assured the jury he would report their recommendation "to the proper authorities."[44] Fitton was to be hanged unless an appeal overturned the verdict or the executive commuted his sentence.

Fitton's family was desperate to stop the law from taking its course, and they favoured an appeal to grant their condemned loved one a new trial. Florence Fitton was too distraught to speak at the trial's close, but Fitton's mother and father both insisted the verdict was unjust. Outside the courtroom, clutching a handkerchief to daub her eyes, Pearl Fitton vowed the family would sell the house to fund an appeal for her son. Her husband, William, collapsed and was helped to his feet. "I wish I could take his place," he cried out. He, too, pledged to save his son from the infamy of a murder conviction. "He's been called every name under the sun but he's my boy and I'll fight this to the end," he swore to a reporter from the *Telegram* who interviewed the couple after the family returned home.[45] Several neighbours who knew the Fittons thought they should strike up a clemency campaign, but Pearl Fitton told them a new trial was more appropriate, since "the judge didn't give the jury any other choice than to bring in murder."[46] Clemency petitioners also contacted David Humphrey, who wished them well but informed them a plea for mercy would only "back up an appeal." From the moment the verdict was announced Humphrey decided to proceed through the courts. He agreed with his client's mother, and he was nearly as blunt as she when he talked to reporters about the startling verdict. Justice Treleaven's charge did not fully present the defence's theory, Humphrey told the press, and he had not properly instructed the jury on the question of intent to murder.[47]

Linda Lampkin's parents' reaction to the verdict differed from that of Fitton's supporters. After Mrs. Lampkin endured swingeing questioning by the defence the couple left town with their remaining daughter, leaving two seats empty in the courtroom for avid onlookers to occupy. When the jury found Fitton guilty of their daughter's murder, a reporter telephoned Raymond Lampkin for his response. He replied that he and his wife were "satisfied that justice has been done," and in their opinion, the judge and jury had given Fitton "a fair trial: that was that." While the condemned man's wife and parents still held out hope that an appeal against the verdict might save their loved one, the Lampkins wished for it all to be over. "When we lost our daughter that was the end for us."[48]

IN ROBERT FITTON'S TRIAL, the odour of victim complicity lingered over Linda Lampkin's reputation like cheap perfume, but it was not strong enough to deter the jury from delivering a verdict that defied expectations: guilty as charged. Back at the opening of York County's April Assizes, the first man the grand jury had committed to trial claimed he had killed his wife accidentally during an argument, and in that trial, the jury took five hours before they found the man guilty of manslaughter, for which the judge sentenced him to ten years in prison.[49] This was the verdict most common in murder trials. In Fitton's trial, the jury deliberated for just over four hours, including a lunch break. Despite their foreman's jitteriness, he managed to confirm the jury found the defendant guilty of murder, not manslaughter, defying the prediction of seasoned court watchers, who would have lost money if they had wagered along with the spectators at Fitton's trial.[50]

The defence's closing statement showed Humphrey had also bet on manslaughter. He did his best to boost his client's chances by bringing out the man's good qualities without risking presenting witnesses for the defence. Were it not for this criminal charge, the defendant was a model citizen, and no one, not even the detectives assigned to Linda Lampkin's murder, had a bad word to say about the "boy." Humphrey set up a contrast between the defendant's character and the victim's. As one of the experts the Parents Action League enlisted to advise on the problem of sex criminals, Humphrey knew that Linda Lampkin neither looked nor behaved like the other girls recently victimized in and around Toronto by unidentified sex killers, and he surmised the men on the jury could see that difference. The jury had reached the wrong conclusion, and Humphrey, assisted by co-counsel and expert advisers, prepared to go into battle to set it right.

According to Justice Treleaven, optimistic advocate of jury trials, the Crown's evidence made it impossible to imagine how the jury could have reached a different verdict. Arthur Klein's full-bore objection to the judge's inadequate instruction on constructive murder proved unwarranted. Humphrey's comparatively mild objection to the charge and his acceptance of the judge's admission of Fitton's statement provided an uncertain platform for an appeal, and he had limited time to transform the points of law that appeared to disadvantage his client into arguments that would convince appellate court judges to set aside the jury's verdict.

5

Contesting the Confession

IN JUNE 1956, A David and Goliath contest, initiated by the aptly named David Humphrey, took place before the justices of the Ontario Court of Appeal. Despite his inexperience in capital appeals, Humphrey and his allies came up with stones to sling. The date the judge set for Fitton's execution – July 10 – allowed six weeks to file a formal notice of appeal.[1] The first hurdle to be cleared was the court's agreement to hear it, but the man selected to represent the Crown was a titan of the bar: William B. Common, Queen's counsel and Ontario's director of public prosecutions. By 1956, Common had two decades of experience arguing before the Court of Appeal and the Supreme Court.[2] As the appellant and respondent prepared their arguments, Fitton remained in the "death cell" in Toronto's Don Jail, where he read comic books and detective magazines.[3] On June 25, the condemned man received good news: the Ontario Court of Appeal had quashed Fitton's conviction and ordered a new trial. The biblical tale played out.

During the trial, Humphrey had not objected to either statement's admission; in fact, the defence had relied on Fitton's statement that the unintended strangulation followed consensual intercourse. Despite this, one of the country's leading experts in criminal law and procedure, G. Arthur Martin, plus Arthur E. Maloney, veteran defender of accused murderers and a barrister who frequently argued appeals on their behalf, advised Humphrey to contest the confession's admission. Maloney provided Humphrey further assistance by lending him one of his juniors, John G.J. "Archie" O'Driscoll.[4] The court found Justice Treleaven had erred through his misdirection and non-direction of the jury on rape and murder, and the majority also determined the Crown had not established the voluntary nature of the accused's second statement. Although the five-judge panel was split on the admissibility of Fitton's confession, and one judge dissented on that basis, the appellants convincingly argued that the judge in Fitton's trial had not fairly presented the defence's theory.

For a brief moment, the Court of Appeal set the convicted murderer on a brighter course by providing the prospect, if retried, of a conviction for manslaughter and a prison sentence, not the death sentence. However, Fitton's release from the death cell was tentative because the Criminal Code allowed the provincial attorney general to appeal split decisions to the Supreme Court if the dissent concerned a matter of law.[5] In Fitton's appeal, disagreement over the distinction between matters of law and fact surfaced when the judges applied it to the confession.[6] Some critics, such as Arthur Maloney, thought the recently revised Criminal Code should have expanded the right to appeal to questions of fact, but they were considering the rules from the point of view of defendants' rights.[7] The same rules allowed the Crown to seek leave to appeal against the Court of Appeal's decision to set the verdict aside, leaving the defence's victory tentative.

APPEALING CAPITAL CONVICTIONS

By comparison with England and many US states, Canada was a laggard in allowing appeals from criminal convictions.[8] Few Canadians aside from lawyers and judges connected to appellate courts gave any thought to the laws respecting criminal appeals, but Wilbert Coffin's conviction for murder in 1954 changed that. The Quebec case became national news because many prominent critics believed the verdict was unjust and tainted by political interference before, during, and after the trial. After the Court of Appeal of Quebec upheld Coffin's conviction, despite gross violations of fairness to the accused, a single judge of the Supreme

Court refused leave to appeal.[9] Sensing a miscarriage of justice, Arthur Maloney called on the minister of justice to act on a section of the code, rarely applied, to refer the case to the Supreme Court. Stuart Garson, the minister, granted Maloney's request, but the majority decided they would have dismissed the appeal had they granted leave to argue it.[10] The federal Cabinet had the discretion to commute Coffin's sentence, but they declined to exercise it.[11] Maloney's failure to save Coffin, a man he was sure was innocent, did not deter him from supporting Humphrey's appeal.[12] No matter how confident Fitton's defence team felt as they crafted their arguments, Coffin's execution on February 10, 1956, was a repellent reminder that dire consequences awaited their client if the Crown prevailed.

An elaborate and shifting set of rules governed criminal appeals under Canada's iterations of the Criminal Code in the first half of the twentieth century.[13] The great majority of decisions by the Court of Appeal in criminal matters concerned sentences.[14] For instance, trial court judges who sentenced convicted rapists to a period of imprisonment had the option to add whipping to the penalty. Prior to the code's revision in 1954, a judge could also sentence a man convicted of rape to death, but that punishment was not mandatory, and any man sentenced to be hanged for rape could appeal on that basis. Another sentence that was appealable was the criminal sexual psychopath sentencing provision, introduced in 1948, because it was up to the trial judge, on the advice of experts, to add an indeterminate sentence on top of a fixed term (and possibly whipping), as both proponents and critics of the statute complained.[15] Murder was different. Capital punishment was the penalty fixed by law, and persons convicted of murder had no legal right of appeal against the death sentence.

The Criminal Code that came into force in 1955 defined the grounds under which appeal courts could grant leave to appeal against verdicts, including murder convictions. Appeals could be argued on questions of law alone, fact alone, or mixed questions of law and fact; however, courts could also grant leave to appeal on "any ground of appeal." When courts heard appeals, they could dismiss them and affirm the verdict; however, if a court found in the appellant's favour, it could quash the conviction and either order a new trial, direct a verdict of acquittal, or substitute a verdict "that in its opinion should have been found."[16] The substitution of verdicts was rare, but in 1938, the Ontario Court of Appeal directed an acquittal for a man convicted of the rape and murder of a thirteen-year-old girl. In that case, Arthur Maloney's older brother, James, represented the accused, and he successfully argued that the trial judge had erred in admitting unsworn statements.[17] William Common's senior colleague was the Crown lawyer who had failed to sustain the accused sex killer's conviction in 1938, but by 1956 there was no question who would represent the Crown as the respondent in Fitton's appeal.[18]

Although appeals against conviction could be considered on multiple grounds, courts of appeal had the power to disallow appeals if errors appeared of little consequence. When Common and the chief justice of Ontario, J.A. Hope, appeared before the special joint committee on the death penalty, they concurred that each appellant "gets fair play and the utmost fair play."[19] Hope went further, stating that "every consideration possible, which one could dream of, is given the accused," especially anyone condemned to death. Although the Criminal Code of 1955 provided wide scope for appeals, Justice Hope set out three principal grounds for appeal in his experience: the evidence did not reasonably support the jury's verdict, the trial judge had misdirected the jury or failed to direct it (non-direction) on an essential point of law, or the judge had made an improper ruling on the admissibility of evidence. Beyond that, courts could grant leave to appeal if they believed "on any ground there was a miscarriage of justice."[20] In Ontario, at least, Hope said the court allowed appeals whenever the tribunal considered that errors at trial amounted to injustice toward the accused. Yet, notwithstanding errors or irregularities in the conduct of a trial, courts could also disallow any appeal if it decided there was "no substantial wrong or miscarriage of justice."[21] Applied in the Fitton case, these rules set the field of play for Humphrey and O'Driscoll to pitch their appeal: the judge had erred, and those errors were sufficiently grave that their client had been unfairly convicted of murder.

TO ERR IS HUMAN

The man who sentenced Robert Fitton to death, Justice Russell W. Treleaven, was no hanging judge. From his appointment to the High Court in 1945 up to Fitton's trial in April 1956, he presided over nine capital trials: four were convicted as charged, two were executed, and two were granted commuted sentences. Aside from these cases, one of Treleaven's murder trials ended with an acquittal, and in four others, the jury found defendants charged with murder guilty of manslaughter. Appeals against conviction were argued on behalf of three of the condemned men, and Arthur Maloney was involved in each of them.[22]

In 1950, Maloney represented an accused bank robber and appealed on the ground that Justice Treleaven had failed to instruct the jury on the possibility of finding the defendant guilty of manslaughter. However, the Ontario Court of Appeal refused him leave to appeal, and Maloney's client was one of the two executed.[23] In his second appeal against a capital conviction in a case over which Treleaven presided, Maloney picked up another trial lawyer's client whose appeal had been dismissed by the Court of Appeal. The Supreme Court of Canada granted Maloney leave to appeal on a matter of law in that case, on the ground that Justice Treleaven had erred when he admitted a confession by the accused and failed to put the theory of the defence properly to the jury.[24] One of Maloney's regular sparring partners, William B. Common, appeared for the Crown, and in this case, he persuaded the Supreme Court justices that the appellant's confession had, indeed, been voluntary. Although one judge (Justice Cartwright) dissented, the March 1953 decision endorsed Justice Treleaven's conduct of the trial, and the conviction was affirmed. Despite the adverse decision, Maloney's client was granted a commuted sentence of life in prison.[25]

Two years before Fitton's conviction, Justice Treleaven's handling of another murder trial cast his judicial competence in a dimmer light. In 1954, two francophone youths (Jean Guy Henaire and Emile Bédard, aged nineteen and seventeen) were found guilty of a robbery murder. In the trial, the Crown alleged the pair had beaten the victim to steal his money, and police testified Henaire confessed he had "made a theft with violence."[26] However, in their joint trial, the lawyer who defended Henaire contended that his client had been drunk and that an older associate had quarrelled with the victim and driven him to an isolated spot, where he was murdered. Justice Treleaven instructed the jury to find the accused men either guilty of murder or not guilty and both were convicted.[27] Two grounds were argued in appeal: the judge had failed to inform the jury that manslaughter was a possible verdict, and he had also neglected to instruct the jury on drunkenness as a defence.[28] As usual, William Common appeared for the Crown, but he stunned the court by agreeing with the appellant. In his opinion, the convicted men deserved either a new trial or substituted convictions for manslaughter because Justice Treleaven's charge had misdirected the jury. "CROWN ADMITS JUDGE WRONG," the Toronto *Star* reported on April 26, 1954.[29] The Court of Appeal followed Common's advice and sentenced Bédard and Henaire to eight years in prison for manslaughter. According to the Clerk of the Court, the decision was "very unusual," and he could not recall a similar case."[30]

The Crown's admonition of Justice Treleaven raised eyebrows in legal circles, and it boosted hope in Fitton's defence camp that the Court of Appeal might use its power to rectify the judge's similar errors in their case. Before they filed leave to appeal, David Humphrey and Archie O'Driscoll checked in with their brains trust: Maloney and Martin. The "only thing that we could see as a defence," Humphrey later recalled, "was in the statement that Fitton had made to the police, which the Crown was very anxious to put in because it cemented the fact that he was the person who murdered her."[31] Arthur Martin, doyen of criminal law, reassured Humphrey it was ethical to present that argument, despite the defence's lukewarm challenge in voir dire to the statement's admission. As O'Driscoll prepared the argument that Fitton's second statement to police was not voluntary, Humphrey beefed up the objections he had raised at trial to argue the judge had not properly presented the defence's theory. After Fitton's defenders submitted their notice of request for leave to appeal, the court granted leave.[32]

Justice Treleaven's charge to the jury had hinted that an appeal might follow their decision, should they find Fitton guilty. Whether he spoke out of false modesty or the bitter memory of his dressing down for non-direction and misdirection, Treleaven opened his charge "humbly and with much diffidence," and he told the jury he hoped he would not "make a mistake" concerning the law on culpable homicide. Lawyers and judges frequently differed in "interpretations of the law," but the jury's job was to consider the facts. "It is very seldom that those decisions [by juries] are disturbed in any way," he commented. Treleaven's recent experience was a reminder that judges' decisions in criminal trials were the ones challenged in appeals, not jurors' verdicts. He advised the jury that "should [he] make a mistake as far as the law is concerned, there is another court to which the matter will be referred and any question of law can be straightened out there." "To err is human," he quipped.[33]

When the special joint committee investigating the death penalty consulted Justice Hope of the Ontario Court of Appeal to explain the role of appeals in capital cases, he made similar remarks about judicial fallibility. Judges, Hope observed, "have all the frailties which go with human nature. We try to avoid them, but after all, we may err. That is why there are all these safeguards after the trial judge is finished."[34] In Fitton's case, two lawyers with scant experience presented arguments to persuade the Court of Appeal to rule as it did in the robbery murder case – to correct Justice Treleaven's errors.

A SUBSTANTIAL WRONG?

In 1956, ten judges served on the Ontario Court of Appeal, and a full panel of five judges heard Fitton's appeal, a sign of the significance accorded to capital cases.[35] It took a long time for younger men to replace the "ancient pre-War judges" who reigned over the first half of the twentieth century. When Justice Hope died late in 1954, a fifty-five-year-old man, Walter F. Schroeder, replaced him, and the presiding chief justice, having served from 1938, was replaced in 1952 by John W. Pickup, aged sixty and appointed directly from private practice.[36] Both men served on Fitton's panel, as did three of their brother judges, each of whom had more experience than Pickup on the Court of Appeal. Although this combination of seasoned judges and recent appointees

The bench of the Ontario Court of Appeal, 1956, pictured in Courtroom 1 in Osgoode Hall. Fourth-in from the left stands Justice Laidlaw, followed by Chief Justice Pickup and Justices Roach and Aylesworth. Justice Schroeder stands at the far right. | Law Society of Ontario Archives

was less ancient than their predecessors, they were not especially innovative or reformist in their thinking. Yet the generation of brilliant defence counsel who emerged in the late 1940s sharpened their awareness of "due process, procedural fairness, the rights of the accused, and errors by prosecutors or by judges in their charges to juries."[37] According to Christopher Moore, when lawyers such as Martin and Maloney appealed against a conviction or sentence, the Court of Appeal took their arguments of judicial error seriously, and their diligence and brilliance set a high standard for the defence bar.

The work of the Court of Appeal began weeks before formal hearings took place in the plush chambers of Osgoode Hall, more august than the shabby city courtroom where Fitton was tried. The panel of judges considered the appellant's memorandum, which set out the grounds for appeal, and the respondent's (the Crown's) argument in favour of affirming the conviction. Like most memoranda, the appellants referred to pertinent sections of the Criminal Code and to case authorities. Appellate Court judges were also expected to read the trial transcript and review the evidence prior to the hearing. Fitton's trial transcript ran to 625 typed pages and cost almost $500 to produce, the bill covered by the Crown. Many pages recorded matters irrelevant to the appeal – such as minute details of Fitton's mail route – although the stenographer, as usual, excluded counsels' closing statements. What mattered most to appeals was the record of objections made by the defence and the Crown at various points in the trial, the voir dire sessions, and the judge's charge. According to Justice Hope, judges studied the full record "conscientiously" to "familiarize themselves as far as possible" with the facts and the law pertinent to the case prior to the hearing.[38]

THE BATTLE BEGINS

On June 19, three weeks before Fitton was due to be hanged, five berobed judges heard the appellant's and respondent's oral arguments. Humphrey opened by arguing, as he had at trial, that the judge should have instructed the jury more clearly to dismiss McLean's testimony that Linda Lampkin had been "raped."[39] This failing meant the jury received inadequate direction on the theory of the defence, that sexual relations occurred prior to the victim's accidental death. O'Driscoll took up less time in arguing that the judge should not have admitted Fitton's second statement on the ground that it was not voluntary.[40] The Crown argued a different view: "No substantial wrong or miscarriage of justice" had occurred, and the appellant had been properly convicted.[41] During Fitton's trial, Justice Treleaven's conduct, including his decision to admit the accused's statement into evidence, had been "entirely beyond reproach," Common offered in praise.[42] The doctor's reference to rape in the trial was an "unfortunate" slip, but the judge had clearly instructed the jury they were not bound by the doctor's opinion. The Crown's evidence proved Fitton had committed "a very vicious assault" and killed the victim to carry it out, which made the offence constructive murder. Common regarded the jury's verdict as proof they understood that the defence's theory of an accidental strangulation could not "possibly be true." In short, Common exclaimed, "The evidence of this case simply screams of intent to kill."[43]

Two of the judges had questions concerning Fitton's treatment by the police before his arrest, but they addressed them to the appellate court veteran, not the novice appellants. Justice Schroeder was troubled that detectives kept Fitton in custody for the better part of a day after he gave his first statement and then proceeded to challenge it: "The police instilled unnecessary fear into Fitton by telling him they didn't believe him and that they had new information." A more pointed challenge to the trial judge's admission of the statement came from Justice Laidlaw, who contended the confession was the outcome of "the police trying to get Fitton to change his story by making a second statement."[44] Once the hearing ended, the judges retired to consider their decision. Five minutes later, Chief Justice Pickup announced the result of their vote: four to one in favour of allowing the appeal based on Justice Treleaven's misdirection and non-direction.

Written decisions of the Court of Appeal were customarily prepared by one judge, and in Fitton's case, the chief justice wrote for the majority. On the matter of misdirection, Pickup agreed with the appellants that the trial judge had discounted the defence's theory (that Fitton had consensual sex and grabbed Linda Lampkin's scarf only to stop her from "kibbitzing") by instructing the jury that the victim had suffered an assault that resulted in her death. Although he acknowledged that Fitton's account "would not appear to have much merit," Pickup also thought the victim's injuries and her ripped clothing did not "prove that the sexual intercourse was without consent." This supposition echoed remarks Pickup had made in a February 1956 decision on a rape conviction, in which he ruled the jury could not regard the victim's dishevelled state and torn underclothing "as being corroborative of the complainant's testimony."[45] The more substantial error in Fitton's trial was the judge's failure to instruct the jury on constructive murder. The chief justice stated that Justice Treleaven should have alerted them to "the vital question: 'Was the tightening of the scarf before, during or after the act of sexual intercourse?'"[46] The majority effectively endorsed the defence's claim, that the strangulation occurred after the "act," and Pickup concluded that the jury, properly instructed, might "reasonably have brought in a verdict of manslaughter instead of murder," even under the terms of section 202.[47]

During the trial, the counsel who objected strongly to Justice Treleaven's handling of constructive murder in his charge to the jury was the Crown attorney, not the defence. By contrast, the majority on the Court of Appeal decided the judge's reference to the content of section 202, oblique as it was, had put the defence at a disadvantage. Pickup stated the Crown had not established that Fitton meant to cause injury to Linda Lampkin when he pulled on her scarf, which made the conviction unsound: "Intent to cause bodily harm is a vital element in the offence of murder under s. 202." The defence's theory was that stopping Linda Lampkin's breath had been an unintentional act after sex, and the majority accepted that sequence. The court also agreed with the appellant that the juror's request for clarification of the definition of manslaughter showed the judge had not provided clear instructions.[48] The majority sided with the appellant on this ground, finding that a substantial wrong and injustice had occurred in Fitton's trial.

The second substantive ground of the appeal – the judge's admission of Fitton's statements – consumed more space in the written decision than it had in the hearing. Plumbing a deep body of law, the majority expounded on the rule, anchored by English common law, that confessions must be voluntary to be admissible. In 1949 the Supreme Court had restated that principle in *Boudreau v The King*. That appeal concerned the investigation of a murder under circumstances akin to the Toronto detectives' extraction of Fitton's confession. In 1947, police in Quebec investigated the shooting death of a man and questioned Gaston Boudreau, a trapper who knew the victim. Although Boudreau divulged he was involved in an affair with the victim's wife, he denied responsibility. Detectives, suspicious, gathered ballistic evidence, and when they questioned Boudreau again, he spontaneously confessed

John W. Pickup in private practice, 1949. | Law Society of Ontario Archives, Fasken Martineau DuMoulin LLP fonds, 2009006–23P

to the homicide. Tried and convicted of murder, the trapper was represented by a lawyer who appealed the conviction.[49] Although the Quebec Court of King's Bench, Appeal Side, upheld the verdict, one judge dissented on a matter of law, and this allowed the defence to appeal to the Supreme Court.[50]

Chief Justice Pickup leaned heavily on *Boudreau* to articulate the majority decision in *Fitton,* and he quoted Supreme Court Justice Ivan Rand at length for his definition of the principle that determined the admissibility of suspects' statements: "What the statement should be is that of a man free in volition from the compulsions or inducements of authority and what is sought is assurance that that is the case. The underlying and controlling question then remains: is the statement freely and voluntarily made?"[51] Pickup also referred to an earlier English precedent, *Ibrahim* (1914), which the Supreme Court of Canada cited in *Boudreau.* The circumstances in that case involved an infantry soldier (Ibrahim) serving under British command, who was detained on suspicion of killing another soldier. When Ibrahim's superior officer asked him why he had done "such a senseless act," the private confessed.[52] Lord Sumner, a Privy Council justice, decided that this question, uttered by an officer exercising authority, did not exert undue pressure on the soldier or place him in fear of consequences when he was already in custody.[53] But each such scenario was distinct.

Although Lord Sumner's definition of voluntariness set some limits on the scope of police power and the techniques of interrogation, the majority in *Boudreau* rejected his appeal. Supreme Court Justice Kerwin thought the mere fact that a detective had issued a warning was "not necessarily decisive in favour of admissibility," yet, at the same time, "the absence of a warning" should not compel the court to rule out a statement given to police.[54] Justice Rand took an equally equivocal stance. On the one hand, he imagined what it must have been like for Boudreau to be questioned by the police: "The arrest and the presence of officers tend to arouse apprehension which a warning may or may not suffice to remove." On the other, Justice Rand warned it would be a "serious error to place the ordinary modes of investigation of crime in a strait jacket of artificial rules."[55] In *Boudreau,* the trial judge properly admitted the suspect's statements. Applied in *Fitton,* however, the Court of Appeal decided Fitton had buckled because detectives had held him in custody and informed him they had evidence that contradicted his first statement. Unlike Ibrahim's major, the Toronto police had abused their authority.

REPRIEVE FOR FITTON

ORDER NEW TRIAL IN LINDA KILLING

THE TELEGRAM

Final Markets Night

Final Sports–Markets

Front page of the Toronto *Telegram,* June 20, 1956. Reports of the successful appeal appeared nationwide through the Canadian Press wire service.

The majority in *Fitton* underscored that the onus was on the Crown to prove that any statement to the police was voluntary. When investigating Linda Lampkin's murder, the detectives should have issued a warning – that anything he said might be used in evidence – from the moment they apprehended Fitton. Consequently, the judge erred by failing to exclude both statements from evidence. The chief justice's opinion of Treleaven's misdirection was sterner than the appellants ventured, and he supported his decision by reference to Rand in *Boudreau,* who had settled that no admission could be used unless it was "free in volition from the compulsions or inducements of authority."[56] The Crown did not affirmatively prove this was the nature of Fitton's statements.[57] The police had compelled Fitton to confess, and the judge had erred in admitting his confession.

Justice Pickup was not known for his commitment to suspects' rights, and he went to some effort in the final paragraphs of the decision to dampen any such assumption. Lest he convey the impression he failed to recognize the duty of the police to undertake "the heavy task of investigating crimes," the chief justice explained he had applied the general rule to the unique facts in Fitton's case. The court directed a new trial for the murder of Linda Lampkin because the police did not obtain a confession according to the rule. Yet Pickup, like Kerwin and Rand in *Boudreau,* concluded by warning that law enforcement must not be hamstrung in their investigation and prosecution of crime. The dissenting judge, Wilfrid D. Roach, took that warning seriously, but when he looked at the particularities of Fitton's case, he thought the conviction ought to be affirmed.

NEVER A PERFECT CHARGE

Of the three senior judges who had been overlooked when the post of chief justice of the Court of Appeal opened in 1952, two of them disagreed with the majority on the admissibility of Fitton's statements, and one, Justice Roach, dissented from the majority. Although he and Justice John B. Aylesworth agreed that Fitton's statements met the threshold of voluntariness, Aylesworth sided with the majority on misdirection, leaving Roach the sole dissenter.[58] Roach agreed with the Crown (the respondent in this decision) that there had been no misdirection in the judge's charge. A jurist who had spent most of his career on the bench, starting with his appointment to the High Court in 1937, Wilfrid D. Roach had extensive experience in criminal law. He was also a trailblazer as one of the first Roman Catholics appointed to the Ontario bench.[59] In trials over which he presided, five defendants accused of murder were found guilty, and none of those convictions was overturned by the Court of Appeal.[60] Three of the men Roach sentenced to death were executed, and two were spared through commutations of their sentences. According to one of his junior colleagues, John D. Arnup (who later served on the Court of Appeal), Roach's attributes made him a suitable appointee to that court in 1944. He was "patient, attentive, polite," and he had "good knowledge of the law and a lot of common sense."[61] Arnup's faint praise applies equally well to Roach's dissent in *Fitton*: while it carried the weight of his seniority, it lacked the gravitas of a brilliant legal mind.

Justice Wilfrid D. Roach, 1961 | Toronto Star Photograph Archives

Prior to Fitton's appeal, Roach had served on two panels that heard appeals by another convicted sex killer, Ronald Sears, in 1946. Having practised in Windsor for many years, Roach would undoubtedly have known about the series of knifings in that city that had engulfed locals in fear of "the slasher." After police arrested Sears, he confessed to two murders and three attempted murders, instigated, he claimed, by his experience of sexual abuse. In September 1946, G. Arthur Martin filed an appeal against the nineteen-year-old's conviction, principally on the ground that the detectives had used heavy-handed tactics.[62] Martin convinced the Court of Appeal that the police had obtained Sears's inculpatory statement unlawfully, and Roach and his brother judges quashed Sears's conviction and ordered a new trial.[63]

After Sears's second trial, in which he was convicted of attempted murder, Arthur Maloney agreed to a request from the court to prepare an appeal. Again, Roach appeared on the panel of appeal court judges, but the circumstances that ended in the conviction led Maloney to an approach that differed from Martin's. In this second appeal, Maloney focused on the trial judge's failure to inform the jury of the need for reasonable doubt over the Crown's circumstantial evidence. On this occasion, Roach rejected that argument, and he mused that if the bar of certainty were set as high as Maloney urged, no jury would ever find a defendant guilty: "Juries ... need not be racked and tortured because of the fact that absolute certainty is impossible. They do their full duty when they bring to bear upon all the evidence presented to them all the mental faculties with which Divine Providence has endowed them."[64]

Maloney's appeal was no match for providence since the decision upheld Sears's conviction for attempted murder, and with that, his sentence of twelve years in prison. A decade after he made that decision, Roach appeared on the panel of judges that heard Fitton's appeal. Applying the same commonsense approach, Roach thought the jurors in this defendant's trial had been morally certain the defendant had murdered Linda Lampkin, and he shared their certainty.

The matter of Fitton's statements to police and their treatment of him prior to charging him with murder raised no concern for Roach. For anyone who kept track of his decisions, his approach to this case, which involved allegations of police coercion, would have come as a surprise. In January 1955, Roach served as a one-man commission into the abuse of suspects by constables on the Toronto force who had roughly handled two men arrested after a rowdy football match in 1954. The officers denied the men their right to consult a lawyer while in custody, and the suspects were held for an inordinate amount of time, Roach found. His report condemned the police: "The suggestion that any detective or other police officer is justified in preventing or attempting to prevent a prisoner from conferring with his counsel is a most shocking one."[65] Roach also criticized the Crown attorney for advising the police to detain the pair until they completed their investigation. By contrast, Roach found it acceptable that Toronto detectives confronted Fitton, announced they were investigating "the rape and murder of a girl," and detained him at police headquarters without counsel for a full day. In Fitton's appeal, Roach thought the suspect had freely answered the detectives' questions. More importantly, the defence raised no objection to the initial statement's admission in the trial, and Humphrey had not challenged the detectives' claim that Fitton had "blurted out" that Linda Lampkin died at his hands.[66] Because the police immediately charged Fitton with murder and cautioned him, they were not at fault, and the judge had properly admitted both statements.

Justice Roach invoked the principles Pickup referenced, and he cited the same authorities on the admissibility of Fitton's statements. However, he dissented because he thought his brother judges were misapplying *Boudreau* and *Ibrahim* to the circumstances of the case. In custody, Fitton told police he had strangled the victim unintentionally after she demanded more sex. He affirmed he gave that statement voluntarily, and he willingly read and signed the statement. Consequently, there was no support for the contention that Fitton "felt under any compulsion or that [his statement] was induced by any fear or prejudice or hope of advantage held out to him."[67] The police did nothing to deceive, threaten, or trick the man. When detectives presented Fitton with evidence that contradicted his first statement, they simply invited his response, and the amount of time that elapsed before Fitton was cautioned (a matter he had treated seriously in his review of the rowdy footballers' detention) did not worry Roach. In his report on that earlier case, he stated: "The police should understand that it is their duty, once they arrest a citizen, to tell him at once the charge on which he is arrested."[68] In their investigation of Linda Lampkin's murder, the Toronto police were covered in glory for charging Fitton with murder.

When Roach turned to Justice Treleaven's charge, he considered it more than fair to the defence, an assessment he made without reference to the Criminal Code or citations to authorities; instead, his dissent was based on his reading of McLean's medical evidence. At trial, the defence had asked the jury to accept a preposterous claim, that Fitton had "sexual intercourse with Linda Lampkin with her full approval," and that after the act was "completed, she was not sexually satisfied and commenced to annoy the accused." The trial judge had bent over backwards to invite the jury to accept the story of a consensual encounter that ended in an accidental death. Roach noted that Justice Treleaven had even stated that the victim might have been a willing, even eager, partner who had "kibbitzed" Fitton to satisfy her – the defence's theory. However, it was also the judge's duty to draw the jury's attention to more credible evidence – the condition of the victim's body, "her torn clothing and the pathologist's evidence as to the cause of death." Roach found the most significant wound on Linda Lampkin's body to be the deep abrasion to her neck. The photograph of that injury was dispositive because it "spoke more eloquently than any words the trial judge could have uttered in explanation of this assault, under either the theory of the accused ... or the theory of the Crown."[69]

The distinction between culpable homicide as defined in sections 201 and 202 of the Criminal Code, the focus of the majority's decision to allow the appeal, barely registered in Roach's dissent. As far as he was concerned, Treleaven had explained the difference adequately to the jury. However, Roach scrutinized the postmortem evidence more thoroughly than the majority. The defence asserted that the sexual intercourse occurred before the unintended strangulation, but Roach thought the evidence did not support that contention. The hemorrhaging from the wounds to Linda Lampkin's "private parts" was "equally consistent with the Crown's theory that the accused was throttling the girl while he was attempting or engaged in the act." Roach agreed with the appellant, that McLean had exceeded his authority when he used the legal term "rape" to describe how Linda Lampkin acquired those wounds. He also thought the judge had been incautious to describe the encounter as an assault. Nevertheless, the evidence convincingly supported Fitton's conviction, and the judge's missteps were minor. Besides, Roach added, "I do not suppose that there has been or ever will be a perfect charge by a judge to a jury."[70]

Compared with the majority's decision, which cited eight authorities and directly quoted passages of the Criminal Code, Justice Roach's dissent skimped on citations and rules to substantiate his dissenting view, and he also skated over the significance of the law regarding constructive murder. This style of argumentation was consistent with his general approach to appellate court work. In 1957, he and Aylesworth spoke at a dinner in Windsor hosted by the Law Society of Essex County in their honour. Aylesworth's after-dinner talk described how each assigned judge conducted a preliminary study to draft reasons for judgment and then conferred with his colleagues. Roach dilated on "the concept of justice [as] the one inspiration and source of all our laws." Justice was not so much a matter of rules, he reflected, than a mark of civilization, which judges were duty bound to foster: "Every law is the idea, carried in the minds of judges and law-making authorities, of what is right and just."[71] Embodying that "moral certainty," which he assumed the jury felt when they found Fitton guilty of murder, Justice Roach dissented because he believed "no substantial wrong or miscarriage of justice" had occurred.[72]

Had Justice Roach sided with his brother judges as he did when he condemned the police for abusing the rights of the accused in the Sears case and the mistreatment of the football rowdies, there would have been no means for the attorney general to appeal the majority decision. "Mr. Justice Roach felt very strongly about the [Fitton] judgement," William Common recalled, decades after the appeal. "He was not a vindictive judge – far from it. He had a great humanitarian streak in him."[73] If

Roach expressed any sense of that streak in his dissent, he saved it for the victim in this case, not the man convicted for her murder.

GRANTED A RETRIAL

News of the successful appeal against Fitton's conviction drew a divided response. Linda Lampkin's father was distraught: "Now we're faced with the ordeal of another trial. It's too bad, especially for my wife." Florence Fitton believed justice had been done since her husband deserved a new trial: "I think he was entitled to one," she insisted. David Humphrey, asked how he felt after the first day of hearings, told reporters he was "nervous over the appeal," but he "optimistically" believed Fitton "would be granted a retrial."[74] A day later, the four-to-one vote in the Court of Appeal meant he and O'Driscoll had saved his client from execution. As for the prisoner, the press reported, "Fitton cried openly when taken from the death cell."[75]

The Lampkins and the attorney general were not the only ones who thought the Court of Appeal had reached the wrong decision. An aspiring Toronto councillor, George Rolland, complained to the minister of justice about the legal "dickering" that led the Court of Appeal to overturn the sentence of a "convicted rapist and murderer." Identifying himself as a "responsible citizen of Canada," he declared that Fitton had "forfeited his own life" when he took the life of "an innocent girl." The decision was dangerous and distressing: "To save him from the rope means to encourage other men to commit similar crimes. To conduct another trial means to impose the horrors of such a trial on the innocent family of the victim, Linda Lampkin, and such an act would be most unfair and unjust to all concerned." For Rolland, the prisoner's "confession to the crime" had been turned into a "riddle in order to provide a little extra business for the defence lawyers."[76] This citizen was wrong on that score since the lawyers representing this client in appeal did not enter the fray for money.[77] However, the writer had good reason to describe the arguments surrounding Fitton's statements as a riddle.

FOR MOST LAWYERS, EVEN veterans of criminal trials, arguing matters of law before appeal court judges was a daunting prospect, particularly when appellants were inexperienced and under-resourced. "The task of preparing a criminal appeal to the Court of Appeal is no tea party," Archie O'Driscoll warned students in a law lecture he delivered thirteen years after he'd had his first taste of appellate work in Fitton's case.[78] Advised by two luminaries of the defence bar who generously advised the lesser legal lights who argued the appeal, he and Humphrey did their mentors proud: the Court of Appeal ordered a second trial, which granted Fitton the opportunity to be tried by a different jury instructed by a different judge. In the meantime, the quashed conviction stopped the countdown on Fitton's execution.[79]

In criminal appeals against conviction, the respondent's task was to convince the court the trial judge's mistakes were inconsequential, an argument William Common was accustomed to making on behalf of the Crown. Despite his failure to persuade the court to affirm Fitton's conviction, all was not lost. Two of the five judges, Roach and Aylesworth, agreed the defendant's statements had been properly admitted in evidence, but Roach split from the majority, having found that the trial judge charged the jury adequately on reasonable doubt and the presumption of innocence.

As soon as the Court of Appeal announced its decision on June 20, 1956, Ontario's attorney general prepared to appeal it. Just as David Humphrey could have pleaded for mercy instead of appealing against Fitton's conviction, the prosecutors could simply have retried Fitton for Linda Lampkin's murder, as the majority decided. Instead, the attorney general armed himself with the Court of Appeal's dissent over a matter of law, and he re-enlisted the director of public prosecutions to seek leave from the Supreme Court of Canada to appeal on that basis. Goliath was down but not out.

6

An Uncommon Appeal

In most criminal cases heard by the Supreme Court of Canada, defendants appealed guilty verdicts or sentences. Although the Crown could appeal acquittals and decisions by courts that quashed convictions or reduced sentences, such appeals were less common.[1] When the attorney general of Ontario, Archibald Kelso Roberts, chose to seek leave to appeal the Court of Appeal's decision to set aside Robert Fitton's conviction for Linda Lampkin's murder, that choice coincided with the apex of intense pressure on the provincial government to take action against sex crime.[2] What message would it send the public if Fitton were retried, found guilty of manslaughter, and given a light sentence? It was also possible a second jury might find Fitton not guilty if a different trial judge were to rule Fitton's confession inadmissible. By contrast, an appeal of the Court of Appeal's decision could be sought on the basis of the dissent and the fact that two judges had agreed with the trial judge – the accused's statements to the Toronto police had been voluntary and therefore admissible.[3]

Appealing to the Supreme Court was a riskless option that wedged open the possibility of restoring Fitton's conviction. Because the Supreme Court of Canada could hear appeals only if dissent in the provincial Court of Appeal concerned matters of law, not fact, appellants first had to convince the court it had jurisdiction (*intra vires*). The ideal man to argue that point was William B. Common, the province's most experienced prosecutor and Canada's leading counsel in appeal.[4] The men who defended Fitton pro bono at trial and in appeal, David Humphrey and Archie O'Driscoll, were rookies, who were under no contractual or professional obligation to respond to the Crown's appeal. Yet, they threw themselves into another round of legal legwork. This time, however, the stakes were higher: if the Crown's appeal was granted, there would be no further legal recourse to save Fitton from the sentence of death.

Jurisprudentially, the Supreme Court's decision to restore the jury's verdict in *Fitton,* delivered on October 24, 1956, affirmed that the police had considerable discretion over the interrogation of suspects but provided ambiguous guidance on the admissibility of confessions.[5] Politically, *R v Fitton* lobbed the mandatory sentence of death from the judiciary into the lap of the federal Cabinet for discretionary review. For Fitton, the Supreme Court's decision reset the clock ticking toward a new execution date – November 21, 1956.

THE SUPREME COURT AND CRIMINAL APPEALS

Unlike Osgoode Hall, the elegant mid-nineteenth-century home of the Ontario Court of Appeal, the Supreme Court was a modernist construction built for postwar Canada. The first sittings in the chambers of the "stately temple of marble" perched "high on a cliff" above the Ottawa River were held in 1946.[6] Yet it was a neoclassic edifice in which black-robed barristers appeared before a raised panel of judges, resplendent in red, each one of them a man from Canada's "founding races."[7] The building befitted the "traditional legal conservatism" that lingered after the war, despite the long-serving chief justice's replacement in 1954.[8] Newer judges and younger faces did not lead to a zest for radical reform, however, and the Supreme Court's 1956 decision in *Fitton* was no exception.[9]

Although appeals to the Privy Council were abolished in 1949, hope for a fresh approach to jurisprudence, unshackled from British precedent

The new Supreme Court of Canada, opened in 1946, was a granite building designed in the classical tradition.

and attuned to Canada's social, economic, and political landscape was confined to the realms of civil and constitutional law.[10] Innovation was also stifled by the regional, linguistic, and religious imperatives that steered prime ministerial appointments to the Supreme Court, nudging "high professional competence" and "mature social understanding" to the back seat.[11] The *Supreme Court Act* set a single criterion for appointees – prior service as a judge of a provincial superior court or at least ten years' membership in the bar of a province.[12] In 1951, law professor and future Supreme Court Justice Bora Laskin conducted a review of the Supreme Court since its establishment in 1875 and he found that just over half the appointees had prior judicial experience and that several were former ministers of justice or attorneys general.[13] Laskin's analysis implied that prior bench service might be taken into greater account as a criterion for selecting future Supreme Court judges, but he did acknowledge that many appointees had been involved in professional societies and universities or had served on tribunals and royal commissions. At the time Laskin wrote, however, only a minority of the judges on the Supreme Court held prior judicial roles, and even fewer were specialists in criminal law.[14]

The nine judges who contributed to *Fitton* in October 1956 reflected federal political priorities over strict merit-based criteria.[15] Chief Justice Patrick Kerwin had one of the longest track records in criminal law, having worked as a Crown prosecutor before his appointment to Ontario's High Court in 1932. In his three years on that bench, Kerwin sentenced four men to death, each of whom was hanged.[16] In 1956, the judge with the longest career in criminal law was Joseph H.G. "Gérard" Fauteux, appointed to the Supreme Court in 1949. After six years as Montreal's Crown prosecutor, Fauteux served as Quebec's chief Crown prosecutor (William Common's counterpart) from 1939 to 1946. His final provincial appointment was to the bench of the Superior Court of Quebec. Robert Taschereau was one of Fauteux's fellow Quebecers. On his appointment to the Supreme Court in 1940, he had no judicial experience, but he mixed his private practice with part-time work teaching criminal law at l'Université Laval. Justice Henry G. Nolan arrived in March 1956 having some judicial service in his background, but only in the field of military law and the prosecution of war criminals.[17] Their five brother justices were appointed from private practice or, in Justice Douglas C. Abbott's case, directly from his post in 1954 as a Liberal minister in Quebec's National Assembly – a decision by Prime Minister Louis St-Laurent which critics condemned as partisan.[18] Like the men he joined on the bench, Abbott had limited experience in criminal matters, but that in itself was uncontroversial since civil and constitutional appeals were the Supreme Court's bread and butter.[19]

From its creation, the Supreme Court was envisaged as the final court of appeal for criminal cases, and Parliament abolished appeals to the Privy Council by statute in 1887.[20] This assertion of judicial authority was challenged in 1926 in *Nadan v R,* in which the Judicial Committee of the Privy Council ruled the statute (incorporated into the Criminal Code) unconstitutional. The Supreme Court of Canada's authority to hear appeals from judgments that conflicted with the judgment of any other court of appeal was *ultra vires,* according to *Nadan,* because the jurisdictional claim interfered with the monarch's

Ernest Lapointe, minister of justice (1921–30, 1935–41) | J. Russell and Sons / LAC C-019104

prerogative to grant special leave to appeal.[21] In 1933, the then minister of justice Ernest Lapointe urged the government to re-enact the Supreme Court's authority as the final court for criminal appeals in keeping with the Statute of Westminster, and the government amended the Criminal Code accordingly.[22] Yet the amendment was more symbolic than substantive since few criminal appeals had reached the Privy Council since 1875.[23] A more significant amendment was incorporated in Lapointe's final days as minister of justice in 1930 – when the attorney general was granted the right to appeal against "any judgment or verdict of acquittal of a trial court" if the appeal concerned a question of law alone.[24] The statute had little impact on the Supreme Court's work, and the court seldom exercised its authority to decide on appeals in capital cases, either from convictions or acquittals.[25] Whenever it did, every such decision was a matter of life and death.

CONFESSING PRECEDENTS

From the mid-1940s, several high-profile capital convictions drew the public's attention to appeals over the use of confessions, and they also stirred up critical political commentary. In 1947, one of Canada's rising stars of the criminal bar, John J. Robinette, represented Evelyn Dick, accused of conspiring to murder her husband. After Dick's conviction for the "torso murder," Robinette appealed against the verdict in the Ontario Court of Appeal, which set aside the conviction and ordered a new trial, as it did later in *Fitton.*[26] The court found that "no caution at all was given before the questioning [of Mrs. Dick] at the gaol, and the accused was not told she was under no compulsion to accompany the officers." In addition, she did not sign a written statement after she was charged.[27] The attorney general could have let the matter lie, but he decided to request leave to appeal to the Supreme Court.[28] The man who argued for the Crown in the Dick case – William Common – contended that the Ontario Court of Appeal had erred by ruling the woman's confessions inadmissible, but Justice Taschereau denied the motion.[29] Tried a second time, Dick was acquitted, and the Crown appealed the acquittal – again, unsuccessfully – although most Canadians, not to mention the Crown, were convinced she was guilty.[30]

In 1947, as prospective revisions to the Criminal Code were being debated, parliamentarians referred to Dick's case and several other notorious criminal appeal decisions to argue that the law concerning confessions required clarification and standardization. John G. Diefenbaker, Conservative MP and former defence lawyer, was troubled that appellate courts frequently mopped up errors made by the police and judges: "When men are convicted of murder and their convictions are quashed on appeal, respect for the administration of justice is undermined." Concerned primarily about the danger of false confessions, extracted by police to solve criminal cases, Diefenbaker identified another danger: "Guilty men should not be permitted to escape because of mistakes made by police." The quashing of Ronald Sears's conviction for a homosexual "slasher" murder in 1946 was further cause for concern since G. Arthur Martin had persuaded the Ontario Court of Appeal that the police had coerced the youth's confession.[31] Whether it was innocent people manipulated into false confessions or guilty people who dodged criminal responsibility because brilliant lawyers argued fine points of law on the admissibility of statements, Canada's rules of interrogation required an overhaul to solve the problem of corrective appeal court rulings.

Toronto Liberal David A. Croll joined Diefenbaker in using Dick's and Sears's appeals to dramatize the "confused and highly unsatisfactory state of the law on this matter." As it stood, he claimed, "there have been grave miscarriages of justice against the person on trial and sometimes in favour of the person on trial." Croll thought Canada should follow England's lead in this important sphere of criminal procedure. In 1907, England had created a special court of criminal appeal, and in 1912 a committee of judges developed rules for the police across England and Wales to follow "before proceeding to interrogate persons against whom there is a suspicion of guilt." Diefenbaker and Croll urged the government to appoint a panel of judges to formulate similar rules for adoption in the revised Criminal Code. But nothing changed.[32]

In Canada, appeal courts and the Supreme Court of Canada as the final court of appeal continued to interpret and pronounce upon the principle of voluntary statements – case by case. Nevertheless, trends in the Supreme Court's rulings emerged through its decisions in the 1940s and early 1950s. Appeals against convictions after trial judges admitted statements given to police without warning tended to produce unanimous decisions, as *Gach v R* (1943) illustrates. This wartime appeal involved a man (Alexander Gach) found guilty in the Winnipeg Magistrate's Court of unlawfully receiving gasoline ration books. Although the Crown had considerable evidence to prove Gach possessed the books, the prosecution of this case hinged on his inculpatory statement. When RCMP officers entered Gach's premises, they told him it would be better to admit he had the ration coupons and to hand them over. Justice Taschereau ruled that the police had "created an atmosphere prejudicial to the appellant," and the court unanimously quashed the conviction because the magistrate had contravened a principle established in British and Canadian law by admitting the accused's statement. Although Gach's offence was minor, the police had trampled over a bedrock dictum: "The appellant should not have been questioned unless properly warned." More broadly, Taschereau continued, the rule set down in *Ibrahim* dictated that "all confessions made to a person in authority, as a result of questioning, are inadmissible in evidence, unless proper caution has been given."[33]

In the postwar period, the Supreme Court continued to turn to British authorities on criminal procedure and to regard British decisions as authoritative, as *Boudreau* illustrated. Every decision in which statements to police were ruled upon cited *Ibrahim v R* (1914). In *Boudreau, Ibrahim* served to affirm the common law principle that questions put by an authority figure to a suspect placed him in fear of consequences and vitiated the admission of his statement, meant to be voluntary. To justify setting aside Fitton's conviction, the Court of Appeal quoted at length from Justice Ivan Rand's interpretation of *Ibrahim* in *Boudreau.* Yet Supreme Court Justice Rand had sided in that case with the majority, who disallowed Boudreau's appeal against his conviction. Based on *Ibrahim,* Rand determined that "arrest and the presence of officers tend to arouse apprehension," but answers to police while in custody were not, "as a matter of law, inadmissible."[34] Seven years later, when the Supreme Court added *Fitton* to its docket, Rand applied the same interpretation.[35]

In *Boudreau,* only one judge – James W. Estey – dissented on what would have allowed the appeal. His reading of Lord Sumner's judgment in *Ibrahim* was more favourable to the accused.[36] In Estey's view, the police obtained an initial statement from Boudreau with no warning, and they followed that admission by subjecting him to a second interview in which they posed questions that abused their power and coerced their suspect. Boudreau's conviction, he stated, should be quashed because his statement was not voluntary: "There has developed a rule of practice that when the police or others in authority have either arrested the accused or made up their minds that he is the party whom they will prosecute then before being questioned he should be cautioned or warned in a manner that will explain his position."[37] In cases where the police failed to follow procedure, Estey thought judges should not admit the suspect's statement into evidence. Justice Rand disagreed with Estey on this critical point. Because the circumstances under which police obtained statements was the determinative consideration, Rand thought the police had acted within the law in questioning Boudreau. The common law principle of voluntariness was a "guard against the danger of improperly instigated or induced or coerced decisions," Rand recognized, but that was a dictum, not an "inflexible rule."[38] In January 1956 Justice Estey died, and his absence from the Supreme Court bench meant that one voice that might have ruled Fitton's confession inadmissible went silent.[39]

A MATTER OF LAW: THE CROWN AS APPELLANT

When it came to defining which lower court decisions the Supreme Court could hear, the Criminal Code provided clear rules, but their interpretation was disputable, as the Dick case showed. Section 597 specified that appeals against conviction were allowable only if dissent in a lower court concerned matters of law. But in the absence of dissent, special leave could be sought from and granted by a justice of the Supreme Court. This rule provided ample discretion for the court to reject appeals whenever judgments in appeal were divided.

This was the challenge Wilbert Coffin faced. After the Quebec Court of Queen's Bench, Appeal Side, affirmed his conviction for murder in 1954, Justice Douglas C. Abbott, a recent appointee with no prior judicial experience, rejected Coffin's application for leave to appeal because he found no substantial issue of law in question in the lower court's decision. Abbott's ruling provoked an outcry, which the minister of justice tried to quell by using his authority to refer the case to the Supreme Court.[40] But not even Arthur Maloney, who presented ten points of law to defend a client in the shadow of death, could persuade the court to consider Coffin's appeal.[41]

After Coffin was hanged in February 1956, the minister of justice, Stuart Garson, tried to avoid another case with the appearance of justice being denied. He introduced a minor procedural change to applications for leave to appeal to the Supreme Court. To obviate the risk of rejection by a single judge, Garson advocated increasing the number of judges required to consider applications for special leave to appeal. In August 1956, the government introduced a bill to amend the *Supreme Court Act* and the Criminal Code by requiring a quorum of three judges to consider leave applications and it raised the number to five in death penalty cases.[42] In the meantime, he brushed aside calls by Maloney and other members of the bar to allow appeals on matters of fact and to provide an automatic right of appeal against capital convictions.[43] As the law stood in June 1956, when the attorney general of Ontario asked his director of public prosecutions to draft an appeal against the setting aside of Fitton's conviction, the Crown had to convince the majority of judges on the Supreme Court that Justice Roach's dissent in the Court of Appeal concerned questions of law, not fact.

In theory, the distinction between law and fact is ontological and straightforward; however, it is complex in application, and the restriction of appeals to the Supreme Court on matters of law made the difference critical.[44] Doctrinally, the facts concern what happened, and however the jury assesses the facts influences or determines a case's outcome; by contrast, questions of law arise when courts apply "statutes, prior caselaw, or legal doctrine" to the facts. Consequently, instances of judicial nonobservance, misinterpretation, or misapplication of the law in trials, particularly jury charges, are law-based grounds for appeal.[45] In Canada, provincial courts had the authority to decide appeals based on mixed matters of law and fact as well as appeals based solely on fact. But not the Supreme Court of Canada.[46] Many defence lawyers, including Arthur Maloney, complained that the confinement of appeals in criminal cases to questions of law was too restrictive since doctrinal distinctions between fact and law had real-life consequences in capital cases.[47] Yet the Crown's requirement to appeal on questions of law alone was equally consequential. If the Supreme Court decided Justice Roach had dissented from the majority on a matter of fact, the Crown could not contest the Ontario Court of Appeal's decision; if they decided it was intra vires, the Crown could find that Fitton's conviction should be restored and with it, the sentence of death.

William B. Common, c. 1954. Common's appearance in the appeal against the quashing of Robert Fitton's conviction was the last in his illustrious career. | Law Society of Ontario Archives, Toronto Lawyers Association fonds, 2022015–058P

To argue that the Supreme Court had jurisdiction, William Common drew on his decades-long experience in crafting factums for the Crown. As a veteran combatant in appeals, he was a polished performer whose appearances in Ottawa were so frequent that he stored one of his Queen's Council gowns in a locker in the building.[48] A year before the Fitton appeal, Common was invited to a forum held as part of the annual meeting of the Canadian Bar Association on "Inequalities in the Criminal Law." One of the topics was criminal appeals, and the gathering was dominated by leaders of the defence bar – G. Arthur Martin, Arthur Maloney, John G. Diefenbaker, and several other prominent advocates of defendants' rights. Although Common considered the panel biased (he referred to Maloney as the "champion of the malefactors"), he agreed with his fellow lawyers on increasing the number of judges required to consider applications for leave to appeal to the Supreme Court.[49] But since dissent in the provincial court enabled appeals, the first capital case appeal the Supreme Court heard after the government's bill received royal assent on August 14, 1956, was the Crown's in *Fitton.*[50]

In nineteen pages, twelve of which covered questions of law, Common concisely laid out the grounds of the Crown's appeal.[51] His factum listed four errors in the majority's decision and presented them as matters of law. The Ontario Court of Appeal wrongly held that the Toronto police had induced or coerced Fitton's inculpatory statement. That court's decision – that the confession was inadmissible – was, perforce, erroneous. The majority also erred in holding that Justice Treleaven did not lay out the defence's theory adequately and failed to direct the jury on the application of the law on murder to the facts of the case. Finally, the Court of Appeal wrongly substituted its "finding of fact for that of the trial Judge."[52]

Common argued that Justice Roach's dissent "meticulously and accurately" articulated his interpretation of the law in line with several Canadian and British civil and criminal authorities, which the majority had failed to follow in quashing Fitton's conviction.[53] In particular, Common's factum stressed that the trial judge should not have excluded Fitton's statements to the police (as the majority held) because failure to give a warning did not render confessions admissible. Even in England, where judges' rules governed police practice, those rules merely guided criminal investigators – they did not dictate precisely how they must conduct every inquiry.[54] According to Common, the Court of Appeal should not have set aside Fitton's conviction since the jury's verdict was not "unreasonable or [could not] be supported by the evidence."[55] Quoting the former chief justice of the Supreme Court, Lyman Duff, Common's factum closed forcefully with a passage from *McCannell v McLean* (1937): "The verdict of a jury will not be set aside ... unless it is so plainly unreasonable and unjust as to satisfy the Court that no jury reviewing the evidence as a whole, and acting judicially, could have reached it."[56] Common concluded that the majority in *Fitton* had overshot the court's authority and violated a sacrosanct principle: the jury is the judge of the facts.

Common's factum fully endorsed Justice Treleaven's conduct of the trial, and he cited passages of the trial transcript to show that Treleaven had fully outlined the defence's theory and explained to the jury the law of murder and its relation to Linda Lampkin's case. Two years earlier, Common had deemed the same judge's conduct of a murder trial so poor that he felt he had to intervene.[57] However, Common complimented Treleaven for the probity of his conduct in Fitton's trial.

The trial judge did not explicitly charge the jury on manslaughter, the factum explained, simply because there was "no evidence which might reduce the crime from murder to manslaughter."[58] To back this up, Common referred to the Criminal Code and a recent English case – *Mancini v DPP* (1942) – which concerned the interpretation of provocation to reduce murder to manslaughter. However, the Crown's factum avoided mention of section 203 of the Criminal Code, which spelled out the grounds on which culpable homicide "that otherwise would be murder may be reduced to manslaughter." This was the section Justice Treleaven refused to read out to the juror who asked for a clearer explanation of manslaughter. And it was one of the grounds on which the Court of Appeal had decided to quash Fitton's conviction. Fitton's defenders, now the respondents, worked to leave that decision undisturbed.

RESPONDING TO THE CROWN'S APPEAL

David Humphrey and Archie O'Driscoll's factum targeted the weakest flank of the Crown's appeal – the claim that the dissent in the Court of Appeal concerned matters of law. Because it was possible to consider the trial judge's application of the law to the evidence as a question of law or fact, the Crown's factum was assailable on that point.[59] The respondents quoted the trial transcript extensively, and they added a string of authorities to argue that the Crown's appeal concerned "not a strict question of law but rather a question of fact, or at least a question of mixed law and fact." One of the authorities they cited, *R v Décary* (1942), was a case in which Gérald Fauteux had appealed for the Crown back when he was Quebec's chief prosecutor and a criminal law lecturer. In that case, Fauteux appealed against the three-to-two decision of the Court of King's Bench, Appeal Side, which had quashed Décary's conviction for national war service violations. As in *Fitton,* there was dissent in the provincial court, but the Supreme Court held it had no jurisdiction to entertain the Crown's appeal because "neither of the judgments of the two dissenting judges of the appellate court discloses a dissent on a question of law within the meaning of section 1023 of the Criminal Code."[60] This was the reasoning the respondents in *Fitton* aimed for.

Humphrey and O'Driscoll also chose to cite an earlier judgment by Robert Taschereau, hoping he might agree that the Crown's appeal in *Fitton* concerned a difference over fact. In *R v Howlett* (1950), Taschereau had refused a motion from the attorney general of Ontario for special leave to appeal against the Court of Appeal's acquittal of a man tried for murder but convicted of manslaughter. Although the Criminal Code allowed the Crown to apply for special leave to appeal against acquittals, Taschereau stated this applied only to questions of law "in the strict sense." In that ruling, he argued this did not cover the admissibility of confessions. The "question as to whether statements of this kind may be admitted or not, are in certain cases questions of law," Taschereau stated, but the issue of inducements by the police "resolve[d] itself to a question of fact."[61] Since a single judge of the Supreme Court could reject a motion for leave to appeal in 1950, Taschereau's rejection of William Common's request meant the Ontario Court of Appeal's acquittal of Howlett stood. The lawyer who had argued against the Crown's request for special leave to appeal in *Howlett* was G. Arthur Martin, who notched up another victory for the rights of the accused. As two of his protégés prepared to oppose Common, Martin may have shared his experience to supply them with further ammunition.[62]

When Humphrey and O'Driscoll constructed their first Supreme Court factum, they placed most of their eggs in the jurisdiction basket, but the respondents saved two for the admission of Fitton's statements and the broader issue of the judge's presentation of the defence's theory, including his handling of the pathologist's description of the victim's injuries. Yet those eggs were cracked by the defence's approach to Fitton's statements in his trial.[63] Humphrey and O'Driscoll reiterated the argument they made before the Court of Appeal – that neither Fitton's initial exculpatory statement nor his written statement had been "free and voluntary." The factum cited *Boudreau* extensively to claim that the conditions under which the Toronto police obtained Fitton's statements were considerably more coercive than they were in the Quebec trapper's case: "No warning whatsoever, of any description, was ever given to [Fitton] until the police had obtained an admission from him." The respondents heaped scorn on the dissent in the Court of Appeal: Justices Roach and Aylesworth had "erred in law" by deciding the statements were properly admitted. They criticized these dissenting opinions because they "shifted the onus on to the respondent to show that incriminating statements given by [Fitton] were not voluntary."[64] Humphrey and O'Driscoll asserted there were plenty of errors in law in the trial and in the dissent that were unfavourable to their client. On top of that, the appellant's grounds were questions of fact, not law. Consequently, the Supreme Court could not consider the Crown appeal.

Many of the decisions the Crown and the respondents cited as authorities in their factums were authored by the men who sat on the Supreme Court bench in the autumn of 1956. For those judges, considering the arguments in Fitton's case was, in part, an exercise in reconsidering their own earlier decisions on the principle of voluntariness and the admissibility of statements to police. But they were not bound by prior decisions (their own or others') when they interpreted the need to protect the rights of the accused versus the need to protect the public.[65] Differences of opinion on that question surfaced in the Supreme Court's decision in *R v Fitton,* but uncharacteristic alignments also emerged among the judges.

THE RIGHTS OF THE ACCUSED

A trio of Toronto barristers – Common, Humphrey, and O'Driscoll – appeared in Ottawa on October 3, 1956, to present their oral arguments. For Common, everything from the forms of address to courtroom furnishings was familiar. He knew the judges personally, and he was a "great friend" of Gérard Fauteux.[66] The two men had been top of mind when the minister of justice, Stuart Garson, appointed an advisory committee in 1953 to review his ministry's management of the remission of penal sentences and the procedures surrounding the commutation of death sentences. Fauteux served as its chairman, and

Common was the committee member who drafted the final text of their report, tabled on April 30, 1956.[67] Several of the other judges, including Justice Taschereau, gave Common pictures of themselves, and former chief justice Rinfret once commented, "There's never been a counsel for the Crown appearing before us like Mr. Common." Later in life, Common claimed, "We established a good reputation for the Crown so much that if I made a statement to a nine judge court in Ottawa, they'd accept it as being gospel."[68] Although Common's record of losses in the Supreme Court makes his boast questionable (as the results of the Dick and Howlett cases dramatized), none of the judges interrupted him with questions when he presented the Crown's case, unlike two of the Ontario Court of Appeal judges, whose decision he had appealed against. By contrast, the novice respondents had a rough ride in the Supreme Court hearing, and Justice Cartwright was the only judge who agreed that Fitton had been denied a fair trial.

John R. Cartwright disagreed with the majority's decision to hear the Crown's appeal, and he also dissented from the majority's decision to restore the verdict. The appeal from the Ontario Court of Appeal's decision was ultra vires, Cartwright argued, because Justice Roach's dissent concerned a question of fact, not law. His reasoning was consistent with his generally supportive approach to the rights of criminal defendants. Called to the bar in 1920 after his distinguished service in the war, Cartwright joined one of Toronto's top firms and appeared frequently for the defence. Although he served as a counsel for the government in the prosecution of individuals suspected of participating in a Soviet spy ring, by the postwar period, his judgments were associated with civil liberties activism in defence of minorities.[69] In 1946, Cartwright represented Japanese Canadians who contested their wartime internment and the extension of deportations through Orders in Council after the war's end.[70] In that decision, he and Justice Rand differed from the majority, led by Taschereau, which upheld the executive's right to extend the deportation orders.[71]

Cartwright's dissent in *Fitton* also aligned with the concerns he had expressed in criminal case decisions after his appointment to the Supreme Court in 1949. In a study of *mens rea* defence cases heard by the

Supreme Court from 1949 to 1961, Paul Weiler found that Cartwright decided in favour of the defendant in every case. Justice Fauteux's decisions landed at the opposite end, and Taschereau agreed with Fauteux in all but two of his decisions.[72] In *Fitton,* Cartwright granted "there may be cases in which the question whether a statement made by an accused is admissible in evidence becomes one of law"; however, he doubted if it could "ever be said as a matter of pure law" that the Crown had fulfilled its obligation to prove statements had been voluntarily made. Consequently, Chief Justice Pickup and the majority of the Court of Appeal were correct to find that the trial judge had erred in admitting Fitton's statements, and Cartwright agreed: this error "was in itself sufficient to require the directing of a new trial." However, Cartwright was the outlier in *Fitton.* The chief justice, Patrick Kerwin, also thought the Crown's appeal was ultra vires, but he found no ground on which to dispute the reasoning of the majority, who simply "read the reasons delivered in the Court of Appeal differently."[73] Common's factum achieved its first objective: seven of the nine judges of the Supreme Court considered the Crown's appeal intra vires.[74]

RESTORING THE CONVICTION AND PROTECTING THE PUBLIC

Adorned in their fur-fringed red robes and perched on their dais, the judges of the Supreme Court exuded authority. For the respondents, the questions Justices Fauteux and Kellock put to them heightened the intimidating atmosphere. In oral arguments, members of the bar were expected to stick to the points they had raised in their factums, but they also had to respond to queries from the bench. Years after O'Driscoll's first appearance, he delivered a lecture for the law society on criminal appeals. His experience as a respondent in *Fitton* taught him that "counsel should listen carefully to questions from the Bench and *immediately* attempt to answer them."[75] Reporters who attended the proceedings described how the judges' questions put the respondents on the spot. More than questions on "fine legal points," they undermined the credibility of the respondents' claims. Justice Roy L. Kellock, who spent two years on the Ontario Court of Appeal bench before his appointment to the Supreme Court in 1944, asked a question that had gone unanswered since Fitton's arrest: "What was meant by the phrase 'kibbitzing around'?" Humphrey was forced to admit he did not know despite his repeated use of the term at trial when he suggested Linda Lampkin had egged on Fitton. But Humphrey tried to capitalize on the opportunity to reassert the defence's theory – that Linda Lampkin had "wanted more" sex and that Fitton "grabbed her by the scarf to 'quieten her.'"[76] Fauteux's question followed, and it gave the strong impression he found the theory preposterous: "You say she (the Lampkin girl) died by accident and in that case the verdict should be manslaughter?"[77] *Yes* was the reply. Although reporters did not describe Fauteux's tone of voice, his written decision suggests it was scathing.

Sounding like he was reapplying for his previous job as a Crown prosecutor, Fauteux tore apart the defence's contradictory position on Fitton's statements, and he panned the notion that Linda Lampkin had consented to intercourse. On this point, all but one of his fellow judges concurred. When he questioned Humphrey at the Supreme Court hearing, Fauteux had already decided the condition of the victim's body and her ripped clothing was "violently inconsistent with any suggestion of consent on her part." In his written statement, Fauteux agreed with Justice Roach that the victim's death by strangulation was not necessarily "divorced from the act of rape," as the defendant had stated and the defence argued. Taschereau, as usual, sided with Fauteux, and he added that the trial judge had properly instructed the jury about "the use that could be made of the expert evidence of Dr. McLean," who had given his opinion that the victim had been raped. Justice Henry Nolan, on the bench for just seven months when the Supreme Court considered the Fitton appeal, highlighted the challenges the investigators had faced. It would be "quite impossible to discover the facts of a crime without asking questions of persons from whom it was thought that useful information might be obtained." Nolan's observation may have reflected his prior experience prosecuting war crimes, but he also found that the defence's theory of consensual sex defied credibility. The jury had properly rejected the defence's theory based on the "pathological evidence ... [and] the description of her injuries, together with the photographs ... showing the condition of her neck and head." Like the others in the majority, Nolan sided with Roach's dissent in the Court of Appeal.[78]

Of the nine justices impanelled for the Fitton appeal, five were veterans who had contributed to the *Boudreau* decision in 1949, including Kellock, Taschereau, Kerwin, and Rand. Each judge, plus the three men appointed subsequently, referred to that decision to decide whether the police had obtained statements from Fitton under circumstances that met the threshold of voluntariness. In the Ontario Court of Appeal, Chief Justice Pickup had relied most heavily on Rand's contribution to *Boudreau* to allow the appeal against Fitton's conviction; however, Rand did not repay the compliment since he thought the majority on the provincial bench had misinterpreted his decision. After he graciously acknowledged it was difficult to interpret "the rule on the admission of confessions," Rand insisted jurists must always consider "underlying considerations material to a determination." When interrogators used or threatened the use of torture, they clearly broke that rule. "Unabashed promises" were also forbidden. But cases such as Fitton's were more difficult to judge because "perplexity arises when much more subtle elements must be evaluated."[79]

In *Boudreau,* Rand had pronounced that statements must be "free in volition from compulsions or inducements of authority." In *Fitton,* he insisted, this did not mean the only statement admissible was a spontaneous one "unrelated to anything as cause or occasion in the conduct of police officers." Since every statement is "willed to be made," Rand reflected, "even the word 'voluntary' is open to question." What mattered most was the "character of the influence of idea or feeling behind that act of willing and its source which the rule seizes upon," Rand stated, and that meant the trial court was best positioned to consider the nature of the suspect's treatment in custody and to assess the accused's maturity and mental state.[80] Consequently, Rand agreed with the majority in *Fitton*: the Court of Appeal had erroneously "enlarged upon" the rule on voluntary statements set out in *Ibrahim* and applied in *Boudreau.*[81]

Turning to the transcript of Fitton's trial, Rand determined the police had not unduly influenced Fitton to make his statements. More significantly, the defence's theory was based on those very statements. The detectives who confronted Fitton at his mail truck garage, who took him to police headquarters, who told him they were investigating Linda Lampkin's murder, and who asked him about his whereabouts and familiarity with her, had simply posed questions "the police might have addressed to any person in the remotest way drawn into the inquiry." Rand conceded their questions had "intimidating or suggestive overtones," but this was an "inescapable" element of any criminal investigation. Furthermore, the respondents' argument that Justice Treleaven should have excluded Fitton's statements was illogical. "Frankly," Rand scolded, the defence had not argued in the voir dire that Fitton's statements were coerced or induced; on the contrary, the defendant's "statement contained the only evidence upon which the defence intended to rely." Rand shot down the final point the respondents raised – the inadequate presentation of the defence's theory – by affirming the principle that the jury must weigh the facts. In this case, the facts had convinced the jurors, after sound instructions from the judge, that Fitton was guilty of Linda Lampkin's murder. "We must credit the jury with ordinary intelligence," Rand insisted.[82]

Among his contemporaries, the Harvard-educated Rand was revered as the brightest mind on the Supreme Court in the postwar decade and as a judge who upheld "liberal views" in alignment with emerging concepts of Canadian citizenship and civil liberties.[83] Although his rulings in criminal cases aligned less consistently than Cartwright's to the rights of the accused, he occasionally made bold pronouncements against the abuse of state power.[84] For instance, in *Cullen v R* (1949), Rand fulminated against the Crown's right to appeal against an acquittal.[85] Cullen was tried for the rape of a seventeen-year-old girl and acquitted at trial, but the Ontario Court of Appeal set that verdict aside and ordered his retrial. Rand objected on principle since he could find no other "common law jurisdiction" that allowed the Crown such powers of appeal. He condemned the Criminal Code for permitting

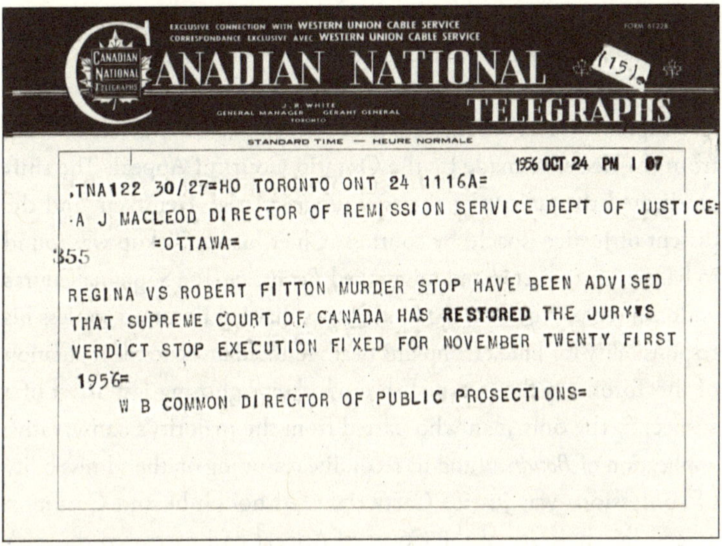

EXCLUSIVE CONNECTION WITH WESTERN UNION CABLE SERVICE
CORRESPONDANCE EXCLUSIVE AVEC WESTERN UNION CABLE SERVICE

CANADIAN NATIONAL TELEGRAPHS

(15)

STANDARD TIME — HEURE NORMALE

1956 OCT 24 PM 1 07

.TNA122 30/27=HO TORONTO ONT 24 1116A=
A J MACLEOD DIRECTOR OF REMISSION SERVICE DEPT OF JUSTICE=
=OTTAWA=

355

REGINA VS ROBERT FITTON MURDER STOP HAVE BEEN ADVISED THAT SUPREME COURT OF CANADA HAS **RESTORED** THE JURY'S VERDICT STOP EXECUTION FIXED FOR NOVEMBER TWENTY FIRST 1956=

W B COMMON DIRECTOR OF PUBLIC PROSECTIONS=

William Common telegrammed the Ministry of Justice in Ottawa as soon as he heard the Supreme Court's decision on October 24, 1956. The word "restored" is in bold. | LAC, RG18-B-1, vol. 1755, "Fitton, Robert," vol. 3, pt. 2

"such a striking departure from fundamental principles of security for the individual." It was "repugnant" for the Crown (again represented by Common) to try an individual repeatedly on the same facts "unless for strong reasons of public policy."[86] The majority in *Cullen* may, indeed, have considered it a matter of public policy that a man who had strangled and beaten a young victim in the course of a sexual assault should not go free on the basis that the prosecutor did not object to the judge's misdirection – the Court of Appeal's ground for setting aside the jury's verdict.[87] In *Fitton,* by contrast, Rand supported the Crown's right to appeal the overturning of the conviction, and he decided the jury's verdict, that Robert Fitton was guilty of Linda Lampkin's murder, must be restored. The wheels of capital justice, clamped over the appeal period, went back into motion. Unless the executive recommended that Fitton's sentence be commuted, he would be hanged for Linda Lampkin's murder on November 21.

THE UNSETTLED LAW ON THE ADMISSIBILITY OF CONFESSIONS

The Supreme Court's decision in *R v Fitton* entailed several role reversals from the decision made by the Ontario Court of Appeal. The shift vindicated the actions of the trial judge, Justice Treleaven, and the dissent of Justice Roach; by contrast, Chief Justice Pickup was found to have misinterpreted and misapplied *Boudreau.* The Supreme Court's endorsement of the interrogation tactics that led Fitton to confess his responsibility for Linda Lampkin's death restored lustre to the reputation of the Toronto police, earned through their lightning-fast arrest of a suspect.[88] The only man who parted from the majority's conservative application of *Boudreau* and its recondite reasoning on the admissibility of confessions was Justice Cartwright. Although he and Common agreed the majority of the Court of Appeal had narrowed the path forward on the rights of the accused, they had different opinions on the implications of the decision. When Common reflected on his role in *Fitton* later in life, he described the decision as a win for the protection of the public because it provided a "great bulwark for those persons who engaged in the investigation of crime."[89] The decision's timing, late in 1956, also capped Common's career since it was the last appeal he argued on behalf of the Crown.[90] Reflecting on his triumph in *Fitton,* he stated: "I couldn't have got a better case for what I was striving for ... to settle the law on the admissibility of confessions."[91]

Yet criticism over the lack of clarity in Canadian rules of evidence and procedure over the admissibility of statements to police did not evaporate in 1956. Complaints that decisions of appeal courts provided hazy and contradictory guidance for the police and jurists persisted, despite the law-and-order orientation of *Fitton.* "You cannot maintain respect for the law," John Diefenbaker proclaimed, "when one court determines that a person shall die for murder and another court determines that because a person happens to appeal he is not guilty of the offence charged because wrongful evidence was admitted."[92] If Diefenbaker was right when he made that complaint in 1947, the Supreme Court's restoration of Fitton's conviction in 1956, after the first appeal decision had reached a different conclusion on the admissibility of his statement, made it no easier for Canadians to feel respect for the law. Common's self-congratulatory appraisal notwithstanding, the Supreme Court's decision in *Fitton* provided ambiguous latitude for investigators unsure about "what course to follow" to elicit admissible statements.[93]

IN SIGNIFICANT RESPECTS, Fitton was more fortunate than most convicted murderers. An Anglo-Celtic man of meagre means, he was represented by two diligent and dedicated defenders who represented him at trial and in appeal and stood up for him after the attorney general appealed the Court of Appeal's quashing of his conviction.[94] They, in turn, had brilliant criminal appeal mentors in G. Arthur Martin and Arthur Maloney. Yet the respondents' strongest shield against the Crown's challenge – the argument that the dissent dealt with matters of fact – shattered. Once that happened, the Supreme Court swooped down on the defence's use of the confession in the trial.

Compared with the intense initial coverage of Linda Lampkin's "sex slaying" in January 1956, reports of the Supreme Court's *Fitton* decision in October were brief. Now the headline read: "FITTON TO DIE NOV. 21."[95] The banner reminded the public that no matter what new experiments might be underway to solve the sex crime problem, the criminal law retained an established solution: death by hanging.[96] The finality of the ruling did not put an end to arguments over the punishment Fitton deserved, however. Doubts over his moral culpability, expressed in the jury's recommendation (with the judge's endorsement) and reiterated in the respondents' factum, found new expression in clemency appeals, drafted in the hope of a commuted sentence.

7

Reversal of Fortune

After Justice Treleaven sentenced Robert Fitton to hang for Linda Lampkin's murder on July 10, 1956, the date came and went due to the defence's appeal against the conviction. Three months later, the restoration of the verdict reversed Fitton's fortunes, and he was taken back to the death cell, steps away from the Don Jail's hanging chamber. David Humphrey could have capitalized on the jury's recommendation to mercy and sought clemency as soon as Fitton was sentenced, but he and his associate opted, instead, for a remedy through the courts. However, the Supreme Court's decision left petitioning for mercy their only option, and Fitton's defenders remained committed to doing whatever it took to prevent the law from taking its course.

Two years prior to Linda Lampkin's murder and Robert Fitton's conviction, the methods and procedures that determined the death penalty's infliction and commutation were scrutinized for the first time. The minister of justice appointed a cross-party committee in 1954 to study three contentious matters the recent royal commission on the Criminal Code had failed to resolve: capital punishment, corporal punishment, and lotteries.[1] The most controversial of these issues was capital punishment. Modelled on the English royal commission on the death penalty, which had just wrapped up in 1953, the Canadian committee heard witnesses who opposed and supported the death penalty's abolition, and it delved into the administration of capital justice by the Department of Justice and the Cabinet. As one committee member jested, they would learn how death penalty cases were handled "from the cradle to the grave."[2]

The committee's final report, published in June 1956, was a letdown for abolitionists because it advocated retaining the death penalty.[3] Since the government was content to accept the recommendation, Fitton's supporters had to plead for mercy. Most sent letters and telegrams to the government, and Fitton's mother poured anguish and rage into her pleas. Humphrey and Archie O'Driscoll used a more formal approach, and it was considerably bolder. Their application (as they called it) included affidavits they had solicited from members of Fitton's jury in an attempt to raise doubt about the verdict's credibility. But each of these pleas had one thing in common: they claimed Linda Lampkin was partly responsible for her death. Adding insult to her fatal injuries, they heaped further blame upon the victim for putting a young man in the maw of the death sentence.

The sex murder of a thirteen-year-old girl in Toronto occurred at a flashpoint in public agitation for law enforcement and courts to take the sex crime problem more seriously. But it also occurred at a time when the administration of capital justice was being exposed and evaluated as never before. What action should follow a jury's recommendation to mercy, especially if jurymen were confused about the law of homicide? Soliciting clemency from the executive was always something of a lottery, but the attempts to reverse Fitton's fortunes a third time marshalled every factor in his favour as they simultaneously disparaged the victim, discredited the judge, and blamed the jury's foreman. The winning ticket was a commuted sentence.

INTERROGATING DISCRETIONARY CAPITAL JUSTICE

Supporters of condemned offenders typically sent letters to Cabinet ministers, the prime minister, and the governor general, sometimes addressing their pleas to "Your Highness."[4] When petitions arrived from political organizations, religious institutions, and professional associations, they included anywhere from a handful of signatures to tens of thousands.[5] The people who processed capital correspondence were clerks in the federal Department of Justice. Its Remission Service was the branch that dealt with applications for parole (tickets of leave), but it also handled official communications and all supplementary material bearing on convicted criminals sentenced to death.[6]

As soon as Justice Treleaven pronounced Fitton's sentence in April 1956, the standard process was followed. The Criminal Code required the trial judge to report on the trial and to send his report to the department forthwith. It was protocol for judges to note whether the jury had recommended mercy and whether they considered clemency warranted.[7] After that point, all deliberations were internal, ending with the meeting of the Cabinet to determine whether the law should take its course. Occasionally, the chief of the Remission Service or a Cabinet minister agreed to meet petitioners in person; however, no petitioner or bureaucrat sat with ministers at the table where they gathered to make life and death decisions.

The seal on the inner sanctum of discretionary justice was partially broken in the mid-1950s owing to the minister of justice's appointment of a Special Joint Committee of the Senate and the House of Commons on capital punishment. Like the English royal commission, the committee ultimately concluded that Canada should retain the death penalty, but it differed by advising the government to keep constructive murder (section 202 in the Criminal Code) as the law of the land.[8] Nevertheless, the Canadian committee recommended several reforms, including exempting youth under the age of eighteen from capital punishment and granting legal appeals as a right for all persons sentenced to death, a reform Arthur Maloney championed.[9] But the majority of the committee's members were content to take the minister of justice and other officials at their word – the review of capital cases for clemency consideration was scrupulous, and executive discretion was tilted, if anything, in favour of the condemned.

One of the reforms the English royal commissioners had considered was a departure from historical ways of managing clemency, rooted in the ancient royal prerogative of mercy. Since the mid-nineteenth century, as bureaucracies increasingly managed petitions and supported executive members of government who recommended commutations and pardons, sovereign mercy had become largely symbolic.[10] Yet discretion over the death penalty remained as hidden and unaccountable as it had been in ancient times. The royal commission heard from witnesses who advocated that discretion over the death penalty should rest with the jury.[11] After all, there was a British common law tradition that granted juries the right to recommend mercy by attaching riders to their verdicts, and this confirmed that their opinions about the appropriateness of prescribed punishment mattered. After finding an accused guilty of a capital crime, the jury, some witnesses argued, could be safely entrusted to determine whether death or a lesser punishment was appropriate. When the English royal commission presented its final report in 1953, it pronounced this reform as a preferable alternative to splitting murder into capital and noncapital degrees.[12] Their report also urged that juries be given the discretion to consider mental impairment or subnormal intelligence as a reason to take the death penalty off the table, and it called for the abolition of the doctrine of constructive malice (the equivalent of the Canadian code's section 202).[13] Despite these recommendations, the government preferred to leave the longstanding administration of capital justice undisturbed.

Like their British counterparts, the Canadian committee set out to study capital case management in 1954, and it was equally curious to hear about possible changes to the status quo. The minister of justice, Stuart Garson, was the politician who instigated the inquiry, and he served as a member of the committee and testified before it. In the second of these roles, he selected several of the witnesses they would hear from. His intention, he declared, was to inform the public of every step in a capital case, from arrest to commutation or execution. The evidence the committee would uncover, Garson hoped, would clear up "misunderstandings" that had led to ill-informed criticism from "newspaper editors and the like." He decided a Crown attorney with experience in jury trials and in "pleading cases before the courts" should testify. In addition, the committee should hear from an appeal court

Stuart Garson, as a Cabinet member and minister of justice from 1948 to 1957, was intimately involved in commutation deliberations. | LAC 3215918

justice "with long years in the trial division." William B. Common was the obvious choice for Crown attorney, and J.A. Hope, chief justice of the Ontario Court of Appeal, was the judge selected to testify. Aided by ministerial staff in the Department of Justice's Remission Service and informed by his personal experience in Cabinet, Garson also testified as to "the way in which the question of commutation of sentences is considered by the Department of Justice" and the executive.[14]

Stuart Garson's tenure as minister of justice began in 1948, a time when the commutation rate (12.5 percent) was close to the lowest it had ever been since Confederation. By the 1950s, however, the ratio of commutations to executions had become roughly equal. In 1953, for instance, twenty-two people were sentenced to death, and nine were executed.[15] Despite these fluctuations in the commutation rate, Garson, Hope, and Common all claimed that executive discretion was and had always been fair-minded. Appearing as a witness, the minister of justice characterized the handling of clemency reviews as the exercise of discretion in the tradition of royal mercy: "There has been a long settled practice in this country that, no matter how friendless and how terrible a rogue a man may be, even if he has no other human being to speak for him at all, his case comes before the whole cabinet and is reviewed in detail just as if he has a host of friends."[16] Because condemned offenders need not apply for clemency, the playing field was the same for an indigent person and a wealthy one.

Justice Hope agreed: there was "no better machinery being set up than what we have now, with the very great care that is taken in screening all the circumstances when it comes to the exercise of the executive clemency or the royal prerogative."[17] Thus, he considered it essential to retain a mandatory sentence but to let the executive consider "any extenuating circumstances."[18] No stone was left unturned to ensure that ministers of the constitutional monarchy made recommendations in the spirit of the royal prerogative, both in policy and practice.

As the director of public prosecutions, William Common's expertise derived from his work on appeals in capital cases rather than on the ultimate outcomes of death sentences. However, Crown attorneys played a critical role by ordering a "mental examination" of prisoners convicted of murder, and they ensured that reports from appointed psychiatrists were forwarded to the Remission Service. As Garson added, if a condemned prisoner was found to be insane, "then he cannot be executed, that is the fixed policy."[19] Common observed that in recent years most persons sentenced to death had appealed, but few capital convictions were overturned (Ronald Sears and Evelyn Dick were notable exceptions). When questioned about the prospect of granting trial judges the right to determine whether it was "too severe to impose the death penalty," Common told the committee that judicial discretion would usurp the jury's functions. Harold Winch, an MP and the committee's fiercest critic of the death penalty, challenged the experienced prosecutor, claiming that was exactly what the Cabinet did, only it exercised its discretion without transparency or accountability. Common replied with a stern rebuke: "No. That is purely an executive action; it is not a judicial action which the Minister of Justice takes. It is an executive action."[20] As an officer of the law, Common operated in a universe of rules and regulations, subject to interpretation, but laws all the same. Executive discretion was lawful constitutionally, but it was not subject to rules.

The joint committee devoted an entire day in March 1954 to hearing from outspoken Toronto lawyer Arthur Maloney, who considered executive discretion not just ruleless but ruthless. As chairman of the Canadian Bar Association's Criminal Justice Committee, he was the only witness the committee called to testify based on his experience in arguing appeals against convictions and petitioning for commutations. A number of flaws in capital justice required rectification, Maloney told the committee. First, judges did not routinely inform juries of the option to add a mercy rider to their verdict, and there were "undoubtedly juries who would recommend clemency if only aware of their right to do so." Second, Maloney thought judges should be required to ask jurors to deliberate over mercy only after rendering their verdicts. He also believed judges had undue influence over executive discretion since they expressed their opinions on the possibility of clemency with no knowledge of the accused outside of what they heard and saw in court. Under the current rules, a judge's report might reach the Cabinet without a recommendation of mercy from the judge or jury, which surely reduced the likelihood that the executive would grant clemency. Finally, Maloney knew that even in cases where juries and judges recommended mercy, their wishes were "not always respected" by the executive. For these reasons, Maloney agreed with the English royal commission – if the death penalty were retained, "responsibility for the death penalty [should] be placed in the discretion of the jury."[21]

Over his career as a lawyer arguing in appeal and pleading for clemency when capital appeals failed, Maloney's impression of capital justice differed from Garson's, Hope's, and Common's portrayals of Cabinet clemency. "The adequate use is not made of the prerogative of mercy," Maloney complained. Based on his own cases and those of other defence barristers, many of whom consulted Maloney for advice on appeals and clemency petitions, he told the joint committee that the executive was unmerciful toward offenders who merited mercy. He had recently represented two convicted murderers denied clemency. One of them, Mervin Hutson, had been sentenced to death for the sex murder of a child in 1953.[22] Because his medical reports were in his capital case file, the Cabinet knew that Hutson had been shot in the head several years before he committed the crime and had suffered from epilepsy and mental instability since his injury. Despite this medical evidence, he was hanged in North Bay in March 1954, just weeks before Stuart Garson addressed the joint committee. Maloney insisted that "there was sufficient doubt in the case of this accused not only to justify but, respectfully, to demand executive clemency."[23] Since the Hutson case was so recent, there was no chance the minister would have forgotten it by the time he informed the committee that insanity was a prompt for Cabinet clemency.[24] If the executive was so concerned about the mental state of offenders, Maloney insisted, it should be "a matter of course" to commute the sentence of anyone suspected of mental impairment or infirmity.[25]

The questions the joint committee put to the defence lawyer provided further insight into how petitioners for clemency went about their weighty task. Because Maloney was on a first-name basis with the minister of justice, he occasionally telephoned Garson, and he appreciated he was always prepared to talk. The minister also agreed to grant Maloney personal hearings when requested. But the number of lawyers who could expect such collegial treatment was tiny, so Maloney explained how an average pitch for clemency was conducted. First, it was necessary to prepare a detailed written account of any extenuating circumstances that might work in a client's favour or any facts beyond the evidence at trial that were important for the executive to bear in mind. Not exactly a legal brief ("because it is not sufficiently formal to be called a brief"), he told the committee his clemency requests mustered as many facts and arguments as possible and presented further documentation where possible. Yet Maloney, one of the country's leading defence barristers, revealed his success rate was just two out of eight of the capitally convicted clients whom he had represented. "It has been my experience that executive clemency is extremely difficult to obtain."[26]

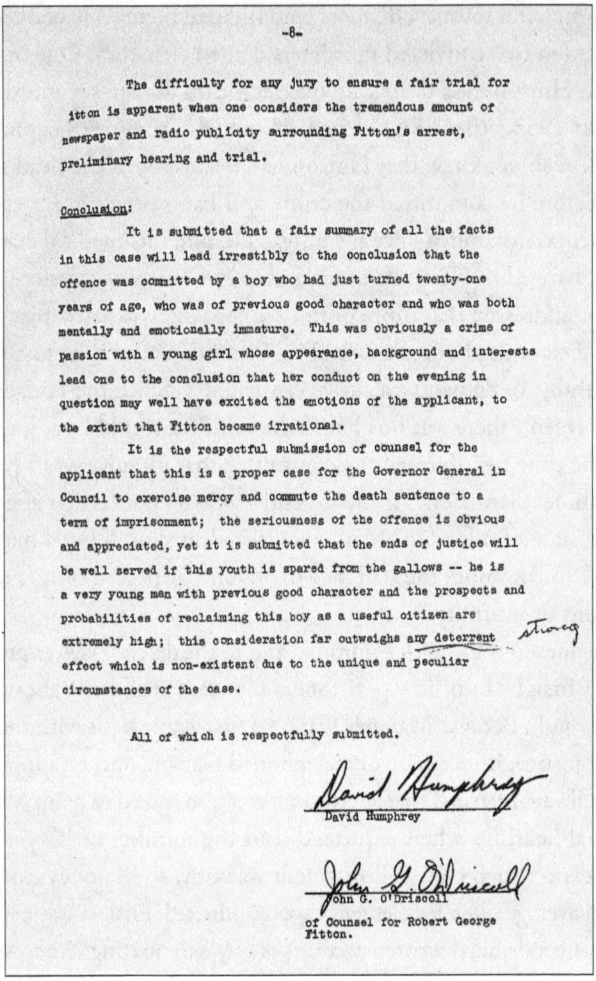

-8-

The difficulty for any jury to ensure a fair trial for itton is apparent when one considers the tremendous amount of newspaper and radio publicity surrounding Fitton's arrest, preliminary hearing and trial.

<u>Conclusion</u>:

It is submitted that a fair summary of all the facts in this case will lead irrestibly to the conclusion that the offence was committed by a boy who had just turned twenty-one years of age, who was of previous good character and who was both mentally and emotionally immature. This was obviously a crime of passion with a young girl whose appearance, background and interests lead one to the conclusion that her conduct on the evening in question may well have excited the emotions of the applicant, to the extent that Fitton became irrational.

It is the respectful submission of counsel for the applicant that this is a proper case for the Governor General in Council to exercise mercy and commute the death sentence to a term of imprisonment; the seriousness of the offence is obvious and appreciated, yet it is submitted that the ends of justice will be well served if this youth is spared from the gallows -- he is a very young man with previous good character and the prospects and probabilities of reclaiming this boy as a useful citizen are extremely high; this consideration far outweighs any deterrent *strong* effect which is non-existent due to the unique and peculiar circumstances of the case.

All of which is respectfully submitted.

David Humphrey
David Humphrey

John G. O'Driscoll
John G. O'Driscoll
of Counsel for Robert George Fitton.

The final page of Fitton's lawyers' application for clemency, November 12, 1956. The pencilled annotation was likely written by Allan J. MacLeod, director of the Remission Service. | LAC, RG 13-B-1, vol. 1755, "Fitton, Robert," vol. 3.

In June 1956, one week after the attorney general announced the Crown would appeal to the Supreme Court against the Court of Appeal's decision to quash Fitton's murder conviction, the joint committee submitted its final report. Although the government accepted its recommendation to retain the death penalty, Parliament had recently amended the Criminal Code to restrict its scope: persons under eighteen were exempted from the death penalty if convicted of murder, and the death penalty was removed for rape. Neither of those changes, incorporated before Fitton's trial, would have made a difference to his case. Robert Fitton was a few years past his eighteenth birthday, but there was every reason to highlight his youth in pleas for the executive to consider clemency. His lack of prior offending, his dull intellect, his medical history, his work record, and the fact he had become a father again while imprisoned were further factors in his favour.[27] However, as Maloney knew from his disappointments as a clemency petitioner, these factors had to be packaged and presented to persuade the executive to commute his sentence. While nothing limited or affected "Her Majesty's royal prerogative of mercy," the joint committee affirmed in its final report, nothing ensured it.[28] The committee's hearings had revealed for the first time the inner workings of executive discretionary justice, but there was still no means to predict the inner logic of a specific decision.

APPLYING FOR CLEMENCY

As David Humphrey and Archie O'Driscoll laboured over their application for clemency, Maloney may have offered them advice; however, the inexperienced petitioners made an unorthodox move: they contacted members of the jury and asked them why they had found Fitton guilty of murder, a tactic their mentors were unlikely to have advised. Humphrey and O'Driscoll submitted an eight-page argument in favour of clemency just over a week before Fitton's execution date. The document was a hybrid text – part legal brief, part pardon tale, part victim blaming.[29] They supplemented it with affidavits from several members of Fitton's jury who were prepared to attest that had they known their recommendation would not prevent Fitton's execution, they would not have found him guilty of murder. Furthermore, these men swore that if they had been granted discretion over Fitton's punishment (as the English royal commission and Maloney advocated), they would have recommended against his execution for the crime. Banking on this post-trial evidence, Humphrey and O'Driscoll hoped to convert it into a convincing application for a commuted sentence of life imprisonment "or for any lesser term of years."[30]

The document Fitton's lawyers sent to the minister of justice drew a stark contrast between the condemned man's good character and the victim's irresponsible behaviour, crystallizing the approach Humphrey took in the trial. On the one hand, Fitton was barely over the age of majority (twenty-one), and he had left school after Grade 8 to earn wages and to contribute to the family budget. His lawyers emphasized that their client was not a bright young man (the psychiatrist who examined him pronounced him a "dull normal" with an IQ of eighty-eight). Yet Fitton faithfully carried out the obligations of a mature family man. "At a time of life when most teenagers are carefree," the application opened, "this applicant was saddled with extremely onerous responsibilities, the burden of which might have been too great for such an immature youth." The implication was that overwork (a schedule of fifteen hours a day, six days a week, plus overtime) had left Fitton vulnerable to committing a sexual indiscretion. The psychiatrist confirmed the prisoner showed no signs of "sexual deviation." A dull man, admittedly, but a normal one who got into trouble because of a seductive girl.[31]

Once again, Linda Lampkin's apparent age and sexual maturity were deployed to diminish Fitton's culpability. Clemency petitions were not governed by any statute or rule of evidence or procedure, and the lawyers' application for a commuted sentence made the most of the genre's latitude. Although the girl was thirteen years old (which would have made her consent to intercourse, had she survived, irrelevant), the lawyers stressed she was "only a month short of being fourteen years of age."[32] More significantly, Linda Lampkin was generally thought to appear and act "much older than her actual age." The petition stretched the truth by stating the defence had "avoided any undue reference to the deceased's background" in the trial, a claim that ignored Humphrey's disparaging comments about the victim and his accusatory questions to Mrs. Lampkin about her daughter's flirtatious behaviour. Now, at the eleventh hour, Fitton's defenders could and did enlarge on the theory that Linda Lampkin contributed to her death. The application set out seven of her alleged derogatory characteristics, which ranged from wearing makeup to allegations that her parents reported her missing on several occasions prior to her death. In this petition, these reasons added up to an argument that her death was the outcome of a "passionate relationship between the deceased and Fitton." Were it not for the girl's "unusual interest in older boys," she would not have died.[33]

After the verdict in Fitton's trial, Justice Treleaven had allowed the jury to be polled at the request of the defence, and each juror confirmed he had found the defendant guilty of murder. The defence doubted that was the full story, and they were curious enough to defy legal custom by asking the jurymen what had transpired during their deliberations. Both the Court of Appeal and Supreme Court decisions referred to one juror's request for the judge to clarify the definition of manslaughter, and Humphrey and O'Driscoll were convinced the verdict was the outcome of a misunderstanding. They contacted "all the jurors," starting with the foreman, John Cole, whom Humphrey had anticipated would be amenable to the defence's theory. He revealed he had persuaded two jurors (who were leaning toward manslaughter) "that if they found him guilty of murder but brought in that recommendation [of mercy], he would not hang."[34] This motivated Humphrey and O'Driscoll to seek further evidence, and they found three jurors who were willing to sign affidavits that confirmed Cole's account. As the date set for Fitton's execution crept forward, each of the three "strongly urged" the executive to commute Fitton's death sentence.

References to the jurors' deliberations and the interactions that led them to a unanimous decision served two purposes for Humphrey and O'Driscoll. First, they asserted that the sworn juror statements indicated that Justice Treleaven's explanation of the law was flawed; second, they showed that some members of the jury thought Fitton was guilty of manslaughter, not murder. The lawyers also admonished one of the jurors who had told them he had found Fitton guilty as charged because he followed the judge's instruction – that a "wrongful act" leading to death constituted murder. "That is not the law," the lawyers declared.

However, if each juror had deliberated under that "erroneous concept," then surely the executive should question the verdict. Although they recognized that the information they provided had "no legal significance," Fitton's lawyers hoped their discoveries about the jurors' skewed understanding of the law would persuade the minister of justice and his colleagues to consider clemency.[35]

In the course of their interviews of Fitton's jurors months after the trial, Humphrey and O'Driscoll also fished for impressions of the victim and her role in the crime. The jury's low opinion of Linda Lampkin appeared in the clemency application to substantiate that they believed she had provoked their client. One juror said his "belief and opinion that the deceased contributed to and aggravated the circumstances by flirting, enticing and encouraging Fitton," led him to believe that Fitton did "not intend to kill the deceased – he lost his head in the heat of passion." Another juror thought that "the deceased taunted and coaxed Fitton to a certain degree," and her actions led him to commit "not a premeditated crime but rather one of passion." One juryman even blamed Linda Lampkin for wearing a scarf, otherwise "this crime might never have happened." To execute this man would make "three children orphans and Fitton's wife a widow," another juror noted in his affidavit in support of clemency. Notably, the lawyers did not correct any of these jurors' misconstrual of the defence of provocation.

In a more arrogant passage of their application, Fitton's lawyers pointed out the "wide division of judicial opinion" in the appellate decisions after Fitton's conviction, the first court quashing it and the second restoring it. Humphrey and O'Driscoll had the temerity to state that the Supreme Court, which ruled that there had been no misdirection or non-direction in the trial judge's charge, had reached the wrong decision, and they used evidence from their interviews with jurors to support their claim. "From the affidavits of the jurymen, it appears that they did act under a misapprehension and in error as to what the law actually is."[36] As a result of the jury's poor instruction and comprehension, "a boy who had just turned twenty-one years of age, who was of previous good character, and who was mentally and emotionally immature" was sentenced to death.

Humphrey and O'Driscoll "respectfully submitted" their application documents to the minister of justice, hoping the executive would agree this was a "proper case" for the exercise of mercy. The "seriousness of the offence was obvious," they acknowledged, but the measured ends of justice would be served if "this youth" served a commuted sentence. The only reason Fitton became "irrational" on the night of January 18 was the conduct of a girl "whose appearance, background and interests" led him astray by exciting his emotions. The character evidence they submitted was meant to show that Fitton's prospects of becoming a "useful citizen" were "extremely high." Surely this potential should "far outweigh any deterrent effect" of carrying out the execution.[37] The Remission Service's stamp on their application showed November 13 as the date of receipt – eight days before the Supreme Court's date for Fitton's execution. But the submission from Fitton's lawyers was not the only one received, nor was it the sole commutation pitch to focus on the jury's recommendation and the victim's responsibility for her death.

FEAR, ANGER, AND FITTON'S FATE

During Fitton's trial, Humphrey had proved adept at drawing out evidence from Crown witnesses, including detectives, who agreed that Fitton's domestic life was stable, his work habits admirable and his demeanour mild-mannered. Several individuals who might have testified in the trial as character witnesses, had the defence risked calling them and leaving them open to cross-examination, stepped forward as petitioners after the Supreme Court's decision. Fitton's mother, his employer, and two ministers wrote to request the commutation of his death sentence; in addition, members of the public who had never met the man joined in with letters and telegrams. Disturbed because they thought Fitton did not deserve to die for the crime, they all agreed that the executive should heed the jury's recommendation to mercy. However, the government also heard from individuals who thought the executive should ignore maudlin mercy pleas.

In sensational trials that attracted intense public interest, lawyers enjoined jurors to consider evidence dispassionately, and it was also customary for judges to warn those in the courtroom against any remonstrations when verdicts were announced. No caution from Justice Treleaven could have stopped Florence Fitton from shrieking and bursting into tears when she heard the verdict. However, nothing restrained pleaders for mercy from venting strong feelings about the impending death of a loved one or a stranger whom they considered a victim of injustice. Out of Fitton's large family his mother, Pearl, was the only one who wrote to the minister of justice, and like most defenders of her son, including his legal representatives, she smeared Linda Lampkin's character in her desperate hope that "God [may] Help ever[y] one to do what is right in his case."[38]

Shortly after Fitton's arrest, David Humphrey had appeared in a Toronto *Star* photo sitting beside the two Mrs. Fittons in their home, and the defence repeatedly referred to the family as respectable and hard-working. At the time of the murder, Fitton's father, William, was in hospital, and without his wages, his son had taken on extra shifts to make ends meet. The lawyers' commutation application repeated that evidence, but Pearl Fitton's plea painted a darker portrait of family life, a melancholy composition designed to induce pity for her and a commuted sentence for her son.[39]

According to his mother, Robert Fitton never had a chance at a happy, healthy life. From the age of ten, his taskmaster father had forced him to carry heavy cement blocks. Her husband was an abusive lout, who "used to swear and call me filthy names for no reason at all. Also, the children." Before she had Robert, Mrs. Fitton had several girls, all of whom got married as soon as they could "to get away from their father." William beat his son so fiercely, "I had to have his ribs strapped." The violence and abuse drove her to move out with her boy, whom she tried to support on her own, but after she lost her job, she was forced to return to her husband: "I though[t] he had changed but no." The stress of living with him led her to suffer "a nervous breakdown," but Robert stuck by her, working any job he could get. Once he earned his licence, he started driving trucks, but he was involved in two accidents. In one, he smashed his hand, and that injury required the partial amputation of a finger; in the second crash, a four-vehicle pileup in

1953 with two fatalities, he ended up with head wounds and ongoing headaches.[40] The one bright spot on this tough trail was his marriage in 1954. Robert "loved his wife and children very much," and compared with her husband, Pearl considered Robert "a good father." For his children's sake, she desperately hoped he would get "another chance." There was no reference to the murder in Mrs. Fitton's letter, save an allusion in the final line: "What went wrong only God knows."[41]

William Fitton talked a good line about supporting his boy after the trial, but he did not write on his behalf. The only men who pleaded for mercy were two Protestant ministers and Robert Fitton's employer. Together, they vouched for his work ethic and his hard life and vulnerabilities. "This man should not be regarded as fully morally responsible for his acts," Fitton's United Church minister urged. Possibly aware of the father's brutality, the cleric urged the executive to consider the young man's "tragic background and lack of mental stability." It was understandable that society required protection from "perverts, yet the execution of this young man will do nothing to accomplish that purpose."[42] In the months Fitton spent in prison, he received weekly visits from the Don Jail's chaplain, who declared he saw no indication that Fitton was capable of "criminal intent." On the contrary, he found him "a meek modest little man" who was under enormous stress due to overwork and his family responsibilities. "And then he meets temptation and falls before it with all its ugly consequences." The chaplain's description of Fitton's "fall" cast him in the biblical role of Adam – everyman, or just about any man who could just as easily find himself in a similar position. By inference, Linda Lampkin, the temptress, was Eve. Having worked in the prison ministry, the chaplain wrote to the man who headed the Remission Service, anticipating his comments would "help you in your decision about [Fitton's] future."[43]

Fitton's boss, the owner of the cartage company that had employed him for several years, requested a personal appointment with the minister of justice, but the Remission Service chief, Allan J. MacLeod, stood in for him at a meeting held on November 8, eleven days before the Cabinet would meet to determine whether to commute Fitton's sentence. As the company's owner, Howard E. Bacon told MacLeod that customer service was very important in the delivery business. Unlike some of his other drivers, who had complaints against them for failing to follow policy, Fitton had no complaints against him. One of those policies was the rule against mail truck drivers offering rides to members of the public. The trial revealed that Fitton had broken that rule on at least one occasion prior to the murder, but Bacon left that out of the conversation. Instead, he emphasized that Fitton's overseers at the cartage firm and his fellow employees found him to be solid, reliable. In the memo MacLeod made of their meeting, he wrote that "Mr. Bacon says he cannot understand what could have prompted Fitton to commit the offence."[44] Like the two ministers of religion who sought mercy, his employer saw his driver as a steady worker, not a murderer. Surely, they concurred, "the ends of justice will be well served if the sentence of death is commuted to one of life imprisonment."[45]

Some Torontonians who had never met Fitton believed he deserved clemency, mainly because he was too witless to have resisted the enticing victim. A group of teachers from Parkdale Collegiate in Toronto's west end wrote to the minister of justice to remind him that Fitton's fellow workers, not just his employer, held the young man "in high esteem." His family believed in him, and even the police felt he was a "decent fellow." However, they believed he ran afoul of the law because he was "not up to par in intelligence." By contrast, the deceased was "developed beyond her years" and had "tempted [Fitton] more than once." Having followed the crime in the papers, they decided the girl "appear[ed] to have asked for trouble by her behaviour – and then to have resisted the attentions of a stupid and inflamed man."[46] Like the schoolteacher who was shocked when she saw Linda Lampkin in Fitton's mail truck before her murder, the thirteen male and female teachers who signed this letter agreed that sexually precocious girls who played with fire inevitably ended up burned.

Although women were at the forefront of organizations, such as the Parents Action League, which rejected the blunt tools of the criminal justice system to solve the sex crime problem, women were as likely as men to hold moral beliefs that girls were responsible for protecting their chastity, and that parents – especially mothers – had a duty to instill this message. Trouble was inevitable, and tragedy was likely if girls appeared and behaved immodestly; whenever that happened, men could reasonably assume sexual consent. After the Supreme Court decision, several women contacted the Fitton family, including one of the Lampkins' neighbours. In a second letter to the minister of justice, Mrs. Fitton reported on tales told to her about Linda Lampkin's riotous and promiscuous behaviour. The neighbour claimed the girl was a pest in local diners and shops because she flirted flagrantly with boys. She was violent and had knocked out a girl's teeth with a baseball bat. She forced other girls to lie for her by saying she was visiting them when she was out late with boys. The night when she doubled back to Jane Street and approached Fitton's truck was not the first time she had streetwalked, hoping to see him.

Each of these allegations (including the woman's wild claim that Linda had ripped her own clothes and strangled herself with her scarf) appeared in Pearl Fitton's final letter on November 18, after she saw her son for the last time. She stated that Robert had asked the girl numerous times to stop asking him for rides. He also told his mother he had no idea she would turn up on the night of January 18. "Why should all the blame be put upon him when she would not stay out of his truck?" Mrs. Fitton asked. As a mother of girls, she knew "what they are like," but she hoped God would "forgive Linda for her part" in her death.[47] This angry, desperate, and demanding letter reached the Department of Justice on November 19, the day the Cabinet met. Penned to elicit clemency, she prayed it would have the desired effect.

ONCE THE SUPREME COURT snuffed out legal options, appealing for clemency was the only means that remained to urge that Fitton's death sentence be commuted. Most Canadians assumed a jury's recommendation to mercy should dictate the course the Cabinet should take, and critics of capital justice argued that juries, not the executive, should have the power to determine the punishment of convicted murderers. Although the special joint committee did not support that proposal, David Humphrey and Archie O'Driscoll attempted to use jurors' affidavits to support their application for a commuted sentence.

Surely Linda Lampkin's provocative behaviour was the cause of this young, otherwise blameless man's predicament?

Most citizens who pleaded for clemency, unlike politicians, criminal lawyers, or Remissions Service employees, had no knowledge or experience of capital case reviews. Fitton's mother, Pearl, behaved as most parents of condemned prisoners did: she wrote personal letters to the minister of justice, disclosing intimate details of her son's burdens and his abusive upbringing. His employer and ministers also had plenty to say about Fitton's prior good character: he was an exemplar of working-class masculine respectability, despite his burdens. By contrast, Fitton's mother and most of the women involved in her son's case – Linda Lampkin's former schoolteacher, the Lampkins' slanderous neighbour, and women who read about the case in the papers – shared his lawyers' opinion, that the victim had put Fitton's life in peril. On the day the Cabinet met, another venomous telegram arrived from a married woman and neighbour of the Fittons. Sent to the prime minister, it read: "HE DID NOT PLAN HIS CRIME HE WAS JUST HUMAN – APPARENTLY BEING TORMENTED."[48] Messages of this nature conveyed a widely shared belief that Linda Lampkin had turned Fitton into a victim, and they reached the prime minister and his Cabinet. But these efforts to save the man from execution fell short of widespread clamouring for commutation, certainly nothing like the hundreds of letters and petitions sent to urge clemency for the two members of the Boyd Gang, who were the last to be hanged in Toronto's Don Jail. Seasoned Cabinet ministers and remissions branch officers knew the difference between a thin file and a thick one. As those men turned to Fitton's case, they harboured feelings of their own – about the crime, the trial, the appeal decisions, and also about the tactics Fitton's lawyers had used to apply for mercy.

8

The Closed Cabinet

"MY PURPOSE TODAY is to attempt to describe and explain how the Governor General in Council in the exercise of the prerogative of mercy decides to commute or not to commute the death penalty."[1] The minister of justice, Stuart Garson, made this pledge before the Joint Committee of the Senate and the House of Commons, which he had established in 1954 to study capital punishment. By the time it presented its final report, Canada's penal optics had shifted. Allegations of a miscarriage of justice lingered after Wilbert Coffin's execution in February 1956, and one month later, the passage of an abolition bill in the British House of Commons fuelled speculation of a similar turn in Canada. But the committee recommended the death penalty's retention, and the government agreed.[2]

When Robert Fitton was sentenced to death on April 28 for Linda Lampkin's murder, a Toronto *Star* columnist who covered his trial spoke to "legal experts," who informed him that "very few – if any" convicted murderers in the past twenty years had "gone to the gallows" if the jury recommended mercy. The reporter believed that was true: "The majority of Canada's murderers have been escaping the noose," even ones without recommendations of mercy.[3] However, the data presented in the joint committee's final report plus the evidence provided by a second inquiry into the Department of Justice's Remission Service (headed by Supreme

Court Justice Gerald Fauteux) revealed more complex patterns of commutations and executions.[4] Wilfully blind to the trends evident in discretionary capital justice, the final reports of these inquiries endorsed the contention that the federal Cabinet made its decisions on the premise that "no two cases are ever the same."[5]

By the time Fitton's fate was decided, the royal prerogative of mercy was long past being one of the "special dignities, liberties, privileges and powers" of monarchs.[6] Executive clemency decisions were made by the prime minister and Cabinet, acting as the Privy Council, and although they still required the governor general's formal approval, he played no part in deliberations.[7] The minister responsible for advising his fellow Cabinet members relied on senior civil servants in the Department of Justice's Remission Service, who began to compile Fitton's case file as soon as his trial closed. The sheaf of reports, letters, and memoranda that comprised the contents cannot solve the mystery of the Cabinet's refusal to act on recommendations to mercy and post-trial pleas for commutation, however. Garson's commitment to revealing the workings of executive discretion did not fully open the curtain of executive discretion.[8] Despite the crumbs of evidence that remain in the form of cursory Cabinet minutes, which suggest the defence's attempt to question the jury's verdict narrowed the prospect of clemency, none but the men inside the Privy Council chambers could say for certain why, on November 19, 1956, the Cabinet advised the governor general of their recommendation that Fitton's death sentence be carried out.

THE ROYAL PREROGATIVE IN ACTION

The release of the joint committee's report on capital punishment, one of three subjects it was assigned to review after a major overhaul of the Criminal Code, was hurried along by pressure from the Opposition leader and the leader of the Co-operative Commonwealth Federation (CCF). The British House of Commons' vote on abolition led both men to urge the Liberal government to allow the same test in the Canadian parliament.[9] Since the joint committee was about to submit its recommendations, the minister of justice could put them off, but another CCF MP proposed an alternative. Would the government consider suspending all pending executions until the committee reported? Stuart Garson refused, declaring that such a move would require the executive to abrogate its duty to enforce the law. "Would it not be possible to do it by commutation, which is the prerogative of the cabinet?" the MP persisted. Garson reiterated that the Cabinet could not suspend the death penalty by applying "those reasons that are ordinarily the basis for commutation."[10] By the time July rolled around, the British House of Lords had scuttled the abolition bill, as anticipated, and the Canadian joint committee advised against abolishing the death penalty.[11] Garson and the Liberal government, of which he was a leading member, were content for Canada to retain capital punishment as the mandatory penalty for murder and for discretion over its infliction to remain an executive power.[12]

The joint committee set aside one section in its final report on the "Royal Prerogative of Mercy," and it drew substantially on the minister of justice's testimony, which detailed the conduct of capital case reviews. They were carried out "principally on established practice," the report observed. The only recent change to that practice was the deployment of ministerial responsibility. The Remission Service remained under the Department of Justice, assigned to ensure that the "same procedure applies to every capital case," but the solicitor general became the minister to whom the chief remission officer reported.[13] W. Ross Macdonald, a Brantford lawyer and Liberal senator, assumed the post in January 1954.[14] From that point, Stuart Garson was no longer the minister who presented capital cases to his colleagues and recommended for or against clemency, but as minister of justice, he remained intimately involved in capital cases, including Fitton's.[15]

A general picture of the documents required by the Remission Service appeared in the joint committee's final report. The transcript and the judge's report were essential, as were jail and medical records, with reports from psychiatrists becoming standard by the mid-twentieth century. Clerks also contacted "police, custodial officers and other responsible sources" for information about "the convicted person's background, character, personality, conduct in prison and other relevant matters." Beyond that, "careful consideration is given to the representation of defence counsel and friends and all points of fact and detail raised are carefully investigated to ensure that no factor favouring clemency is overlooked."[16] The criteria that activated the exercise of the royal prerogative of mercy were inferred, not delineated; instead, the final report stated that the Cabinet recommended commutation "in all cases where extenuating circumstances of a substantial nature exist or the degree of moral culpability" seemed to warrant clemency. Arthur Maloney, a defender of many clients sentenced to death, reached a different conclusion – the Cabinet was miserly with mercy. But the final report and its retentionist recommendation followed the ministerial mantra.

The Department of Justice's revelation that some types of murder and murderers were less likely than others to be considered worthy of clemency was not contentious in the final report; in fact, the committee decided that these disparities proved that Cabinet discretion was judicious, not capricious. The executive could apply a more commonsense notion of blameworthiness than the courts had to follow to determine whether a crime had been committed with "design and premeditation unqualified by any extenuating circumstances."[17] One example Stuart Garson offered the committee was the crime of infanticide, and in almost all cases involving capitally convicted women, the Cabinet used its discretion to commute the death sentence.[18] By contrast, the Cabinet typically denied clemency if it found a murder was "deliberately committed either to facilitate the commission of another crime or to avoid arrest following another crime." Yet even in cases of robbery murder, the executive was "not bound by the same strict rules as a court and jury in giving effect to them." Sometimes capitally charged offenders convicted of constructive murder involving robberies could strike the Cabinet favourably, especially if the culprits were young or displayed a lower degree of "moral culpability."[19] Sometimes not.

Among the many elements that contributed to decisions for or against commuting the death sentence, a recommendation to mercy was just one, and the role it played was significant, not dispositive. This was confirmed by the joint committee's team of "legal experts" – bigger and better qualified than those whom the *Star*'s reporter consulted. The Remission Service produced several tables of case dispositions based on its records. From 1920 to 1949, 577 individuals were condemned to death in Canada, and 135 of them received a recommendation for mercy. A further forty-two cases were resolved by verdicts that set aside convictions, convictions on lesser charges, or acquittals. Only 18 percent of capitally convicted offenders were executed if the jury recommended mercy. Maloney's claim that convicted murderers who sought clemency without a recommendation had a low chance of commutation turned out to be correct: 63 percent of offenders in that category were hanged.[20] The joint committee rightly regarded this evidence as proof that the jury's support for clemency was not "automatically accepted as grounds for commutation." Clearly, there were other grounds the Cabinet could and did consider more compelling.[21]

The final report supported both the retention of the death penalty and Canada's definition of murder, and it confirmed that executive discretion was a sound means to set the punishment appropriate for the crime and offender. It was certainly better than splitting murder into degrees to distinguish deliberately planned murders from those committed with intent but without premeditation. The committee considered these statutory definitions, common in American states, unworkable and unjust because some planned homicides were not deliberately cruel (mercy killings and suicide pacts were their examples), whereas some unpremeditated homicides were "reprehensible because they arise from a wanton disregard of human life." The committee observed that Cabinets treated "killings involving grave moral culpability" as most deserving of the law's harshest penalty and decided it was best for the executive to sift such cases from ones involving less moral culpability. Besides, the final report concluded, "The present distinction between murder and manslaughter is quite clear and straightforward." [22]

At least one of the jurors in Robert Fitton's trial – the man who asked the judge to clarify the distinction in the two forms of culpable homicide – would have disagreed, had he read the committee's report. Fitton's defenders plus all but one judge on the Court of Appeal strongly disagreed: in their view, Justice Treleaven had misdirected the jury on the distinction. Despite these differences of opinion, the Supreme Court's restoration of the verdict transformed Fitton into a statistic in the table of the Cabinet's denial of clemency in 1956.

COMMUTATIONS AND EXECUTIONS BY NUMBER

The English royal commission set a high standard of compiling and analyzing data to chart rates of murder and execution, and Canada's joint committee followed its lead when it studied the country's records.[23] Both inquiries consulted Thorsten Sellin, the leading authority on the statistical analysis of crime and punishment in this period and "a relentless champion of scientifically sound criminology."[24] By the 1950s, it was possible to compare the small number of nations and states that had abolished the death penalty with those that retained it, and Sellin studied this information to determine whether capital punishment deterred murder. Neither the British nor the Canadian investigators accepted Sellin's conclusion that there was no proof of the death penalty's unique capacity to deter murder.[25] The Canadian joint committee, like the English royal commission, took greater stock in the opinions of "those having responsibility for law enforcement."[26] Their first-hand experience convinced them capital punishment was an effective and essential deterrent, and their anecdotal accounts proved more persuasive than Sellin's statistics. Canada's committee concluded the numbers did not add up in favour of abolition.[27]

Despite its doubts about the relevance of statistics that questioned the death penalty's deterrent potency, the joint committee solicited and studied data on the disposition of capital cases. The figures, provided by the Remission Service, exposed variations over time and by type of murder in discretionary decision making on capital cases. One of the tables in the final report showed the number of males and females sentenced to death from 1867 to 1954, divided according to those executed and those whose sentences were commuted. The fact that women were substantially more likely than men to be spared drew little comment, but the committee recommended that executive discretion remain the means by which to dispense mercy for women, case by case, rather than exempting all females from the death penalty statutorily.

The final report also glossed over data that showed swings in commutation and execution rates over time. During the Depression, clemency plummeted, and although the proportion of commuted sentences had increased by the 1940s, the quotient of executions fluctuated from year to year.[28] As late as 1952, ten of out of eighteen persons sentenced to death were hanged.[29] Another table broke down commutation and execution rates by type of homicide, and these figures confirmed that sex murderers were more likely than other sorts of murderers to be executed. Between 1920 and 1952, a total of twenty-nine men were sentenced to death for murders involving "sexual assault," and the Cabinet granted clemency to just five of their cases. During its hearings, the committee showed more concern about murders committed in the course of robberies (which made up the largest category of capital offenders in the first half of the twentieth century), but the data it requested confirmed that the executive was more likely to recommend clemency in robbery murder cases.[30] Thus, the final report revealed clear evidence of patterns in the exercise of executive discretion without challenging the official line that the executive considered each case on its merits.

The hearings of the joint committee raised the hood on the components of capital case reviews, and the Department of Justice's evidence indicated that circumstances aside from those disclosed played on Cabinet ministers' minds when they considered the possibility of commutations. Yet, if anything, the final report's recommendation that Canada retain the death penalty firmed the Cabinet's preparedness to recommend that the law take its course. Between its publication in June 1956 and the Cabinet meeting on November 19, when Fitton's sentence was the first item on the agenda, three men were executed, and the executive granted just one commutation, demonstrating the government's resolve to retain the death penalty. These numbers, combined with decades of evidence of mercilessness toward sex killers, made Fitton's chance of commutation far lower than the *Star* reporter or his defenders had anticipated.

THE CHARACTER OF THE CASE FILE

Although the joint committee chose the safe road of recommending the death penalty's retention with no change to the definition of murder, there were several reforms it advised the government to consider in the spirit of equitable justice. One was to make it obligatory for the Crown to fully disclose its evidence to the defence; another was to ensure that all persons accused of murder had access to "competent experienced" counsel.[31] The committee also found merit in Maloney's calls for automatic appeals of capital convictions and his advocacy of the right of persons found guilty of murder to appeal to the Supreme Court, no matter whether there was dissent over a question of law. However, none of these recommendations, had they been implemented before Fitton's arrest, would have prevented his case from appearing before the federal Cabinet. The Crown attorney, Arthur Klein, disclosed his case, and Humphrey provided a dogged defence, advised by the country's leading counsel. Fitton's extraordinarily dedicated legal team had represented him from the moment of his arrest to the Supreme Court hearing. Despite these factors in Fitton's favour, the outcome of his case hung on the Cabinet, not legal proceedings. Yet the final appeal decision and the dissent in the provincial Court of Appeal complicated his clemency bid, leaving him vulnerable to the eddies and currents of executive discretion.

According to its defenders, the royal prerogative was "a necessary and indispensable feature of the mandatory sentence of capital punishment for murder" precisely because it differed from the legal reasoning required of judges at trial and in appeal. The Criminal Code set death as the mandatory punishment for murder, and judges reminded jurors they must prevent sympathy from standing in the way of their verdict, as Justice Treleaven did in Fitton's trial. But judges and jurors could recommend mercy, and the executive had the power to act on it, ensuring "the severity of the punishment can be mitigated in appropriate cases."[32] The process that determined whether such recommendations might be put into effect in Fitton's case required the Remission

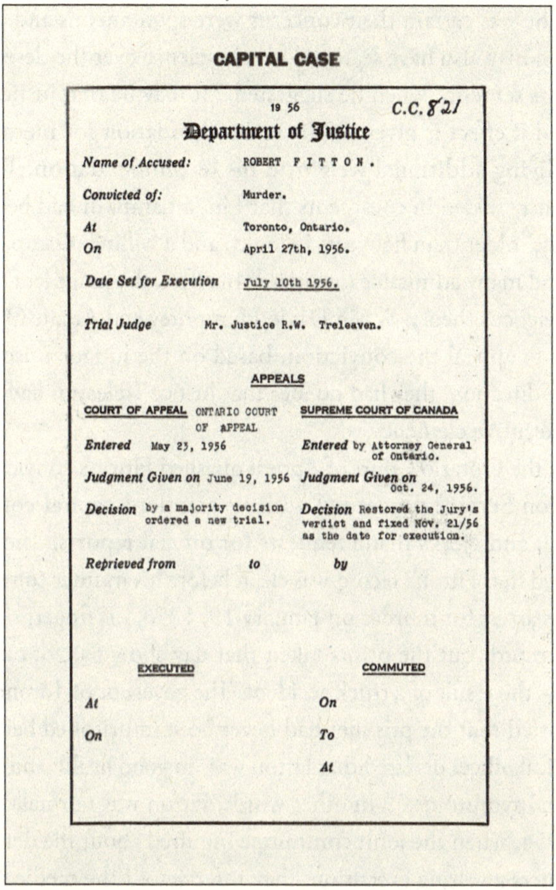

CAPITAL CASE

19 56 C.C. 821

Department of Justice

Name of Accused: ROBERT FITTON.

Convicted of: Murder.

At Toronto, Ontario.

On April 27th, 1956.

Date Set for Execution July 10th 1956.

Trial Judge Mr. Justice R.W. Treleaven.

APPEALS

COURT OF APPEAL ONTARIO COURT OF APPEAL	SUPREME COURT OF CANADA
Entered May 23, 1956	*Entered* by Attorney General of Ontario.
Judgment Given on June 19, 1956	*Judgment Given on* Oct. 24, 1956.
Decision by a majority decision ordered a new trial.	*Decision* Restored the Jury's verdict and fixed Nov. 21/56 as the date for execution.

Reprieved from *to* *by*

EXECUTED	COMMUTED
At	*On*
On	*To*
	At

Top page of Fitton's capital case file | LAC, RG13-B-1, vol. 1755, "Fitton, Robert," vol. 5

Service staff to assemble a case file, starting with the standard request for a report from the judge on the trial and its outcome.

Justice Treleaven's report to the Department of Justice fully supported the jury's wish that Fitton be spared the mandatory punishment for murder. "I am inclined to think that it was a sincere recommendation and not in any way just a matter of form," he commented. Since he had not informed the jury they could add a recommendation to their verdict, he was certain their concerns were spontaneous and genuine. Treleaven may also have searched his conscience over the deservedness of Fitton's sentence when he suggested, "It may be that justice would be served if effect is given to the recommendation for mercy by the jury." Giving additional weight to his recommendation, Treleaven gratuitously tossed in comments that Linda Lampkin had been a "bit boy crazy," older than her years in looks, and a willing pickup, whereas Fitton had many admirable qualities.[33] In effect, the judge lent credence to the defence's theory. When David Humphrey and Archie O'Driscoll decided to appeal the conviction, based on the judge's misdirection and non-direction, they had no idea that Justice Treleaven had strongly urged executive clemency.

Until the Ontario Court of Appeal quashed Fitton's conviction, the Remission Service proceeded with its standard capital conviction protocol, and clerks made requests for official reports. The RCMP confirmed that Fitton's record was clean before his murder conviction.[34] Until his arrest for murder on January 19, 1956, his fingerprints were not on record, but the prints taken that day show part of one finger missing – the result of a truck accident. The governor of Toronto's Don Jail reported that the prisoner had never been imprisoned before, and the medical officer declared that Fitton was "in good health and showing no mental symptoms."[35] In other words, Fitton was normal.

In 1954, when the joint committee inquired about the demeanour of prisoners awaiting execution, they interviewed the medical officer, doctor W.H. Hills, who told them he found that condemned men "were always polite and properly behaved."[36] Fitton struck him in the same way. Although the remission chief also requested an examination by a psychiatrist, Kenneth Gray had examined Fitton at David Humphrey's request shortly after Fitton's arrest, and the Remission Service deemed that sufficient while the appeal was pending.[37] Neither the doctor, Fitton's counsel, nor prison officials considered Fitton mentally disturbed, and he was certainly not a sexual psychopath.

Although Fitton also struck the Toronto police as a normal man, the report sent by the city's chief of detectives, Alexander "Archie" Cathie, described him as a culpable criminal who deserved the death

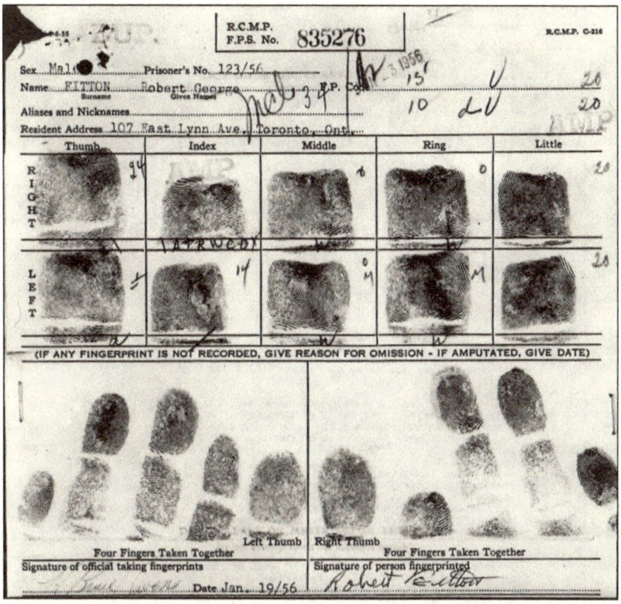

R.C.M.P. F.P.S. No. 835276

R.C.M.P. C-216

Sex Male Prisoner's No. 123/56

Name FITTON Robert George

Surname Given Names

Aliases and Nicknames

Resident Address 107 East Lynn Ave., Toronto, Ont.

	Thumb	Index	Middle	Ring	Little
RIGHT					
LEFT					

(IF ANY FINGERPRINT IS NOT RECORDED, GIVE REASON FOR OMISSION - IF AMPUTATED, GIVE DATE)

Four Fingers Taken Together — Left Thumb — Right Thumb — Four Fingers Taken Together

Signature of official taking fingerprints Date Jan. 19/56

Signature of person fingerprinted Robert Fitton

Robert Fitton's signature appears at the bottom of the fingerprints that show the amputation of his right forefinger. | LAC, AC, RG13-B-1, vol. 1755, "Fitton, Robert," vol. 1, pt. 1

sentence. Cathie, a Scottish-born Presbyterian, had joined the Toronto police force in 1921 and rose to the rank of detective in 1930.[38] In 1955, when Judy Carter was abducted, Cathie headed the investigation that failed to turn up the girl's killer. He had also investigated the murders of two "new Canadian" women who were strangled (one of them was also sexually assaulted) in 1954.[39] In those cases, the police suspected the strangler was a "dark-skinned" foreigner, but again, no charges were laid.[40] By contrast, Cathie's detective force cracked the mystery of Linda Lampkin's murder in record time. Far from a strictly factual report, Toronto's chief detective expressed distress over the crime and disgust toward the criminal who committed it.

Compared with the trial judge's disparagement of the victim's character, Cathie portrayed Linda Lampkin as her parents described her – as "a schoolgirl" and a "child." He also referred, demurely, to the pathologist's evidence that the deceased was "of previous chaste character,"

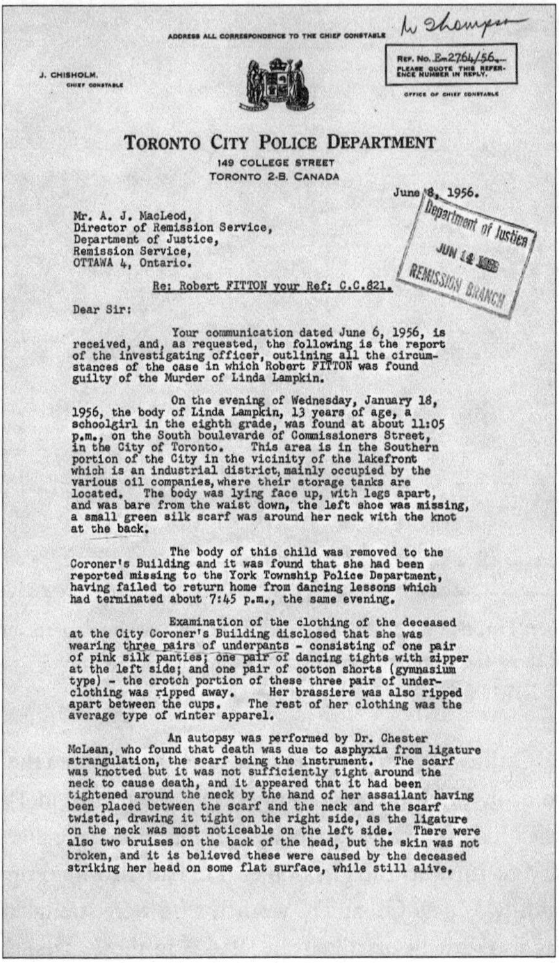

ADDRESS ALL CORRESPONDENCE TO THE CHIEF CONSTABLE

J. CHISHOLM,
CHIEF CONSTABLE

REF. No. E-2764/56.
PLEASE QUOTE THIS REFERENCE NUMBER IN REPLY.

OFFICE OF CHIEF CONSTABLE

TORONTO CITY POLICE DEPARTMENT
149 COLLEGE STREET
TORONTO 2-B. CANADA

June 8, 1956.

Department of Justice
JUN 14 1956
REMISSION BRANCH

Mr. A. J. MacLeod,
Director of Remission Service,
Department of Justice,
Remission Service,
OTTAWA 4, Ontario.

Re: Robert FITTON your Ref: C.C.821.

Dear Sir:

Your communication dated June 6, 1956, is received, and, as requested, the following is the report of the investigating officer, outlining all the circumstances of the case in which Robert FITTON was found guilty of the Murder of Linda Lampkin.

On the evening of Wednesday, January 18, 1956, the body of Linda Lampkin, 13 years of age, a schoolgirl in the eighth grade, was found at about 11:05 p.m., on the South boulevarde of Commissioners Street, in the City of Toronto. This area is in the Southern portion of the City in the vicinity of the lakefront which is an industrial district, mainly occupied by the various oil companies, where their storage tanks are located. The body was lying face up, with legs apart, and was bare from the waist down, the left shoe was missing, a small green silk scarf was around her neck with the knot at the back.

The body of this child was removed to the Coroner's Building and it was found that she had been reported missing to the York Township Police Department, having failed to return home from dancing lessons which had terminated about 7:45 p.m., the same evening.

Examination of the clothing of the deceased at the City Coroner's Building disclosed that she was wearing three pairs of underpants - consisting of one pair of pink silk panties; one pair of dancing tights with zipper at the left side; and one pair of cotton shorts (gymnasium type) - the crotch portion of these three pair of underclothing was ripped away. Her brassiere was also ripped apart between the cups. The rest of her clothing was the average type of winter apparel.

An autopsy was performed by Dr. Chester McLean, who found that death was due to asphyxia from ligature strangulation, the scarf being the instrument. The scarf was knotted but it was not sufficiently tight around the neck to cause death, and it appeared that it had been tightened around the neck by the hand of her assailant having been placed between the scarf and the neck and the scarf twisted, drawing it tight on the right side, as the ligature on the neck was most noticeable on the left side. There were also two bruises on the back of the head, but the skin was not broken, and it is believed these were caused by the deceased striking her head on some flat surface, while still alive,

Alexander M. Cathie, chief of detectives, used the chief constable's letterhead to write the Toronto police's report on the "circumstances of the case." | LAC, RG13-B-1, vol. 1755, "Fitton, Robert," vol. 5

and he reiterated that her birth certificate proved she was thirteen years old. "Like other girls of the same age," he commented, Linda had gone out with boys, but this did not mean she was a sexual delinquent. When he turned to the evidence that she had ridden in Fitton's truck before her death, Cathie took it to indicate that "she felt she could trust the accused and that she may have gotten into his truck on the night in question to be driven home."[41] There was no hint of the moral disapproval many witnesses expressed when Humphrey cross-examined them about the "pickup." Detective Cathie's report pulled no punches about Fitton's responsibility: this offender was a vicious man who had assaulted and murdered an innocent child.

Although Cathie did not consider Fitton a mad sexual pervert, he saw him as a man given to sexual cruelty. The terms and diagnostic categories in vogue to describe sexual abnormality (such as sexual psychopathy or sadism) were not in Cathie's lexicon; instead, he described the criminal and his crime in a style evocative of Victorian melodrama. According to Cathie, once Fitton had the girl in his truck, the route he took led to a dimly lit "quiet lonely location" where he carried out the deed:

> It is quite evident that his lustful intentions reached such a peak that his determination to satisfy his craving brought him to the level of bestiality in its lowest form, at which time he tore the crotch out of three pairs of panties, as well as ripping apart the brassiere, worn by the deceased, at which time he raped her, and then she died as a result of the pressure induced by the accused twisting her scarf.[42]

Cathie repeated there was "no evidence that could despoil the character of the deceased girl, who, as stated before, was a virgin." In his account, Linda Lampkin was not a "pretty brunette" who looked like a starlet: she was a girl, raped and murdered, whom police discovered at the side of a road, "lying face up, with legs apart, and was bare from the waist down."[43]

Like the other official and unofficial commentators on this murder – men and women who gauged the gravity of the crime according to the victim's sexual reputation – Toronto's chief detective considered Linda Lampkin's morality pertinent. But Cathie used a different gauge: the victim was a trusting, virginal child despoiled and assaulted by a scoundrel. When Remission Service clerks read Cathie's letter, they made coloured pencil marks to highlight his moral appraisal of Fitton, suggesting they took his condemnation seriously as they prepared Fitton's case file for the solicitor general and the Cabinet. Still to come were the drier decisions of the Court of Appeal and the Supreme Court.

PRECEDENTS ARE PARTICULARLY IMPORTANT

After Fitton's conviction was quashed, the Remission Service suspended its compilation of documentation for Fitton's capital case file, and he was transferred into the general population wing of the Don Jail. However, the Supreme Court's ruling, which fixed a new execution date – November 21, 1956 – sent Fitton back to the death cell and triggered a second round of inquiries by the Remission Service. In addition, it led to the filing of clemency pleas, most of them mailed or telegrammed to the minister of justice. Shortly before the Cabinet meeting, the service informed W. Ross Macdonald, the solicitor general, of all communications relevant to his recommendation.

In January 1956, just when the outcome of Wilbert Coffin's case was about to be determined, a member of Ottawa's press gallery wrote a feature on the management of capital cases and Macdonald was one of the officials he interviewed. The journalist, John Bird, titled his story, "Cabinet's Toughest Tasks Are Death Sentence Reviews."[44] One of Macdonald's predecessors, possibly Stuart Garson, told Bird he found making decisions in capital cases "the most burdensome of all loads of office." Even if the condemned man was "clearly a thug ... you feel you are the last thing standing between that man and the hanging," he disclosed. When Bird interviewed Macdonald, he said he agreed with his predecessor: having spent two years on the job, he admitted he found his obligation to make recommendations "trying" and "worrying." Fortunately, he had learned he could rely on the chief of the Remission Service, A.J. MacLeod, for advice.[45] The journalist also "cornered" the branch chief to question him about his role: "Square-shouldered, with steady greyish eyes," MacLeod showed the reporter a foolscap-length list of names of persons sentenced to death as of January 7, 1956, and

Wilbert Coffin's name topped the list of eleven men.[46] MacLeod gave Bird a dry, administrative account of his division's work, and he insisted he and his staff were up to the task: "It is really a matter of preparing all the relevant information and factors in each case ... Thoroughness counts and precedents are particularly important."[47]

One month after Bird's exposé was published, Wilbert Coffin was hanged, and five more men were executed in the following ten months, two of them after Fitton returned to the death cell. Would these "tough" decisions set a precedent when his name rose to the top of MacLeod's list midway through November?[48] The question was on the minds of his lawyers, trying to come up with whatever it would take to keep the man from becoming the sixth.

Because the Supreme Court allowed just under a month from its decision to Fitton's revised execution date, the Remission Service had to move quickly to update the file. A second report on the condemned man's physical and mental status was necessary, and the governor of the Don Jail was asked to supply it. The jail was also responsible for making the arrangements for the execution. Hills provided a new report, but nothing had changed other than Fitton's age – he was now twenty-two. MacLeod asked William B. Common to arrange a psychiatric evaluation of the prisoner, and the man he chose for the task was Charles S. Tennant. A forensic psychiatrist in the provincial Department of Health, Tennant was one of the experts who testified before the Royal Commission on the Criminal Law relating to Criminal Sexual Psychopaths, one of several inquiries underway after the Criminal Code's revision. In February 1956, he testified that one cause of the sex crime problem, especially sexually sadistic violence, was the reading of crime comics. To prove his theory, Tennant showed the commissioners incriminating excerpts from the diary of Peter Balcombe, executed in 1954 for the mutilation murder of his girlfriend.[49] Reporters who covered Fitton's incarceration observed that he, too, had a taste for crime comics, but Tennant did not think that meant this prisoner was a sexual psychopath. "I could not find anything to suggest that he was suffering from any mental illness, and he was certainly not mentally defective," he reported to Common.[50]

The most significant appraisal in Tennant's report, from the point of view of the Remission Service, was that Fitton was "quite able to instruct counsel." The handling of mental abnormalities in persons accused and convicted of murder was a major concern in the joint committee's investigation, and it was studied in detail in the royal commission on criminal insanity.[51] The Remission Service provided statistics to the joint committee to document capital cases in which insanity had been raised at trial as a defence to murder, and Stuart Garson commented on the results. Between 1937 and 1952, the Cabinet granted clemency in more than half of such cases (forty-three of seventy-two); however, Garson said he had "no hesitation" in saying the Cabinet had also commuted the death sentence in cases where some lesser form of mental aberration seemed to have affected the perpetrator's "control over his conduct." If a condemned person appeared to have committed homicide "under great mental stress or emotional strain," the Cabinet tended to "exercise clemency by way of commutation." No matter "how heinous his crime may have been," Garson reassured the committee, this tendency prevailed.[52] Arthur Maloney rejected the minister's characterization, based on his experience of defending men whose mental impairments had clearly met the minister's criteria yet they were executed. Evidently, some criminals committed crimes too "heinous" to warrant clemency.

When David Humphrey first agreed to represent Fitton's defence, he suspected his client might suffer from some mental disorder. To assist him, he asked Tennant to observe the young man during his trial, but the doctor had found nothing noteworthy. Humphrey made the best of this by using Fitton's normality to ground the defence's theory of the events that led to Linda Lampkin's death. This ordinary if dull "boy" was no match for the sexually precocious girl who inflamed his sexual desires. Exhausted by his work and overwhelmed by his family responsibilities, he could not resist a type of temptation that any normal man would struggle to resist. Humphrey and O'Driscoll's lengthy clemency application, addressed to the minister of justice, reinforced this characterization of Fitton to set up the prospect of his returning to a respectable productive life. However, the marginalia that

Remission Service officials pencilled on the lawyers' submission suggests their anodyne description of the convicted murderer did not have the desired effect.

RECOMMENDING THE LAW TAKE ITS COURSE

The Remission Service's primary mission was to operate the ticket-of-leave program – the forerunner to the federal parole system and the focus of the Fauteux inquiry, which made capital case file preparation an additional and episodic burden.[53] Their "heavy task" was to take disparate content and summarize it for ministerial review. A.J. MacLeod's senior clerk in the Remission Service, Frederick W. Thompson, was the second-in-command who prepared draft condensed summaries of capital case files, and both men marked up documents as they read through them. The final report of the Fauteux inquiry praised the "Director and officers of the Service" for their "high degree of intellectual and moral rectitude."[54] As they worked through Fitton's file, Thompson and MacLeod reviewed the full transcript, the trial report, the judgments in appeal, the exhibits (including photographs), and all correspondence – official and otherwise.

Thompson's initials appear on numerous documents in Fitton's file, but the trail of pencil marks on Humphrey and O'Driscoll's clemency brief appears in MacLeod's hand. The seasoned head of the Remission Service went on the hunt for errors. When he read the passage that claimed Fitton had told the police "he had no intention of killing [the victim] but only meant to scare her," MacLeod wrote, "Didn't say this." Against the line that said the detectives believed the first exculpatory statement, MacLeod pencilled: "Turned out to be untrue." The lawyers also said the police "believed Fitton was attempting to tell the truth," but MacLeod, having read the transcript, disagreed: "Stat't [statement] was untrue in material facts." The remission chief also corrected the defence's allegation that the Lampkins had reported their daughter missing on several occasions (it was just once). Most significantly, MacLeod disputed Humphrey and O'Driscoll's contention that the foreman had manipulated his fellow jurors. He also dismissed the applicants' claim that the jury acted "under a misapprehension" of the definition of murder: "Not so," MacLeod wrote. In the passage where Fitton's defenders stressed his capacity for useful citizenship, stating it "far outweighs any deterrent effect which is non-existent due to the unique and peculiar circumstances of the case," MacLeod stroked a line under "any deterrent" and wrote "strong." His adjective could have meant "compelling"; more likely MacLeod meant "overcooked."

Humphrey and O'Driscoll followed the usual course in clemency appeals by emphasizing their client's redeeming qualities, but they combined that with a legalistic argument that commuting Fitton's death sentence would follow precedent. They may also have known that the minister of justice had told the joint committee that guiding principles governed executive discretion and that precedents were important. To make that point, they referred to a recent case, that of Annunziato Tripodi. Sentenced to death in 1954 for the strangling murder of his wife, Tripodi's plea for clemency was granted in June 1955.[55] There were many similarities between his case and Fitton's, according to Fitton's lawyers. Both men had been provoked by the behaviour of a female victim, the only difference being that Tripodi killed his allegedly unfaithful wife. Like Fitton, he was represented pro bono by counsel who appealed his conviction, and the Ontario Court of Appeal quashed the conviction and ordered a new trial. In both cases, the Crown appealed the decision and obtained leave to appeal from the Supreme Court, which restored the conviction in a split decision.[56] Up to that point, the legal course of the two cases was identical, and Humphrey and O'Driscoll thought the outcome for Fitton should mirror Tripodi's.[57]

Any close observer of capital case dispositions would have known that the Italian-born convicted murderer seemed a far less likely candidate for clemency than Fitton. Tripodi was a recent immigrant, a stroke against the man at a time when Anglo-Celtic Canadian bigotry against "new Canadians" was rife. He was a thirty-three-year-old man, not a "boy," as the defence repeatedly called Fitton. Finally, in Tripodi's trial, the jury did not recommend mercy. As far as Fitton's lawyers could see, the only reason why the Cabinet had commuted his sentence was the "wide division of judicial opinion" in the appeals and the reasoning of judges who had favoured granting Tripodi a new trial. When MacLeod reached that passage in Humphrey and O'Driscoll's letter, he dismissed it: "Commutation not granted for that reason."[58]

Having worked in the Remission Service's senior ranks, MacLeod may have known the reason, but he definitely knew the all-male executive was often inclined to grant clemency to men who killed their wives upon learning of their infidelity: the Remission Service's statistics confirmed the pattern.[59] Biased notions of the alleged lack of impulse control in "foreigners" could also sway Cabinets toward clemency, and this might also have happened in Tripodi's case. Whatever the actual reason, MacLeod's blunt correction assured the solicitor general there was no cause to regard the commutation of Tripodi's sentence as a precedent to recommend clemency for Fitton.

As the responsible minister, Macdonald was free to read case files in their entirety, but the contents of the average file of the 1950s – two or more thousand pages of transcripts in multi-day trials, judgments in appeal, correspondence, newspaper clippings, and petitions – made the Remission Service's preparatory work essential to guide the minister. The final memorandum of Fitton's capital case was produced a week in advance of the Cabinet meeting on November 19, and it opened, as usual, with a summary of the case's journey.[60] In this instance, it began with Fitton's arrest and documented the twisted course his case took through the appeal process that had recently restored the original trial verdict.

Clerks always placed the condensed summary at the top of case files, and they followed a standard template: trial particulars; prisoner's name and description; victim's name and description; crime (and evidence thereof); facts in evidence; defence; and verdict (including deliberation of jury and any recommendations by jury or judge). However, the red and blue ink marks that appear on several documents pertinent to the appeal indicate where the solicitor general's concerns led him. The last section of the file covered appeals and decisions, and these were the only documents – the grounds for appeal and the reasons for decisions in the

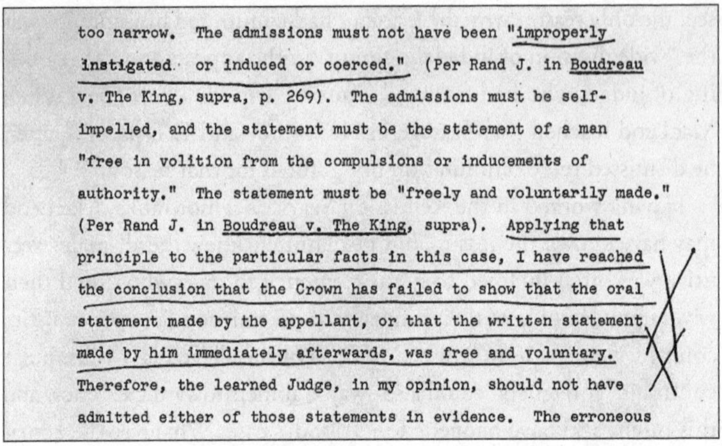

too narrow. The admissions must not have been "improperly instigated or induced or coerced." (Per Rand J. in Boudreau v. The King, supra, p. 269). The admissions must be self-impelled, and the statement must be the statement of a man "free in volition from the compulsions or inducements of authority." The statement must be "freely and voluntarily made." (Per Rand J. in Boudreau v. The King, supra). Applying that principle to the particular facts in this case, I have reached the conclusion that the Crown has failed to show that the oral statement made by the appellant, or that the written statement made by him immediately afterwards, was free and voluntary. Therefore, the learned Judge, in my opinion, should not have admitted either of those statements in evidence. The erroneous

Ink markings, penned by the solicitor general, W. Ross Macdonald, on Justice Pickup's reasons for allowing the appeal against Fitton's conviction | LAC, RG13-B-1, vol. 1755, "Fitton, Robert," vol. 4

Court of Appeal and the Supreme Court – that he marked up. "Sometimes a point will be made in the argument on appeal by some more acute mind, a counsel or the judges themselves, that will shed quite a new light upon the question of commutation itself," Macdonald's predecessor, Stuart Garson, told the joint committee.[61] As the solicitor general flipped through the pages of Fitton's file, holding his ballpoint pen, he searched for legal points on which to base his recommendation.

The solicitor general's comments and underscorings appear only around passages of the transcript and evidence relevant to Fitton's responsibility for Linda Lampkin's death. There is no way of knowing for certain what he meant by his markings, but Macdonald's pen highlighted the defence's theory and the claim, repeated in the clemency bid, that the victim had consented to the sex and provoked Fitton to grab her by her scarf. Two large X's appear next to the lines on Ontario Chief Justice Pickup's decision that the Crown had failed to show that Fitton's oral and written statements were "free and voluntary." Perhaps the X's simply indicated that Macdonald found the judge's point important. However, his recommendation that the law should take its course, combined with the Cabinet's quick approval, suggests the solicitor general decided the ruling that quashed Fitton's conviction was wrong and the decision to restore it right.

THE CABINET CONCLUDES

The best clues to the Cabinet's denial of clemency do not appear in Fitton's case file but in the records of the Privy Council. The clerk of the Privy Council served the governor general as secretary to the Cabinet, and it was his duty to keep a record of executive proceedings that required official confirmation as Orders in Council. Cabinet recommendations for or against the royal prerogative of mercy fell into that category.[62] During the Second World War, ministerial executive decision making grew, and this increased the formality of Cabinet meetings.[63] From that point, it became standard for agendas and papers to be distributed in advance, and minutes were taken of the proceedings, known as Cabinet conclusions. Despite their cursory nature, these minutes (stamped "Secret") record the decisions made in capital cases, and they refer to the points ministers raised as they deliberated.[64] Many of these minutes have not survived in the archival record (Tripodi's case is an example), but Fitton's did.[65]

The Cabinet minutes for November 19, 1956, indicate that the solicitor general opened by describing Fitton's crime in Chief Detective Cathie's terms (the "rape" and murder of a "young girl" carried out in a "lonely place"). When Macdonald raised the fact that Humphrey and O'Driscoll had solicited affidavits from jurors, the minutes registered disapproval. Several days earlier, the Remission Service had added three more juror affidavits to Fitton's file, sent by his lawyers, and on November 14, MacLeod sent the solicitor general a memo to inform him of the affidavits, making it likely they discussed the matter before the Cabinet meeting. Although the minutes do not identify which minister or ministers criticized the defence's ploy as "most improper," it could have been Stuart Garson, since Humphrey and O'Driscoll sent their clemency correspondence to the minister of justice. There is no reference in the Cabinet minutes to any discussion of the Ontario Court of Appeal's decision to quash Fitton's conviction, but they do refer to the

The Privy Council chamber, 1953. Prime Minister Louis St-Laurent is seated in the chair at the table's centre. Stuart Garson, the minister of justice, is seated fourth from the front, on the left. | LAC 196460

Supreme Court's ruling, which "confirmed the verdict of guilty." All the fine legal points about constructive murder – a bone of contention in Fitton's trial, gnawed at further in the appeals – went up in a puff of pipe and cigarette smoke in the Privy Council chambers. Fitton's previous good character also disappeared. "After consideration of all the facts presented" (the standard phrase used to introduce Cabinet decisions), the solicitor general's recommendation that the law take its course received unanimous approval from his colleagues.[66]

The Cabinet members who met to review Fitton's case, like every review of a capital case, made their decision on a narrow selection of facts, sifted by the Remission Service and served up economically by the minister. The requisite Order in Council was passed as PC (Privy Council) 1956-1711 and the Cabinet turned to the next item on its agenda – Canada's support of international relief for Hungarians. In the Canadian Bar Association's forum on abolition in 1954, the same year the special joint committee began its investigations into the death penalty's administration, J.J. Robinette, the lawyer who had saved Evelyn Dick from the gallows twice, observed that open trials allowed the public to see the evidence against suspects and their defences at trial, and newspapers covered the arguments for and against appeals and the reasons why courts allowed or dismissed them. Yet no one knew "on what principle some murderers have had their sentences commuted and some have not."[67] The Cabinet doors remained closed on November 19, 1956.

IN FITTON'S TWO APPEALS – the first at the defence's request and the second at the attorney general's – judges provided reasons for their decisions, agreeing with or dissenting from their brother judges' application of common law doctrine, statutes, and cited authorities. By contrast, the decisions of the Cabinet in the exercise of executive discretion were not subject to appeal, although ministers knew their decisions could attract criticism. When Stuart Garson established a joint committee on capital punishment in 1954, he hoped it would assure the public that deliberations over the death penalty were conducted with probity. By the time the committee's final report appeared in June 1956, the controversial execution of Wilbert Coffin had sown skepticism over the supposed fairness of executive discretion. Nevertheless, the reports of the joint committee and the Fauteux inquiry into the Remission Service, tabled in May 1956, had nothing but praise for the bureaucrats and ministers who carried out their "tough tasks." And they accepted the Minister's observation that "no two convicted murderers are ever exactly alike."[68] Finding no cause to change course, the government reaffirmed its commitment to retaining the death penalty, just before the Supreme Court restored Fitton's conviction for murder and reset his execution date.

Although the minister of justice went on record to state that the Cabinet usually granted clemency if the jury made that recommendation, he was careful to add that they "weigh[ed] it in the light of all the facts" unique to each case, parroting the stock phrase that accompanied final decisions.[69] However, the Department of Justice's records and the tables produced by Remission Service clerks revealed unambiguous patterns of decision making for and against clemency. A recommendation to mercy was a buffer against severity, but it was no guarantee, particularly in sex murder cases. Four justices of the Court of Appeal and two Supreme Court judges believed the jury's verdict had been tainted by the judge's misdirection and non-direction, but one dissenting judge and the majority of judges in the country's highest court ruled otherwise. Fitton's defenders tried to turn the jurors' misunderstanding of the law of murder into a weighty "fact." However, their strategy backfired. Although the Cabinet's decision that Fitton's sentence be carried out did not ignite a firestorm of protest, as their denial of clemency for Coffin did, it gave ample reason for Fitton's loved ones, critics of the death penalty, and believers in the defence's theory that the homicide had been accidental to question whether the government retained the death penalty to deter crime – as it affirmed – or solely to exact vengeance.

9

A Second Fatality

THREE HUNDRED TORONTONIANS gathered on the grounds of the Don Jail on the night of November 20, 1956, having heard that Robert Fitton would be hanged just after midnight. No executions had occurred in the city since 1952, and reporters circled, looking for an angle on the crowd's "morbid curiosity." One "attractive girl" explained why she was there: "Well, I guess he's getting what he deserved."[1] David Humphrey and Archie O'Driscoll did not share her view, and their visit to the jail on that drizzly, cold evening served a different purpose: to inform their client he had no hope of a last-minute reprieve. Dosed with a shot of morphine, Fitton was led to the hanging chamber, wrists cuffed, ankles bound. After the hangman placed a black hood on the condemned man, he felt the rope slip over his head and tighten around his neck. Then the trap door opened beneath his feet. The coroner, the official who had filled out Linda Lampkin's death certificate eleven months earlier, was the same man who held a hasty inquest into the death of Robert Fitton. The cause of this second fatality was different: judicial hanging.[2]

In the mid-1950s, Canada conducted the first major inquiry into possible alternatives to capital punishment, signalling the possibility that it might progress to modern forms of correction and treatment and "do without the penalty of death for murder."[3] Yet supporters of abolition comprised a small, if vocal, minority of Canadians.[4] The final report of the special joint committee of the Senate and the House of Commons, submitted five months before Fitton's execution, advised the time had not come to dispense with the death penalty, although the committee had misgivings over the uncertainties of hangings.[5] As it transpired, the government did not pursue alternatives, and this decision to stick with the status quo, combined with the prevailing low rate of commutations for convicted sex murderers, ultimately outweighed the recommendations to mercy advocated by Fitton's jurors and trial judge. The Cabinet's refusal to grant clemency angered Fitton's loved ones and members of the public who spoke out against the executive's decision. When they wrote to the government, they received the stock response: "Cabinet gave the most serious considerations of the case."[6] There was nothing modern or scientific about this hanging or the discretionary deliberations that led to its infliction.

Once justified as a cornerstone of general deterrence and moral instruction, public executions were prohibited in Canada in the late nineteenth century.[7] The hidden conduct of hangings was one of the reasons the joint committee sought information from officials directly involved in carrying them out. Two decades earlier, a smaller inquiry on the same subject conducted a similar investigation, but they did not call "Mr. Ellis," the chief hangman, as a witness. After much debate, the man who carried out executions in Quebec testified before the joint committee in camera, alleging his work was foolproof. Toronto's sheriff and the Don's surgeon, two men who played central roles in Fitton's execution, conveyed greater credibility when they detailed how troubling they found their duties. Enterprising reporters dug up further information on the hanging from insiders willing to talk anonymously: guards who worked in the Don Jail and the man who carried out Fitton's execution. Cabinet members sometimes admitted they found it tough to render decisions in capital cases, but these officials had it tougher. They took part in intimate rituals that stirred deep feelings: they talked with the condemned, looked him in the eye, touched his body. Fitton's family could only imagine what he felt in his last moments, and any distortion to his neck after hanging on the rope for over twenty minutes was hidden since the coffin was sealed. Yet the attractive girl's comment – that Fitton's hanging was just deserts – was a sentiment most Canadians shared.

EXECUTIONS, COMMUTATIONS, AND APPEALS IN POSTWAR CANADA

After the Second World War, there were many sectors of Canadian law and justice in which the Liberal government of Louis St-Laurent committed to progressive change. Modernizing and streamlining the Criminal Code was one example. New provisions, informed by postwar psychiatry, were introduced to improve the treatment of sexual psychopaths. The revised code excluded infanticide and rape from the death penalty. And the government sponsored numerous inquiries into the statute on criminal sexual psychopathy, the defence of criminal insanity, the Remission Service, and the prospect of abolishing the death penalty. Yet, as Philip Girard shows, the "shadow of the Cold War" darkened Canadian politics in this period: fear of espionage and fifth columnists held back the movement for civil liberties, as critics of the government and suspected sexual subversives discovered.[8] That shadow extended to the imposition of the death penalty. In the postwar decade, the proportion of executions to death sentences hovered just over 50 percent, but sex murderers were executed at a much higher rate.

Stuart Garson, sworn in as minister of justice and attorney general on November 15, 1948, headed the department that managed capital case reviews; and he was the minister who corresponded with lawyers, judges, and members of the public who took an interest in capital cases. At his first Cabinet meeting, held three days after his appointment, a capital case appeared on the agenda, concerning a sex killer accused of sodomizing pubescent boys and convicted of murdering one of them in Winnipeg in 1946.[9] Having recently left his post as premier of Manitoba, Garson would undoubtedly have followed the prosecution of the accused, Michael Vescio, who appealed his conviction unsuccessfully.[10] The Manitoba Court of Appeal denied Vescio's appeal against his conviction, and the Supreme Court dismissed his appeal against that decision, a fact the Cabinet bore in mind in recommending that the law take its course.[11] From Vescio's execution in 1948 to Fitton's eight years later, Garson was directly involved in the deliberations that resulted in seventy-six hangings, an average of one every six weeks.[12]

Of the eight executions carried out in 1956, the year Fitton was hanged, the most controversial was Wilbert Coffin's, which followed a failed appeal to the Quebec Court of Appeal and an adverse judgment by the Supreme Court after a referral. In the five months that preceded Coffin's execution, Canada's hangmen were inactive. One reason for the hiatus in hangings was the number of appeals lodged, which diverted capital cases that would otherwise have proceeded directly to clemency reviews.[13] From the late 1940s, appeals were lodged after most capital convictions, and top-flight criminal defence lawyers, such as G. Arthur Martin and Arthur E. Maloney, frequently argued for the defence.

In 1956, six of the twenty-three people under sentence of death in Canada appealed successfully, and had the attorney general of Ontario decided not to appeal against the provincial Court of Appeal's decision to quash Fitton's conviction and order a new trial, Fitton would have been the seventh. Capital appellants whose appeals were dismissed were still eligible for clemency from the executive, but seeking relief through the courts did not enhance condemned offenders' chance of a commuted sentence. By contrast, three of the convicted murderers who did not appeal against their convictions were granted clemency in 1956.[14] In Arthur Maloney's view, the executive was too prone to interpret appeals denied by the courts as cause to refuse clemency. When Stuart Garson appeared before the joint committee, he claimed that the Cabinet was unbound by legal decisions. Again, Maloney disagreed: in his experience, the executive "ignore[d] the duty to apply totally different considerations to those that are applied by the jury and appellate courts."[15] The Department of Justice's statistics made Maloney's claim more plausible than Garson's. Cabinets clearly took cues from appeal court decisions, especially those of the Supreme Court, that murder convictions were sound, even when there was dissent, as there was in Fitton's appeals.

Recommendations to mercy (their presence or absence) strongly influenced the likelihood (or unlikelihood) of clemency, which was evident in the distribution of commutations and executions in the year

Fitton was hanged (see Table 1 on the following page). Nevertheless, recommendations by the jury, the judge, or both did not dictate Cabinet decisions. Evidence of capital case dispositions in 1956, the year the joint committee and the Fauteux inquiry reported, shows that Arthur Maloney's and other abolitionists' concerns over the Cabinet's disinclination to commute without a recommendation were well founded. In 1956, the executive granted clemency in nine cases, eight of which included a mercy recommendation; by contrast, none of the men executed in 1956 received a recommendation to mercy, with one significant exception: Fitton.

An execution that proceeded in the face of a mercy recommendation was not unprecedented, but 1950 was the last time that had occurred, and it involved an offender quite unlike Fitton, aside from his age. In that year, twenty-year-old William Lusanko was convicted of a robbery murder in Winnipeg and hanged at Headingley Jail despite the jury's recommendation to mercy. The Crown argued that he had bound and smothered a sixty-five-year-old woman whose home he and a "gang of bad young men" had burgled and robbed.[16] The jury did not explain why they added a mercy rider to their verdict, but their recommendation may have been based on Lusanko's youth. Other possible reasons were the involvement of his alleged accomplices and the fact that the chief witness against Lusanko was a jail informant. In the judge's opinion, these concerns were insignificant, whereas the condemned prisoner's lengthy criminal history made mercy inappropriate. Lusanko had been "in trouble since he was eleven years old," the judge stated, and the man's record included multiple counts of theft, housebreaking, and auto stealing. "He and his companions are a menace to the whole neighbourhood," the trial report stressed. On that basis, the judge concluded: "There is no ameliorating circumstance ... which gives any ground as a reason for the exercise of executive clemency, and I cannot recommend it."[17]

In the absence of an extant minute of the Cabinet meeting that endorsed the judge's opinion, its impact is difficult to discern. However, the red underscoring of that damning passage in the judge's report plus the large red asterisk mark that appears beside his recommendation to deny clemency suggest it swayed the Cabinet to act against the jury's

Table 1 **Offence and offender characteristics, Canadian executions, 1956**

Name of accused	*Execution date*	*Type of homicide/victim*	*Appeals filed and decided*	*Mercy recommendation*	*Age at offence*
Wilbert Coffin	February 10	Robbery (firearm)	1 dismissed; 1 denied	No	48
Robert Graham	May 22	Male acquaintance	2nd trial (jury disagreed in first)	No	24
Robert Ducsharm	June 15	Male acquaintance	2nd trial; 1 quashed; 1 no leave granted	No	24
Peter Morrison	July 17	Robbery (firearm)	1 dismissed	No	23
Ovila Boucher	October 10	Robbery (axe)	1st appeal dismissed; 1 quashed; 1 dismissed; 1 Supreme Court overturned; reconvicted	No	32
Clifford Ayles	November 6	Robbery (stabbing)	1 dismissed	No	26
Robert Fitton	November 21	Sex murder (strangulation)	1 quashed; 1 restored verdict (Supreme Court)	Yes	21
Edmond Gagné	November 29	Intimate female partner (strangulation)	No appeal	No	20

Source: Information gathered from Lorraine Gadoury and Antonio Lechasseur, "Persons Sentenced to Death in Canada, 1867–1976: An Inventory of Case Files in the Fonds of the Department of Justice," National Archives of Canada, 1994.

recommendation. But the basis for the denial of executive clemency for Lusanko differed from the Cabinet's decision to let Fitton's death sentence stand. This young, respectable, hard-working man with no criminal record and a recommendation to mercy supported by the trial judge must be hanged.

SEX KILLERS AND SEVERITY

Fitton's conviction and the Supreme Court's upholding of the Crown's appeal occurred in the context of the government's affirmation of its commitment to retain the death penalty. The introduction of a statute on the treatment of sexual psychopaths in 1948 made no difference to this trend, and few sex murderers were considered anything other than criminally responsible. The hanging of Fitton in 1956 made him the thirteenth sex murderer executed after the end of the Second World War. When news of Linda Lampkin's murder first broke, a Liberal backbencher addressed Parliament about the need to enforce the penalty of death. More dangerous than the sexual psychopath, MP Russell Reinke thought, was the "sane person who wilfully and methodically sets out to carry out this act." The Lampkin murder was committed by the type of criminal who, "after committing this foul deed, kills his victim for the purpose, I suppose, of hiding his identity." Psychiatric treatment was not the answer: "The penalty is there and must be meted out severely to act as a deterrent to others." Reinke's speech drew applause from both sides of the house.[18] Another Liberal who doubled as a political columnist, Elmore Philpott, shared his colleague's view.[19] A Vancouver MP, Philpott worried that "more and more people assume that evil people commit sinful acts because of some strange combination of circumstances over which they have no control." Yet, he claimed, "the vast majority of people who commit sexual crimes are completely aware of what they are doing and are completely responsible for their acts."[20]

In Toronto, the last execution before Fitton's was the double hanging of two members of the notorious Boyd Gang, both convicted of the murder of a sergeant on the city's police force. Their execution surprised few who were familiar with stated government policy. A staff reporter for the Toronto *Daily Star* claimed a former Cabinet minister had told him that "it was a foregone conclusion that two men who were partners in crime at the time of a murder of a police officer in the performance of his duty would not get clemency from the federal cabinet."[21] When Stuart Garson testified before the joint committee, he freely admitted that "such types of murder will deserve a lower rate of commutation, generally speaking, than will those murders which arise out of family and lovers quarrels, jealousy, and the like."[22] However, Garson said nothing about murders involving sexual violence to explain why men sentenced to death for those types of crimes were granted the lowest rates.[23]

After Garson was sworn into the Cabinet, six men convicted of sex murder were denied clemency before Fitton, although none of them was hanged in Toronto. The last man executed in the city for a murder involving a sexual assault was Harry O'Donnell, convicted in 1936 of the murder of an unmarried and respectable stenographer, Ruth Taylor. James C. McRuer, future chief justice and chairman of two royal commissions – the one on the law relating to sexual psychopaths and the one on the criminal insanity defence – was the prosecutor in O'Donnell's trial. After the jury convicted him, with no recommendation to mercy, O'Donnell's lawyer appealed, but the Court of Appeal dismissed the appeal, and the Supreme Court denied leave to appeal. Shifting to a plea for clemency, the lawyer tried to persuade the executive that his client's confession of a long history of sexual voyeurism, stalking, and sexual assault was reason enough to consider him mentally abnormal and therefore deserving of mercy. However, the psychiatric reports the executive ordered pronounced the man to be criminally responsible, and the Cabinet found that evidence persuasive. After O'Donnell was hanged in the Don Jail on May 5, 1936, Toronto's next sex murderer, pronounced to be normal, but with no history of sexual deviancy, stepped into the Don's death chamber.[24]

INSIDE THE DEATH CHAMBER

The procedures surrounding executions and the method of hanging were two of the joint committee's chief concerns as it conducted research and questioned witnesses about capital punishment in practice. Two decades earlier, Canada had conducted a similar inquiry into executions by various means, both ancient and modern. In 1936, a bill was introduced to replace hanging with lethal gas. Rather than debate the bill, the Liberal government agreed to appoint a committee to investigate the penalty of death in January 1937. The inquiry looked into allegations of faulty calculations of the drop and misplacements of the rope that had resulted in prolonged strangulations or decapitation (notably the case of Tommasina Teolis's ghastly execution in Montreal in 1935), but they recommended retaining the British tradition.[25] The veteran chief of the Remission Service was one of the witnesses who strongly supported hanging over other methods because he approved of the "ignominy" of hanging – a time-tested deterrent and a cornerstone of Canadian criminal justice.[26] In March 1937 the committee's final report appeared with only one major recommendation: central places of execution in all provinces to reduce the likelihood of "unfortunate mistakes" in local jails and to avoid stirring up the public in small towns.[27] Like many such recommendations concerning capital punishment, the government did not act on it.[28] Nevertheless, the committee confirmed that Toronto's Don Jail, with its interior execution chamber, had operated with no "untoward incident."[29]

In small towns, labourers erected temporary scaffolds in jail yards, and the sawing of wood and the hammering of nails preceded executions. When the surgeon of Welland County Jail testified before the joint committee in 1954, he said he felt this percussive prelude was "a living death for the condemned and intensifies the depression suffered by the staff and inmates."[30] Toronto's jail was different. At the time of its construction in 1864, "the Don" was the largest jail in North America, with an official capacity of cells for five hundred prisoners, including a small wing of cells for prisoners sentenced to hang. In 1908, a converted lavatory with a trap door that opened to a lower room replaced the outdoor scaffold.[31] According to York County's sheriff, the conduct of internal hangings was "way ahead of the old system" at the Don, which had required the condemned to walk through the jail to the yard. This was "enough to break down the strongest man."[32]

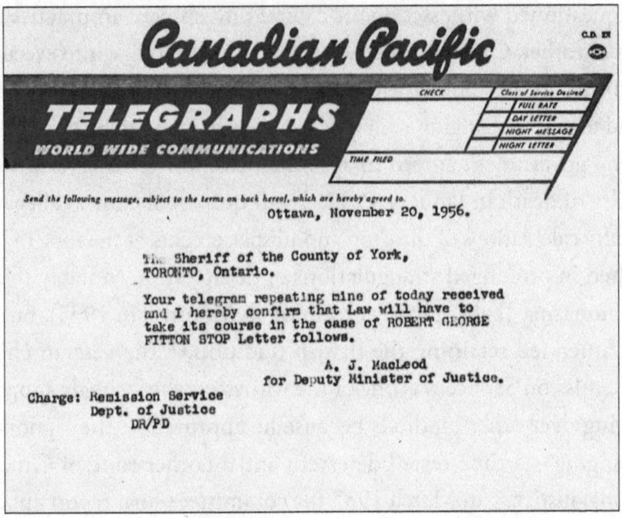

Canadian Pacific
TELEGRAPHS
WORLD WIDE COMMUNICATIONS
CHECK
Class of Service Desired
FULL RATE
DAY LETTER
NIGHT MESSAGE
NIGHT LETTER
TIME FILED

Send the following message, subject to the terms on back hereof, which are hereby agreed to.

Ottawa, November 20, 1956.

The Sheriff of the County of York,
TORONTO, Ontario.

Your telegram repeating mine of today received and I hereby confirm that Law will have to take its course in the case of ROBERT GEORGE FITTON STOP Letter follows.

A. J. MacLeod
for Deputy Minister of Justice.

Charge: Remission Service
Dept. of Justice
DR/PD

After the Cabinet denied Fitton clemency on November 20, 1956, the Remission Service wired the sheriff of York County to make arrangements for his execution. | LAC, RG13-B-1, vol. 1755, "Fitton, Robert," vol. 5

In Canada, sheriffs were not involved in catching criminals, as they were in many parts of the United States; rather, they were officers of the court who had a duty to carry out orders and ensure that orders were conducted according to the law.[33] To set an execution into motion, the Remission Service sent a telegram to the sheriff of the locality to make the necessary arrangements. On November 20, 1956, Colonel J.D. Conover, the sheriff of York County, received a message ordering him to ensure that the hangman, acting as his deputy, would carry out Robert Fitton's execution at midnight the following day.

The 1937 death penalty inquiry and the mid-1950s joint committee both studied the bureaucratic management, procedures, and personnel involved in the condemned prisoner's last day. Throughout their proceedings, they recorded the toll executions took on the men involved. Toronto's deputy sheriff, Stephen Wills, having served twenty-four years on the job and having witnessed eleven executions, appeared before the 1937 committee. Each hanging was traumatic because he feared a decapitation every time, although he said he had never had the misfortune to witness one at the Don Jail.[34] In his era, executions took place at 8 a.m., after the prisoner's breakfast, and he testified that spiritual advisers were allowed to attend the night before. Some stayed the night, but they always accompanied the condemned to the death chamber. In Wills's experience, the jail governor made it a rule to visit the prisoner to see if he desired a "hypodermic" containing morphine, and such requests were always granted. In the last moments, the sheriff asked the prisoner for any final words before he instructed the hangman to pull the lever and release the bolt on the trap door. "Everything goes very quickly," Wills commented, and the time it took from the opening of the trap door to the prisoner's death varied, in his experience, between twelve and seventeen minutes. In one execution, he saw the hangman yank on the prisoner's suspended body after the drop, attempting to hasten death because he had overestimated the length of the hanging rope. Although Wills thought it would be "more humane" to replace hanging with lethal gas, a method that had recently been introduced in some US states, he had nothing critical to say about the conduct of the final rituals.[35]

By 1954, a new generation of officials involved in hangings at the Don Jail told the joint committee that executions had become infrequent in Toronto. Despite this, Sheriff Conover and the surgeon of the Don Jail, W.H. Hills, the men who would serve in Fitton's execution, testified at length.[36] The doctor said he had witnessed four executions, and the sheriff said he had seen two, involving a total of three men (Jackson and Suchan were hanged together). Conover began by explaining why there were so few executions in the city. Over his nine years on the job, fifty-nine murder trials had been held in Toronto, and just five of those trials ended in convictions. Of that number, two received commuted sentences, and three were executed. Ten trials either ended in an acquittal or the defendant was found to be insane. By far the most common outcome (forty of the fifty-nine trials) was the verdict of guilty of manslaughter – the verdict Fitton's lawyers had anticipated.[37] Conover thought that Toronto jurors were reluctant to find accused murderers guilty since the penalty of death was mandatory. Whatever the reason, these numbers meant he rarely had to contact the official hangman to arrange for a hanging at the Don Jail at the prescribed date and time.

The duty to fill out the paperwork necessary to certify death, a statutory requirement in all executions, fell to the Don's surgeon, Doctor Hills.[38] As the jail's physician, Hills was primarily involved in maintaining the health of prisoners, including the condemned, whom he came to know. "As time goes by," Hills reflected, most of the men became "friendly, co-operative and pleasant."[39] By the mid-1950s, greater effort was made by the staff to reduce prisoners' anxieties. As the execution day approached, the doctor provided sedation if requested, and he also offered the prisoner a shot of morphine with hyoscine (an antispasmodic), although some did not desire it.[40] In Hills's opinion, "the clergyman probably does more" to comfort men facing imminent execution, but as a physician, he found the switch to pronouncing a prisoner's death after tending to his health "an unpleasant duty." As soon as the hangman called out that the prisoner appeared to be dead, the doctor mounted a step ladder and placed a stethoscope "on the man's heart." The joint committee members were surprised to learn that after the body drops, "the heart beats very strongly and loudly. The rate is hastened." Harold Winch, the most committed abolitionist on the committee, asked Hills to explain: "After the hanging the rate is faster, and then slower, and the sound remains loud and presently the rate becomes slower and the sounds become quieter and quieter ... The heart beat becomes irregular and slows until it stops."[41] In a macabre embrace of the prisoner's body, the doctor teetered on a ladder, listening to the prisoner's life fade away. This part of his job, Hills told the joint committee, this "operation," went against "all his teaching, training and experience."[42]

The members of both inquiries into capital punishment sought accurate information about the efficiency of hanging to assess the viability of alternative methods. If it took a long time for a heart to stop beating, and if the prisoner died by suffocation rather than a quick severing of the vertebrae, it might be time to try a more modern technique.[43] Hills admitted he had made "no records of such times" between the drop and death, but his notes on the hangings he had attended indicated he could still hear "heart sounds" between twenty-two minutes and forty-five minutes after the trap door opened. Winch was troubled by this evidence. Was death by hanging instantaneous, he asked the doctor. "No," was the reply.[44] Furthermore, Hills observed that hanging caused the neck of the deceased to become "angulated and lengthened." Although he thought the cause of death of the four men whose hangings he had attended "appeared to be primarily fracture of the neck," Hills admitted that "strangulation would have to be considered as a secondary cause, although probably not the actual cause of death."[45] In fact, there was no way to say for certain since autopsies were not performed on the bodies of executed prisoners. Hills's final responsibility was to ensure "that the body is interred without being viewed by an unauthorized person or even relatives."[46] Once the doctor signed the death certificate, it was the coroner's duty to conduct an inquest to confirm the cause of death. Aside from the undertaker, who embalmed or cremated the remains, the doctor was the last person to see the body and touch it in the grim intimacy of the execution chamber.

Toronto's sheriff and the Don Jail's doctor referred numerous times to "the hangman," whom both committees considered calling as a witness.[47] The members of the 1937 committee decided against it, with the majority convinced that such a witness would be "biased" and have a "one-sided opinion."[48] W. Ross Thatcher, who, like Winch, was a Co-operative Commonwealth Federation MP who opposed the death penalty, strongly urged the joint committee's chairman to call on one of Canada's executioners to provide a statement and appear as a witness. In his opinion, "it might remove a great deal of mystery" about the mental suffering of everyone involved in an execution, not just the condemned. Sheriff Conover admitted he felt a "sense of strain" whenever an execution date approached. His role in the preparations made him feel "sort of tense to a certain extent, or nervy." Hills disclosed that he took "a little phenobarbital" to quell his nerves. As a former boxing champion, he told the joint committee he could take a great deal of physical pounding, but it pained him deeply "to see anyone suffer."[49] Several joint committee members felt uneasy about meeting a hangman in person: "There is something terrible about it ... I think this would bring on a morbidity before this committee to which I am opposed," Liberal MP Maurice Boisvert revealed. Senator Nancy Hodges felt similarly: "It seems to me a very gruesome thing." When Thatcher heard this, he taunted them: "You bet!"[50] He or Winch may have had a hand in encouraging the man who carried out executions primarily in Quebec to request an opportunity to appear before the joint committee. In May 1954, a subcommittee recommended that he appear to answer questions in camera.[51]

Six senators and fourteen MPs were escorted to an RCMP administration building in Ottawa on May 11, 1955, to hear directly from a man who, by that point, had carried out some two hundred hangings since his work began in 1926. "Camille Branchaud" (the hangman's *nom de métier*) appeared with an officer in Montreal's sheriff's department who read out his statement in English for the mainly anglophone joint committee. Using jail reports of the condemned prisoner's height, weight, and age, Branchaud reported that he used his table of calculations to determine the length of the rope (stretched). To "avoid strangulation," he tied the rope with five rings, applied Vaseline, and adjusted the noose "to assure the immediate break of the spinal vertebrae at the base of the neck." No "accidents" had occurred in his practice, Branchaud asserted, and he claimed that spinal fracture was the cause of death in 99 percent of the executions he carried out. As soon as the trap door was sprung, there were "no signs of consciousness," and the time to death (stoppage of the heart) averaged from twelve to fifteen minutes, with ten minutes the shortest and twenty-two minutes the longest in his experience. He disputed Hills's testimony that forty-five minutes could elapse before death. Yet Branchaud's report provided no evidence to verify his assertions, since Canada, unlike England, did not carry out postmortem examinations of executed prisoners. In addition, the hangman insisted that the details of his practice, from the tying of knots to the length of the drop, were "of a confidential nature."[52]

Having heard unsettling accounts from the Don's physician and York County's sheriff, members of the joint committee questioned hangman Branchaud and tested his claims as a professional tradesman. A.J.P. "Pat" Cameron, a Liberal MP who represented one of Toronto's west end ridings, asked whether 99 percent had possibly died from "pressure on the carotid arteries," thereby producing "cerebral anaemia or loss of blood to the heart."[53] The technical language flummoxed the witness. On rare occasions when death was not instantaneous and strangulation occurred, Branchaud blamed incorrect weights provided by prison officials. Stuart Garson pressed him on the precise placement of the rope needed to ensure the fracturing of specific cervical vertebrae, but the hangman's answer was rubbery: "We always put the noose underneath the left ear so the string of the heart is broken, or the nerve to the heart is broken." This garbled explanation was more than a problem of translation, the abolitionists on the joint committee suspected. Thatcher pounced, asking Branchaud to confirm if it was true "there is no way the hangman can so adjust the rope to break ... any particular vertebrae." The hangman, through his translator, agreed. Branchaud gave the committee further reason to determine that executions in Canada were replete with uncertainties. In his experience, he found that officials involved in an execution sometimes arrived at the event intoxicated, and they continued drinking, unable to carry out their duties. Asked if he had ever reported a drunken coroner or prison doctor to the authorities, Branchaud replied: "No ... everything stays within the walls of the prison."[54]

In the course of the joint committee's debates over the prospect of hearing from one of the men who carried out the death sentence in Canada, the question of morbidness came up frequently. They, and many of the witnesses they interviewed, referred disparagingly to members of the public as morbidly curious about capital punishment. If the committee were to talk to an executioner about his work, were they any different? One member urged his fellow MPs and senators to carry out their task, no matter how distasteful: "While it may be morbid listening to his evidence, we have had the prison doctor and the sheriff and after all, executions are conducted in our society and let us not be hesitant about going right to the root of the thing. As long as we are going to execute people we require an executioner."[55]

Their refined feelings and sensitivities disturbed by first-hand accounts of putting capital offenders to death, the joint committee members differed from their counterparts on the 1937 capital punishment inquiry on the question of execution methods. In their final report, tabled in June 1956, the joint committee advised that Canada replace death by hanging with more technically advanced methods. The government accepted their recommendation to retain the death penalty, but it ignored their advice, preferring to stick to the ignominious tradition of death by hanging. This meant that Conover and Hills had to brace themselves for another bout of strain and nervousness behind the Don Jail's walls when the notice came to prepare for Robert Fitton's hanging.

FINAL CONTACT

As Allan MacLeod flipped through the list of officials he had to inform that the Governor General in Council had not seen fit to "interfere with the death sentence passed upon Robert George Fitton," he started with York County's sheriff (responsible for securing the hangman's service) then moved down to the RCMP commissioner, the attorney general of Ontario, the director of public prosecutions, the Crown attorney (who had prosecuted Fitton), and the judge (who had pronounced that sentence). MacLeod also informed David Humphrey and Archie O'Driscoll, and he wrote, as a courtesy, to Fitton's mother and his boss. The only people on that list who visited the prisoner in his final hours were his lawyers.

The Supreme Court's decision required that Fitton be transferred from the overcrowded shared cells in the general population block back

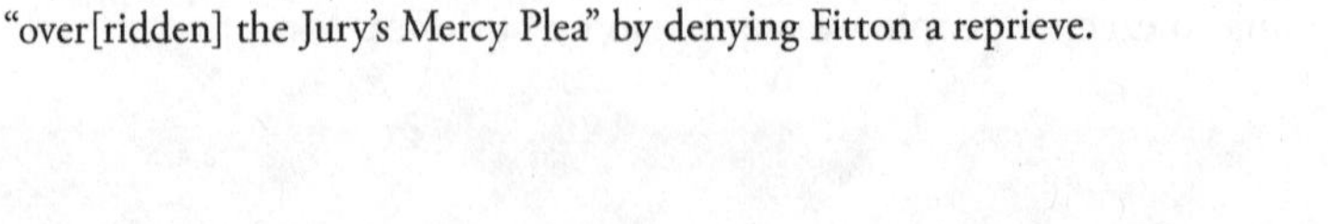
THE TELEGRAM

The Pink Tely
Night
Final Sports – Markets

81ST YEAR
48 PAGES
TORONTO, TUESDAY, NOVEMBER 20, 1956
PRICE 5 CENTS

NO REPRIEVE -- FITTON DIES TONIGHT

The Toronto *Telegram* on November 20, 1956, reported that the Cabinet had "over[ridden] the Jury's Mercy Plea" by denying Fitton a reprieve.

to the solitude of the death cell, where the light was never extinguished and a guard kept watch around the clock. All visitors had to be authorized, and they were barred from entering the cell or coming into physical contact, the only exception being clerics. That rule was strictly enforced, according to Colonel Hedley Basher, the deputy minister in charge of Ontario's prison system. When he appeared before the joint committee, he said it was customary for a spiritual adviser (chosen or provided), a family member, and defence counsel to receive permission to visit in the hours leading up to the execution.[56] The last member of the Fitton family to visit him was his mother, Pearl, who saw her son on November 19. The no-contact rule struck her as heartless: "I couldn't even touch his hand. They wouldn't even let me kiss my own son goodbye. I can never see him again."[57]

Fitton's defence counsel met their client for the last time in the early evening of November 20. Humphrey was aware that the man's family was "very religious," but he also drew on his personal faith to offer the young man solace, telling Fitton, "What they are going to do at midnight tonight, that is their business. You will be involved, but you are going to meet Jesus tonight at midnight and that is what I want you to look forward to. So whatever anybody else thinks, you have made your peace with God."[58] Although Humphrey drifted from his church and religious faith later in life, he reflected many years later that he spoke to Fitton from the heart that night: "At the time, I meant it very sincerely."[59] Humphrey also knew that the family's Pentecostal minister and the Don Jail's chaplain were willing to minister to Fitton up to the moment the hangman pulled the lever.[60] Recalling his client's demeanour on that night, Humphrey thought the condemned man was resigned to his fate: "He seemed matter of fact, and, to me, I didn't notice any fear in him." But anyone who read the papers knew Fitton's wife, Florence, felt differently. Nineteen years old and nursing her third child, she was angry and perplexed. "All along, the lawyers and everybody have been telling us Bob wouldn't die. He was going to be all right, maybe get 10 years. And now this news."[61]

A story circulated that Fitton had told his lawyers he would have hired J.J. Robinette, one of the country's highest-profile defence barristers, if he had to go through the ordeal of another trial, but Humphrey insisted the rumour was false. In his recollection, Fitton was as genuine in his appreciation of his counsel's efforts as he was when he told the young man to make peace with his saviour. According to Humphrey, Fitton "did thank me very much for doing what I tried to do for him." But there was no more a lawyer could do as midnight approached, and his defenders bid Fitton goodbye.

THE LAST WALK

At Toronto's Don Jail, reporters were barred from attending executions, a policy of long standing. As far back as 1937, the branch chief in the Remission Service testified before the capital punishment inquiry that reporters were no longer allowed to view executions up close as they had in the nineteenth century. Consequently, the press relied on informants in the jail. One guard told the *Telegram* he had come to know Fitton since he arrived. In the early months of his incarceration, the prisoner was "morose and sometimes sullen," but "as the hours got closer he seemed quite cheerful."[62] When Fitton left his cell to walk the twenty paces to the death chamber, he appeared subdued, possibly on account of the morphine. Another insider informed the press that Hills had offered Fitton a "hypodermic." When members of the 1937 committee inquired about morphine's effect on the condemned, they assumed it was a sedative. "No, no, no sedative is ever used," Toronto's deputy sheriff corrected them.[63] One committee member, a Liberal MP who had trained as a doctor, described morphine's effect more poetically: "Morphia means the bliss of peace to a man; without anything else."[64] Sedation was to be avoided since it risked making it difficult to rouse the prisoner from his cell and it also risked requiring guards to drag or carry the condemned to the chamber. It appeared, however, that the dose of "bliss" given to prisoners varied substantially, from half a grain of morphia to three-quarters of a grain.[65] When Hills offered Fitton a shot, he declined at first but changed his mind. At about 11 p.m. on November 20, as the execution party awaited the hangman's arrival, he dosed the prisoner with half a grain of morphine and hyoscine.

This tense interior drama had a more raucous external counterpart that grew as members of the public assembled on the muddy grounds in front of the jail. The late hour of the execution and the drizzly weather failed to deter the crowd – mainly youths. All they could see was the jail's gloomy facade; yet their presence, steps away from the enclosed execution chamber, made them participants in the hanging. The prohibition against direct witnessing did not dampen public interest in executions, something officials involved in the hanging considered shameful. Welland County's jail doctor told the joint committee that a crowd of five hundred had gathered in Cornwall, Ontario, on the night of Peter Balcombe's execution in May 1954.[66] When the double hanging of Jackson and Suchan occurred in the Don Jail in December 1952, between two and three thousand people gathered. Events of this sort could be eliminated, the doctor urged, if Canada conducted executions away from population centres.[67] The joint committee included that recommendation in its final report – yet another reform the government ignored.[68] This meant Fitton's execution would take place in the same city where he had raped and murdered Linda Lampkin.

Sequestered from the assembling crowd, the Fittons' pastor and the jail's chaplain attended Fitton before the guards came for him. Two weeks earlier, Reverend Malcolm P. Smith had written the chief remission officer on behalf of the family to urge the Cabinet to consider clemency: "There has never been any question about his guilt or about the horribleness of his crime," he acknowledged. Yet Fitton was not a career criminal (as Lusanko, Suchan, and Jackson were), and the pastor thought the young man had no criminal intent: "He seems to be entirely free of any premeditation to murder."[69] Once the Don's chaplain heard the law would take its course, the only thing left for him to do was to accompany the prisoner to the execution chamber and recite the Lord's Prayer. When Doctor Hills, the prison physician, testified before the joint committee on the time required to position the prisoner on the trap door he estimated it was about the same as the time the chaplain took to recite the customary prayer: "A very few minutes. You cannot get through the Lord's Prayer in seconds."[70] After the minister's "Amen" and the sheriff's order, the hangman pulled the lever at 12:06 a.m.

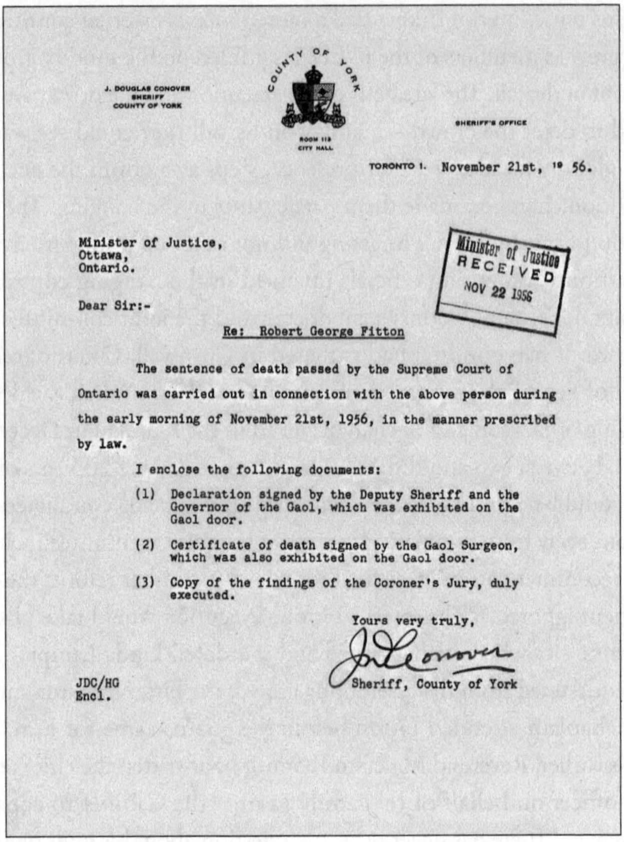

J. DOUGLAS CONOVER
SHERIFF
COUNTY OF YORK

COUNTY OF YORK

ROOM 113
CITY HALL

SHERIFF'S OFFICE

TORONTO 1. November 21st, 19 56.

Minister of Justice,
Ottawa,
Ontario.

Minister of Justice
RECEIVED
NOV 22 1956

Dear Sir:-

Re: Robert George Fitton

The sentence of death passed by the Supreme Court of Ontario was carried out in connection with the above person during the early morning of November 21st, 1956, in the manner prescribed by law.

I enclose the following documents:

(1) Declaration signed by the Deputy Sheriff and the Governor of the Gaol, which was exhibited on the Gaol door.

(2) Certificate of death signed by the Gaol Surgeon, which was also exhibited on the Gaol door.

(3) Copy of the findings of the Coroner's Jury, duly executed.

Yours very truly,

J D Conover

Sheriff, County of York

JDC/HG
Encl.

Sheriff Conover to Minister of Justice, November 21, 1956 | LAC, RG13-B-1, vol. 1755, "Fitton, Robert," vol. 1, pt. 3

"Ghouls. That's all they are. What do they come for?" a veteran guard asked, expressing his anger toward the impromptu outdoor audience for the event. "It's disgusting," he told a reporter. Members of the crowd who remained after midnight would have seen two notices posted on the jail's enormous door: the declaration that Robert Fitton had been hanged, and the certificate of his death, the final act in the drama. When reporters submitted their reviews of the night's performance, they conveyed the guard's feelings, but they added greater detail. "Cars, mostly filled with teenagers lined the street," a *Telegram* reporter ob-

Officials pronounced the youths who gathered at the Don Jail for Robert Fitton's hanging as "disgraceful." | Toronto *Telegram,* November 21, 1956

served, and most of the boys sported "Presley-type hair-cuts and black windbreakers." The photograph that illustrated the story showed one youth with a trumpet standing beside several other young men, not much younger than Fitton, who appeared in a festive mood. "A few youths joked and a drunken woman laughed," but the rest of the crowd was subdued. The *Daily Star* was more critical of the young spectators: "LEATHER-JACKETED TEENAGERS LAUGH AND JEER OUTSIDE DON JAIL DURING FITTON EXECUTION." Yet that story also commented that rowdy youths made up a small minority of the assembly. Most stood by in silence and then left after the postings appeared at 12:32 a.m.[71]

While journalists disapproved of citizens' readiness to spend a cold, rainy night standing outside a jail while a man was executed, neither they nor their editors questioned their right and obligation to carry out their professional form of witnessing. Like the sheriff, the guards, the physician, the spiritual adviser, the coroner, and the hangman, the press had a part to play by communicating what the crowd could not see. A reporter for the *Daily Star,* whose editor opposed the death penalty, spoke with a guard who revealed that "Fitton walked handcuffed from his death cell between two guards and according to the few witnesses he displayed considerable courage ... Behind him walked the hangman." The *Daily Star* also managed to track down that man, the

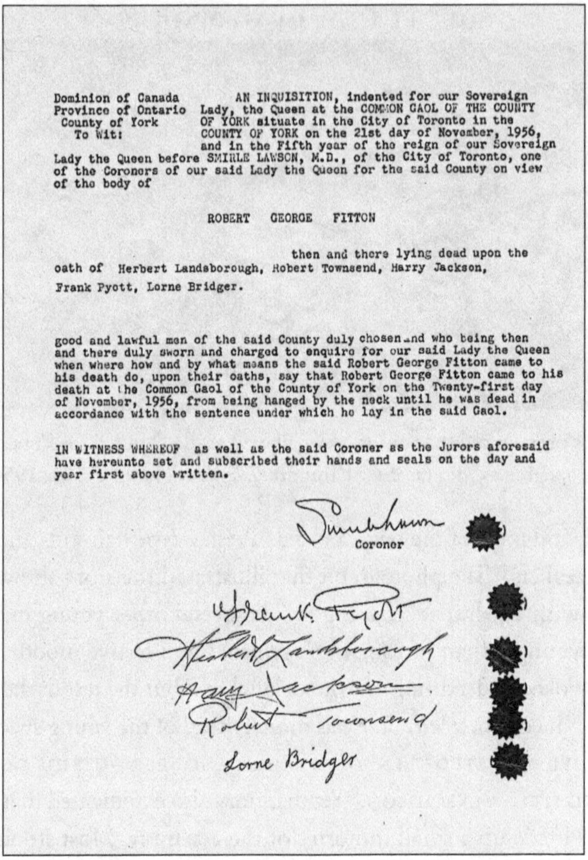

Dominion of Canada
Province of Ontario
County of York
To Wit:

AN INQUISITION, indented for our Sovereign Lady, the Queen at the COMMON GAOL OF THE COUNTY OF YORK situate in the City of Toronto in the COUNTY OF YORK on the 21st day of November, 1956, and in the Fifth year of the reign of our Sovereign Lady the Queen before SMIRLE LAWSON, M.D., of the City of Toronto, one of the Coroners of our said Lady the Queen for the said County on view of the body of

ROBERT GEORGE FITTON

then and there lying dead upon the oath of Herbert Landsborough, Robert Townsend, Harry Jackson, Frank Pyott, Lorne Bridger.

good and lawful men of the said County duly chosen and who being then and there duly sworn and charged to enquire for our said Lady the Queen when where how and by what means the said Robert George Fitton came to his death do, upon their oaths, say that Robert George Fitton came to his death at the Common Gaol of the County of York on the Twenty-first day of November, 1956, from being hanged by the neck until he was dead in accordance with the sentence under which he lay in the said Gaol.

IN WITNESS WHEREOF as well as the said Coroner as the Jurors aforesaid have hereunto set and subscribed their hands and seals on the day and year first above written.

Smirle Lawson
Coroner

Frank Pyott
Herbert Landsborough
Harry Jackson
Robert Townsend
Lorne Bridger

Coronial inquest on Robert Fitton, listing the five male jurors and the coroner, November 21, 1956 | LAC, RG13-B-1, vol. 1755, "Fitton, Robert," vol. 5

mysterious figure who carried out the execution. Speaking incognito, "Ontario's hangman" said he was a former Royal Canadian Air Force squadron leader, who, unlike Branchaud, was paid on a fee-for-hanging basis. The official said his job as a mechanical engineer paid enough that he "didn't need the money," which implied he regarded executing convicted murderers as a form of public service, similar to serving in war. When the reporter asked how long it had taken for Fitton's heart to stop, the hangman said twenty-four minutes, which the doctor's report confirmed.[72] Reporters also spoke to Fitton's mother. Although she did not witness her son's execution, she told them he "had a strong heart. I wish it was a weak one and he'd die before midnight."[73] But that was not to be. According to Hills, the last audible beat of Fitton's heart occurred at 12:30 a.m., when he pronounced him dead.

Before Fitton's body was placed in a sealed casket, the coroner, Smirle Lawson, carried out the legal requirement to hold an inquest. This brief inquisition, held within the jail, simply confirmed "where and by what means" Fitton had come to his death. After twenty-four minutes suspended by the noose, his neck was likely "angulated and distended," but there was no postmortem to confirm whether the drop broke his cervical vertebrae. The "good and lawful" jurors merely confirmed the obvious: the cause of Fitton's death was "being hanged by the neck in accordance with the sentence" of death. It was customary for executed prisoners to be buried in the jail yard unless the family intended to claim the body, and that was the Fitton family's wish.[74] On November 21, a funeral home picked up the casket from the jail, the scene of their loved one's death.

ANGER AND TRAGEDY

Responses to Fitton's hanging unleashed emotions that differed from the feelings expressed in earlier accounts of Linda Lampkin's murder and Robert Fitton's trial and appeals. Abolitionists were as angry as Fitton's family. Not only did the government reject the opportunity to do away with the death penalty, after considerable documentation of its biases and inequities; now, in Fitton's case, the Cabinet had also refused to follow the jury's recommendation to mercy. People who were not bound up in politics or criminal law reform also considered the execution a travesty of justice, and they wrote to the government (the minister of justice and the prime minister) and to the papers to express their dismay. Florence Fitton, who lost her husband to a system that seemed set against him, was not the only person who felt a sense of bitter bewilderment. According to the joint committee's final report, the death penalty was the most effective means of deterring murder;

yet the same report declared that over half the murders prosecuted in recent decades had been crimes "committed under compulsion of overwhelming passion or anger, where no deterrent could have been effective."[75] Although Robert Fitton's execution ended his life, it left a lingering question: If this hanging could not deter similar crimes, what purpose had it served?

Members of the public frequently called upon the government to justify its decisions in capital cases, but people who complained about Fitton's execution received nothing but formulaic letters drafted by bureaucrats in the Remission Service. Several last-minute clemency pleas arrived as preparations were already underway for the execution: "BELIEVE GRAVE INJUSTICE BEING DONE IN CASE OF FITTON AND DEMAND IMMEDIATE POSTPONEMENT AND FURTHER REVIEW OF THE CASE BY THE CABINET," one Torontonian wired the prime minister.[76] On November 20, the Remission Service received a letter from the minister of a United Church not far from the Fitton's home. "There are quite a large number of citizens of Toronto who feel that even at this date, the sentence ... should be commuted." Although "society must be protected against such perverts," he acknowledged, "the execution of this young man will do nothing to accomplish this purpose."[77] At the time he telegrammed, he thought there was still a glimmer of hope that "this tragic injustice" might be averted, but the Cabinet had already made their decision when the message was processed. The reply the cleric received bore the solicitor general's signature: "I regret to advise you that no action can be taken in respect to your request."[78]

Complaints about the administration of justice received slightly more considered responses from government officials. An elderly mechanic from north Toronto placed Fitton's execution in the context of recent murder prosecutions, verdicts, and punishments. Based on that evidence, his execution was anomalous, the writer believed, and he demanded an explanation: "What most people here are wondering is why Robert Fitton, a boy with a wife and three children, should be the only one to be executed, especially, since the jury had recommended mercy." Another man, John E. Saul, wrote to the minister of justice the morning after Fitton was hanged. "Never before in all my life, and

I am 72, have I ever seen such bitterness over a hanging." The writer further claimed that "everyone" assumed the Cabinet would never "override the stated wishes of this jury." Consequently, "the blood of this unfortunate life is on our hands."[79] Stuart Garson forwarded the letter to the solicitor general, who sent a response, likely composed by the Remission Service: "I can assure you that ... the Cabinet gave the most serious consideration to all the circumstances in this case, including the various representations which were made in connection with it."[80] Neither an answer to the writer's question nor a balm for bitterness, the response articulated the fiction of fair and equitable executive discretionary justice.

Compared with the flood of news that followed the discovery of Linda Lampkin's body and the capture of the suspect in January 1956, coverage of the outcome reduced to a trickle, but it was pointedly critical. Saul's letter to the minister included a clipping of an editorial published on November 21 in the Toronto *Daily Star*, the sponsor of the public forum on sex crime early in 1956. Its editor, Harry C. Hindmarsh, followed the paper's "Atkinson Principles," which encompassed exposing injustice and advocating for working people.[81] Opposition to the death penalty was consistent with those principles, and Fitton's execution was a prompt for the *Daily Star*'s editor to question the law, not just the Cabinet's decision. Titled, "An Eye for an Eye," the editorial made no attempt to minimize the gravity of the crime for which Fitton had paid with his life – the "sadistic and horrible murder of thirteen-year-old Linda Lampkin" that had "outraged and revolted the public" back in January. The hanging of the man convicted for her murder had avenged "the dead child," but Hindmarsh asked, "Should vengeance be the sole aim of justice?" His question was rhetorical:

> [Fitton's] execution must rest uneasily on the conscience of many. For when a fellow human being is deliberately put to death by the state everyone is involved. In a sense, hanging represents a failure by civilized man to face up to the complex social and moral problems out of which crime grows. Blindly, we demand revenge for murder. But what do we ever gain from it?[82]

The paid circulation of the Toronto *Daily Star* was the largest of any paper in the country: four hundred thousand in 1956.[83] Hindmarsh's editorial aimed to persuade its subscribers that vengeance would never solve the "problem of violent crime, or sexual deviation and murder."[84] Some required no convincing: "Twelve good men of the jury recommended mercy toward Robert Fitton, but none was shown by those more fortunate and of higher station," a reader wrote in a letter to the editor.[85] However, if the *Daily Star*'s readers were representative of their fellow Canadians, over half of them would have considered the loss of Fitton's life a boon for deterrence and a demonstration of just deserts.[86]

At least one Torontonian believed beyond the shadow of a doubt that the man who murdered Linda Lampkin deserved to die: the foreman of the jury, John Cole, a man of David Humphrey's and his mentor's acquaintance, whom they had naively assumed would sway his fellow jurors in Fitton's favour, had done the opposite. In an interview late in life, Humphrey revealed that Cole's disgust toward his client and his anger at being approached by the defence was far stronger than he and O'Driscoll had disclosed in their lengthy application for clemency. The lawyers had good reason to keep Cole's rejection of their request to support clemency to themselves. When O'Driscoll contacted the foreman along with "all the jurors, hoping to find out if there had been sympathy," Cole was enraged: "John swore at him and told him to get in touch with his lawyer. And, in any event, he said, 'I hope they hang him by his private parts. He deserves to hang.' So I was very upset with this guy."[87] When Cole ran into Humphrey months after Fitton's execution, he offered to shake hands, but Humphrey refused: "No, John, I am afraid I can't shake your hand. My client did it in passion; you did it in cold blood."[88] Fifty years after Humphrey agreed to represent Fitton, his anger toward the man who had played a critical role in his client's conviction for Linda Lampkin's murder was still hot.

BY CARRYING OUT THE execution of Robert Fitton, the executive acted on the sentiments expressed by backbenchers Reinke and Philpott, who felt, as most Canadians did in the mid-1950s, that sane killers must die for their crimes. Backed by the recommendation of the joint committee that Canada retain capital punishment, the government held to the conviction that the death penalty deterred murder most effectively when carried out. The people closest to Fitton – his family, his lawyers, his pastors – did not view him as a sex killer: they saw a normal man, flawed but not malevolent. They believed he deserved clemency, as the jury had recommended and the trial judge had supported. The Cabinet was aware of those recommendations but was not bound by them. Despite the unprecedented level of inquiry into executive discretion, the administration of capital cases and the criteria by which the Cabinet separated individuals deserving of clemency remained opaque, as were the reasons Fitton met his death in the Don Jail's execution chamber.

The disposal of prisoners' bodies after execution was the last step in the cold-blooded orchestration of judicial hanging. The sealing of the casket further obscured the violence done in the name of justice since the sheriff had to ensure the casket was not opened after it left the jail.[89] Seven hours after the hangman pulled the lever and launched Fitton to his death, his casket was taken to a chapel where his mother could pray by her son but not see him or touch him.[90] His internment in Resthaven Cemetery in the city's east was a private affair, unlike the public church service and official cortège that led to Linda Lampkin's burial. Her murder had occurred in a frenzy of sexual violence. Fitton's was carried out in accordance with the law. Both were indictments of the failed campaign to prevent sex crime.

Unfinished Business

ON A CHILLY NIGHT in January 1956, the fates of Linda Lampkin and Robert Fitton were set in a violent sexual encounter that took place in the bag-strewn hold of a Royal Mail truck. The formal legal legacy of that incident lies in two appeal court decisions, cited by appellants, jurists, and academics. *R v Fitton* has supported opposing interpretations of evidentiary standards for confessions and criminal intent since the decisions by the Ontario Court of Appeal and the Supreme Court divided on those critical fault lines. From a legal perspective, the case is an unconventional landmark: rather than setting a clear precedent, it illuminates the ongoing struggle to define how the voluntariness of suspects' statements should be determined and, equally, the challenge of appraising the requisite intent for murder.[1] The case's second legacy lies beyond the realm of jurisprudence, located in its relevance to the history of the death penalty, its changing scope, and its shifting politics. The Cabinet's decision to let the law take its course after the Supreme Court restored Fitton's conviction sharpened Canadians' attention to the vagaries of capital justice, and its timing, several months after Wilbert Coffin was hanged, added recruits to the ranks of abolitionists. Yet the abolition of the death penalty in 1976 failed to quell public support for capital punishment.[2] The third legacy of the legal response to Linda Lampkin's murder springs from its illustration of the criminal justice system's masculinist underpinnings, which feminist activists began to identify in the 1960s. Focusing on trials and appeals associated with the prosecution of lethal and nonlethal sexual violence, they called out patriarchal laws and chauvinistic courts that appraised the culpability of male perpetrators of sexual abuse and assault through the victim's sexual respectability. The feminist critique of victim blaming resulted in legal reform by the 1970s.[3] Yet solving this problem, like the other legacies of the Lampkin-Fitton case, remains unfinished business.[4]

CONFESSIONS, CONSTRUCTIVE MURDER AND THE CONSTITUTION

Prior to the adoption of the *Canadian Charter of Rights and Freedoms* in 1982, most legal and constitutional experts agreed that collective security took precedence over the rights of the individual, and Fitton's conviction and punishment made that clear.[5] William B. Common was the first of many commentators to interpret the Supreme Court's decision in *Fitton* (the final case of his long career as director of public prosecutions for Ontario) as approval of Canadian police interrogation practices, which British and US legal authorities restricted. In a 1957 symposium on "law and police practice," sponsored by the American journal *Northwestern University Law Review,* one contributor who trained police in the United States praised *Fitton* because it endorsed the admissibility of confessions induced through prolonged interrogations, false friendliness, and accusatory questions. The detectives who asked Fitton to come to police headquarters the morning following Linda Lampkin's murder used each of these techniques. The policing expert who wrote the article wished that US courts would adopt the same approach to improve American crime fighting: "Consideration should be given to the fast moving series of events which confront the policeman at the time of the crime, and the practical difficulties facing him in his subsequent efforts to solve the crime."[6]

Unlike commentators who thought courts in the United States were unfairly "handcuffing the police," prominent Canadian legal experts took a dim view of the national difference.[7] Respected criminal law authority, G. Arthur Martin, sided with the Ontario Court of Appeal's decision because he thought the trial judge had erred in admitting Fitton's statements into evidence. His 1961 article on the subject of police interrogations was especially critical of Supreme Court Justice

Ivan Rand's insistence that absolute voluntariness could never be expected in the production of confessions. More broadly, Martin warned that the *Fitton* decision set a troubling precedent by signalling that Canada was "taking a more liberal attitude than heretofore with respect to lengthy police interrogation providing that the questions are not such as to imply a threat."[8] A cross-national overview of the law of confessions, published in the *Harvard Law Review*, concurred: *Fitton* confirmed that "Canadian courts seem even less willing [than English courts] to use exclusionary rules as a device to control police conduct." That study's comparative analysis of countries founded on the same legal principles concluded that "there is probably little question that the police in Canada are less restricted than in many other common law countries."[9] In 1982, just before the Constitution's patriation, future Supreme Court justice Beverley McLachlin stated that *Fitton* set out "strong disapproval" of "false or exaggerated claims of other incriminating evidence" to extract confessions. Yet, she cautioned, it did not rule out the police using "aggravated forms of trickery."[10]

After Chief Justice Brian Dickson retired from the Supreme Court in 1990, he reflected that the Charter had introduced judicial responsibility to review legislation on constitutional grounds, which imposed on the government a new obligation to "enact legislation consistent with the rights and freedoms [the Charter] enshrines."[11] From 1982, a framework was in place for the protection of citizens against the state, including section 7 of the Charter, which guarantees the constitutional right to the "life, liberty and security of the person." Nevertheless, many scholars argue the Supreme Court's post-Charter decisions have done little to shore up the principle of protection against self-incrimination. For instance, in *Oickle* (2000), Justice Frank Iacobucci reprised Rand in *Fitton* by stating: "If a trial court properly considers all the relevant circumstances, then a finding regarding voluntariness is essentially a factual one and should only be overturned for 'some palpable and overriding error.'" The majority held that the common law confessions rule was broader in its protections than the Charter provided but that both served the "twin goals of protecting the rights of the accused without unduly limiting society's need to investigate and solve crimes."[12] Similarly, in *Spencer* (2003), the Supreme Court ruled that any evidence of an inducement to confess must be considered regarding its "strength" and its impact on "the particular individual and his or her circumstances" in the "overall contextual analysis into the voluntariness of the accused's statement."[13] Hamish Stewart cautions that even when a suspect's will is not overborne through police interrogation, an individual's "genuine reasons for speaking to a person in authority may have been undermined by inducements or oppression."[14] Despite the Charter's guarantee of the right to silence, critics claim the common law rule excluding involuntary confessions, not the Charter, offers "the suspect's best protection against coercive interrogations."[15] If Fitton had been tried in the post-Charter era, the judge may have come up with more grounds than Justice Treleaven could find to exclude Fitton's confession from evidence, but the appellate courts' preparedness to abide by the trial judge's determination of voluntariness has not shifted substantially since 1982.[16]

Unlike the law of evidence concerning confessions, the Canadian concept of constructive murder was controversial from the late 1940s, when Parliamentarians' concern over robbery homicides led to a broadening of the Criminal Code's definition.[17] By contrast, the British parliament followed one of the recommendations made by the Royal Commission on Capital Punishment by abolishing "constructive malice" in the amended *Homicide Act* (1957), the year after Fitton's execution. This emboldened critics of Canada's law to urge lawmakers to rid the Criminal Code of section 202.[18] Legal scholar John Ll. J. Edwards criticized Canadian politicians for failing to correct the misstep Parliament had made in 1947 when it expanded the Criminal Code's definition of murder to include homicides that occurred regardless of whether the offender means "death to ensue or knows or not that death is likely to ensue" by committing another offence. Writing in 1959, Edwards argued that England had "shown the way by taking the bold step of abolishing the doctrine altogether," and he called on Canadian lawmakers to follow suit.[19] However, it took forty years from the 1947 revision of the Criminal Code for his call to be heeded.

The Supreme Court began to "whittle some of the harsh edges" off the constructive murder law in the *Vaillancourt* decision of 1987 which found that it violated section 7 by imposing the "harsh stigma and punishment of murder" for a homicide committed without intent.[20] The court moved further in *Martineau* (1990), which invalidated constructive murder because the statute violated the constitutionally required *mens rea* of subjective knowledge of death.[21] This was a foundation stone of justice, the chief justice declared: "In a free and democratic society that values the autonomy and free will of the individual, the stigma and punishment attaching to murder should be reserved for those who choose intentionally to cause death or who choose to inflict bodily harm knowing that it is likely to cause death."[22]

Yet again, a dissenting opinion in this post-Charter decision hearkened back to *Fitton.* Justice L'Heureux-Dubé emphasized that proof of the objective foreseeability of death was consistent with fundamental justice. Moreover, "no other common law jurisdiction" had adopted subjective foresight as the "exclusive standard for murder." In her opinion, the "heinous" nature of murder meant its punishment need "not be proportionate to the *mens rea* alone."[23] Despite L'Heureux-Dubé's endorsement of constructive murder's policy objective – to deter violence during the commission of other crimes – *Martineau* established that subjective knowledge of the likelihood of death must be proven beyond doubt to find fault for murder, although it took Parliament almost twenty years to amend the Criminal Code accordingly.[24] Since 2019, convictions for murder under section 229(c) remain stigmatic, and onerous terms of imprisonment and slim prospects for parole for the offence are severe. But convicted murderers no longer face the mandatory penalty of death.

THE PLAY OF DEATH PENALTY POLITICS

In the year of Linda Lampkin's murder and Robert Fitton's execution, abolitionists faced a setback when the special joint committee of the Senate and the House of Commons recommended that Canada retain the death penalty. Some who deplored Fitton's execution registered it as a reason to oppose the death penalty. "We do not believe in capital punishment, especially since Wilbert Coffin's death," a letter writer to the *Star* declared. "But if we did, the death of Robert Fitton would certainly have changed our opinion, especially after hearing it took him 24 minutes to die."[25] By the late 1950s, a broader mood shift against the death penalty had taken place: "Public Opinion Swinging against Noose," the pro-abolition *Star* announced.[26] The case's significance to abolitionist politics increased as the legislative and policy framework of capital punishment shifted. If Fitton had been tried under the same judge and jury post-July 1961, he may have been convicted of "non-capital" murder, after the government of Prime Minister Diefenbaker amended the Criminal Code to restrict "capital murder" effectively to premeditated murder and the killing of law enforcement agents and prison officials.[27] By 1963, Fitton would not have faced execution even if a jury had found him guilty of capital murder since a period of de facto abolition began that year, followed by the passage of Canada's first legislated moratorium on the death penalty in 1967. Fitton's execution was not the sole generator of Canada's turn to abolition, but along with other controversial capital cases, it provided kindling that fired up activism against the state's coercive powers over citizens, lit by political and legal elites committed to civil and human rights.[28]

In 1956, the federal government justified its decision to retain the death penalty as the endorsement of public opinion, but over the next twenty years, it introduced a series of reforms in the absence of popular support.[29] Several weeks before Fitton was hanged, one of the female MPs who had served on the joint committee, Marie Ann Shipley, explained why she supported the death penalty: "If the threat of capital punishment saves the life of one innocent victim ... that would be sufficient justification for its retention."[30] The minister of justice agreed with the chairman of the joint committee: Canadians were not ready to support abolition in 1956. But was the public ready for the federal government to enact a Bill of Rights in 1960? Did Canadians want Parliament to create two categories of murder – capital and noncapital – or to require judges to inform jurors of their right to recommend mercy?[31] After the federal election of 1963 led the Liberals to form a government, did the public call for the Cabinet to practise de facto abolition? Tentative abolition ensued in 1967, when Parliament introduced a five-year moratorium, which it followed up in 1972; and Canada finally abolished the death penalty in 1976, even though support for the death penalty was much higher in the mid-1970s than it had been twenty years earlier, when Fitton was executed.[32]

In the lead-up to de jure abolition, retentionists and abolitionists agreed on one thing: the informal retreat from capital punishment, which began in the early 1960s, was indefensible.[33] By commuting all but a tiny number of death sentences, the Cabinet's handling of capital punishment appeared ever more aleatory, and the death penalty became a political liability. On the one hand, the introduction of noncapital murder in 1961 pared down the number of death sentences; on the other, this concession to the police lobby raised expectations that every person convicted of capital murder would surely be executed.[34] In 1962, the double execution of an Anglo-Celtic police killer (Ronald Turpin) and an African American (Arthur Lucas) found guilty of a murder connected to the drug trade (the men were hanged back to back in the same chamber where Fitton had been executed) reassured retentionists that Canada had not done away with capital punishment. But these men were the last in the country to be hanged.

After 1963, every convicted murderer, including vicious career criminals and killers who stalked and killed numerous victims, was spared. This era of de facto abolition made the execution of Fitton appear especially harsh, not a wrongful conviction (as Wilbert Coffin's and later Steven Truscott's were believed to be), but arbitrary, cruel.[35] One of the young lawyers Arthur Maloney mentored, R. Roy McMurtry, recalled in his memoirs that he had visited Fitton after his conviction at the Don Jail, possibly at Maloney's suggestion. McMurtry's illustrious legal career included serving as Ontario's attorney general, but toward the end, he could still recall the impact of Fitton's execution for the "rape and panic murder" of Linda Lampkin. Because he concluded that the killing had been neither deliberate nor planned, the Cabinet's refusal to commute Fitton's death sentence shocked him: "His youthful face haunted my dreams for many months."[36] Beyond its emotional impact, the hanging proved to McMurtry that capital punishment was inflicted disproportionately on the "poor and the friendless."[37]

In 1976, Parliament abolished the death penalty by a slim margin of seven votes, but campaigns to reinstate it undercut the victory from the start.[38] When the second moratorium on the death penalty was about to expire, opinion polls showed that support for the death penalty was highest for murders of serving police officers, at close to 80 percent.[39] The Canadian Association of Chiefs of Police kept stoking that sentiment. Hoping to haul the death penalty back into use, the association lobbied politicians to support their objective.[40] Abolitionists boldly asserted that 1976 would stand as the end date for the death penalty in Canada, but the fragility of abolition became apparent in 1987.[41] A free vote took place in Parliament that year on a reinstatement motion, supported by populist politicians, and despite its defeat, public support remained strong.[42] Subsequent opinion polls confirm majority support for the death penalty endures, expressed increasingly through pledges of respect for victims' rights.[43]

THE SHIFTING POLITICS OF SEXUAL ASSAULT

In the mid-1960s, the federal government introduced a cluster of reforms that shattered moral certainties, including the liberalization of divorce and the decriminalization of homosexuality, and feminist criticism of the criminal justice system's patriarchal grounding arose simultaneously. Second-wave feminism transformed grassroots activism into demands for changes to the rules of evidence bearing on sexual violence, and activists politicized the treatment of rape victims. This version of political action starkly contrasted with the campaigns and goals of the "housewives" of the early 1950s, who demanded that the government do more to protect children and women by detecting and treating sex criminals. Feminist analysis of sexual victimization also differed from that of legal and medical experts, whose research and treatments inspired Canada's first sentencing regimes for sexual psychopaths and institutions tailored for their diagnosis and treatment. Two foundational notions set feminist lobbying apart: first, the insight that evidently normal males – men such as Fitton – posed a greater danger to women than did strangers; and second, that the treatment of victims by the police, the courts, and the media in cases of sexual violence made it imperative to change the laws of criminal evidence so that offenders, not victims, were on trial.

The prosecution of Robert Fitton for Linda Lampkin's murder was a prime demonstration of the issues that would soon galvanize feminists into action. It was perfectly legal and culturally acceptable in 1956 for the defence in Fitton's trial to insinuate that the thirteen-year-old had been an eager pickup who lured the defendant into a passionate, consensual sexual encounter.[44] Tropes of temptation and conquest were ubiquitous in this period, and they infested popular culture, high art, and conservative religious teachings as well as the criminal law. No matter the severity of Fitton's verdict and sentence, his execution had nothing to do with supporting girls' and women's sexual autonomy, a keystone of feminist politics from the 1960s.

According to the charge against Robert Fitton, Linda Lampkin was a murder victim; nevertheless, her alleged promiscuity and mature looks raised doubts about his moral culpability.[45] By challenging the medical evidence of her ripped clothing and genital injuries as evidence of a brutal assault, the defence undermined her credibility as a victim, a common defence tactic in prosecutions for rape.[46] The trial judge and all but a few of the men who sat on the benches of the Ontario Court of Appeal and the Supreme Court were receptive to the "boy crazy" characterization of the murdered girl. If she had survived the assault she suffered on January 18, her attacker could have been charged with rape or with sexual intercourse with a female under the age of fourteen – both offences punishable by a maximum of life imprisonment, with whipping a possible added punishment at the judge's discretion. Yet evidence of trials for underage sex, attempted rape, and rape in the 1950s confirms that the likelihood of his being convicted or suffering a stiff sentence if found guilty would have been minuscule.[47] In the trial for Linda Lampkin's murder, in the appeals against Fitton's conviction, and in the petitions for clemency, this victim was rendered responsible, at least in part, for her own death.

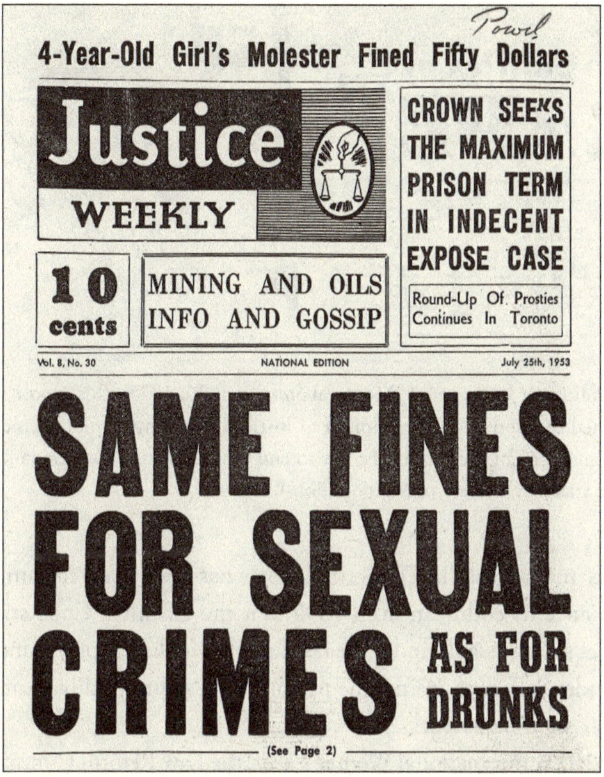

4-Year-Old Girl's Molester Fined Fifty Dollars

Justice WEEKLY

CROWN SEEKS THE MAXIMUM PRISON TERM IN INDECENT EXPOSE CASE

Round-Up Of Prosties Continues In Toronto

10 cents

MINING AND OILS INFO AND GOSSIP

Vol. 8, No. 30 NATIONAL EDITION July 25th, 1953

SAME FINES FOR SEXUAL CRIMES AS FOR DRUNKS

(See Page 2)

Justice Weekly, July 25, 1953. The scandal sheet frequently objected to light sentences for indecent assault and rape. | Courtesy of Thomas Fisher Rare Book Library, University of Toronto Libraries

Sexist contortions that twisted victims into dangerous liars and dissemblers were not peculiar to the Lampkin-Fitton case: they occurred again and again in trials involving sexual violence, provoking frustration and anger in antirape activists.[48] Although the revised and updated Criminal Code of 1955 set severe penalties for sexual violence against females, critics argued they were rarely enforced relics of the patriarchal notion that sexual violence compromised a complainant's value to her father or husband.[49] Similarly, the Criminal Code's severe penalty for sex with a girl under the age of fourteen reflected the value of chastity

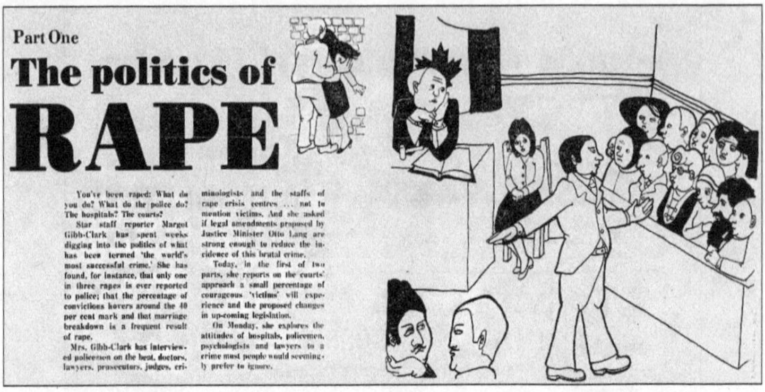

Part One

The politics of RAPE

You've been raped: What do you do? What do the police do? The hospitals? The courts?

Star staff reporter Margot Gibb-Clark has spent weeks digging into the politics of what has been termed 'the world's most successful crime.' She has found, for instance, that only one in three rapes is ever reported to police; that the percentage of convictions hovers around the 40 per cent mark and that marriage breakdown is a frequent result of rape.

Mrs. Gibb-Clark has interviewed policemen on the beat, doctors, lawyers, prosecutors, judges, criminologists and the staffs of rape crisis centres ... not to mention victims. And she asked if legal amendments proposed by Justice Minister Otto Lang are strong enough to reduce the incidence of this brutal crime.

Today, in the first of two parts, she reports on the courts' approach a small percentage of courageous 'victims' will experience and the proposed changes in up-coming legislation.

On Monday, she explores the attitudes of hospitals, policemen, psychologists and lawyers to a crime most people would seemingly prefer to ignore.

"The Politics of Rape," pt. 1, Montreal *Star*, April 26, 1975. This exposé was published in response to the Minister of Justice Otto Lang's announcement of the government's reform of the law to end retraumatizing complainants in rape trials. | Courtesy of Margot Gibb-Clark

to girls' marriageability. The criminal law has been updated numerous times since its codification in 1892, but the Criminal Code still categorizes sexual assault under the heading that includes "public morals," not under "offences against the person," as assaults, bodily harm, and murder are designated.[50]

By 1975, International Women's Year, the Law Reform Commission of Canada and a growing body of feminist legal scholars had lobbied Canadian legislators for years to make rape convictions more certain and to stop trials from being a "degrading and devastating ordeal for the complainant."[51] In response, the government introduced statutes to narrow the scope of questions put to complainants on their prior sexual activities, and it removed the requirement for corroboration.[52] In 1982, the Criminal Code replaced "rape" with "sexual assault" of various degrees, a proposal feminist criminal law experts had advocated, to emphasize the crime's violent character.[53] Yet barely credible defence claims of "honest belief" of consent continued to persuade juries to acquit men tried for sexual assault, as affirmed in 1980 by *R v Pappajohn*.[54] Many judges still treated complainants as collusive, at best, or as fabricators, at worst, and a dubious approach to the credibility of victims meant the ideals feminists articulated were only partially fulfilled.

Nevertheless, activism remained robust in the 1980s as women marched by the thousands demanding to "Take Back the Night" and shouting, "No Means No."[55]

Take Back the Night button, 1986 | Rise Up Feminist Archive

As a murder victim, Linda Lampkin could not consent to the trial's exposure of her interest in dating boys, her use of makeup, or the walks she took to bump into the defendant on his postal pickup route. Instead, a procession of others, from the Lampkins' neighbours and the local press to Supreme Court justices, judged her behaviour harshly. The only person to state under oath that the victim was a normal girl was her mother, Barbara Lampkin. At the preliminary hearing and the trial, she described her daughter as a child budding into her teens who had been hungry to live life to its fullest: she was a good girl. The pathologist confirmed the victim's virginity, and the Crown provided Linda Lampkin's birth certificate to prove her age at death – a child of thirteen. But these facts barely registered in the din of moral condemnation.

Feminist sexual assault reform advocates hoped that advances in forensic analysis and improved legal services would make it easier to prove complainants' accounts and support victims through the prosecutorial process. However, the insecure funding of rape crisis work and elevated expectations of evidence based on laboratory analysis of sexual assault kits have yet to "transform cultural systems that maintain and support sexual violence."[56] In the decades that followed Linda Lampkin's rape and murder, political activism, statutory changes, and scientific advances have made modest headway in the battle against "rape culture."[57] And increasingly divisive splits between feminists who support the criminal punishment of men found guilty of sexual assault and feminists who advocate non-carceral alternatives provide unclear pathways for policy reform.[58]

Linda Lampkin's school photograph, likely taken six months before her death. | LAC, RG 13-B-1, vol. 1755, "Fitton, Robert," vol. 2

The emergence of sexual consent educational programs is a reminder that the enduring objective is prevention, an elusive goal. Had it been reached by 1956, Linda Lampkin could have fulfilled her dreams, and Robert Fitton could have died a natural death.[59] But January 18, 1956, was a night neither of them could take back. At the time of Fitton's judicial hanging, most Canadians believed, as the majority continues to believe, that the state has the right to impose death as the penalty for murder. His execution, based on a contested confession and the Criminal Code's definition of constructive murder, amplified opposition to the death penalty as more and more Canadians began to see capital punishment as vengeance, not as a deterrent to murder. They were right. Hanging Linda Lampkin's killer did not enhance girls' safety or their freedom to pursue their dreams, sexual or otherwise.

Notes

OF GRAVES AND GALLOWS

1 Elise Chenier, *Strangers in Our Midst: Sexual Deviancy in Postwar Ontario* (Toronto: University of Toronto Press, 2008), 69; and Carolyn Strange, *The Death Penalty and Sex Murder in Canadian History* (Toronto: University of Toronto Press / Osgoode Society for Canadian Legal History, 2020), 162.

2 Strange, *The Death Penalty*, 97–98.

3 Chenier, *Strangers in Our Midst*, 33–43.

4 Toronto *Star*, January 20, 1956.

5 "Police Say Suspect 'Breaks' after Hours of Grilling," Toronto *Daily Star*, January 20, 1956.

6 On the targeting of immigrant and refugee men through assumptions of the sexual and political dangers they posed in postwar Canada, see Franca Iacovetta, "The Sexual Politics of Moral Citizenship and Containing 'Dangerous' Foreign Men in Cold War Canada, 1950s–1960s," *Social History / Histoire sociale* 33, 66 (2000): 361–89.

7 Toronto *Daily Star*, January 20, 1956.

8 Library and Archives Canada (LAC), RG 2, Privy Council Office, series A-5-a, vol. 5775. Although Cabinet meetings were not fully minuted, this collection of "Cabinet Conclusions" provides insight into the inner sanctum of discretionary power. Strange, *The Death Penalty*, 236–37.

9 Louis Riel and the North-West Resistance have been explored in many histories. On the impact of his fate in Canadian history and identity, see Jennifer Reid, *Louis Riel and the Creation of Modern Canada: Mythic Discourse and the Postcolonial State* (Winnipeg: University of Manitoba Press, 2012).

10 J.M. Bumstead, "Another Look at the Riel Trial for Treason," in *Canadian State Trials*, vol. 3, *Political Trials and Security Measures, 1840–1914*, ed. Barry Wright and Susan Binnie (Toronto: University of Toronto Press, 2009), 411–50.

11 In 2021, the *Canadian Historical Review* devoted a special issue to Riel. See, in particular, Douglas Owram, "The Myth of Riel," *Canadian Historical Review* 102, 1 (2021): S81–S98.

12 On efforts to pardon Riel and their rejection by most Métis leaders, who wanted the stain of Riel's execution to remain, see Jean Teillet, "Exoneration for Louis Riel: Mercy, Justice, or Political Expediency – A Colloquy on Metis Rights," *Saskatchewan Law Review* 67, 1 (2004): 359–92.

13 "The Queen v. Fitton," April 23, 1956, transcript, in LAC, RG 13, Department of Justice, RG13-B-1, Capital Punishment Case Files, vol. 1755, "Fitton, Robert," pt. 1, 3 (hereafter Fitton capital case file).

14 *R v Fitton,* [1956] OR 696, 702.

15 Justice Nolan, "R. v. Fitton," *Canada Law Reports* (1956): 968.

16 Carolyn Strange, "Stories of Their Lives: The Historian and the Capital Case File," in *On the Case: Explorations in Social History,* ed. Franca Iacovetta and Wendy Mitchison (Toronto: University of Toronto Press, 1998), 25–48.

17 On the historian's task of "feeling" oneself into past time, see Thomas A. Kohut, *Empathy and the Historical Understanding of the Human Past* (New York: Routledge, 2020), 9–10.

18 Mary Louise Adams, *The Trouble with Normal: Postwar Youth and the Making of Heterosexuality* (Toronto: University of Toronto Press, 1997); Cynthia R. Comacchio, *The Dominion of Youth: Adolescence and the Making of Modern Canada, 1920 to 1950* (Waterloo: Wilfrid Laurier Press, 2008; and Joan Sangster, *Regulating Girls and Women: Sexuality, Family and the Law in Ontario, 1920–1960* (Toronto: Oxford University Press, 2001).

19 The royal commission was appointed in December 1953. It held hearings in Toronto on February 9–13, 1956. Canada, Royal Commission on the Criminal Law Relating to Criminal Sexual Psychopaths, "Report of Meetings Held at Toronto," LAC, R1064-0-9-E, RG33-131.

20 Canada, *Reports of the Joint Committee of the Senate and House of Commons on Capital Punishment, Corporal Punishment and Lotteries* (Ottawa: Queen's Printer, 1956).

21 In 1941, the head of the Remission Service produced a manual to document capital case procedures, but it was not a public document. See Carolyn Strange, "Comment: Capital Case Procedure Manual," *Criminal Law Quarterly* 41, 2 (1998): 184–97.

22 On the statistically significant low rate of clemency for sex murderers, see Strange, *The Death Penalty,* 5.

23 Constance Backhouse's analysis of rape cases in the 1950s shows that judges frequently countered compelling evidence of sexual assault with narrow doctrinal interpretations of the untrustworthiness of uncorroborated testimony

by complainants. See *Carnal Crimes: Sexual Assault Law in Canada, 1900–1975* (Toronto: Osgoode Society for Canadian Legal History, 2008), 181–92.

24 The maximum penalty for rape and underage intercourse was life and a whipping: Canada, *Criminal Code,* SC 1954–55, c 51, ss 135, 138. For girls under the age of fourteen, consent was not a defence to the charge. Backhouse, *Carnal Crimes,* 317n45.

25 Michael C. Gizzi and R. Craig Curtis, "What Is a Landmark Case? Ranking Search and Seizure Cases Using *Shepard's Citations,*" *Criminal Law Bulletin* 49, 2 (2013): 2–3.

26 See, for example, Philip Handler, Henry Mares, and Ian Williams, eds., *Landmark Cases in Criminal Law* (Oxford: Hart, 2017), 5–7.

27 Determination made by examining decisions in all capital cases appealed to the Supreme Court (through its database of cases) against the outcome of cases (using LAC's database of capital cases).

28 Eric Rauchway, "In Retrospect: Landmark Law Cases in American Society," *Reviews in American History* 35, 1 (2007): 155.

29 Rauchway, "In Retrospect," 156. See also Handler, Mares, and Williams, *Landmark Cases,* 2.

30 See Hamish Stewart, "The Confessions Rule and the Charter," *McGill Law Journal* 54 (2009): 517–46; Lisa Dufraimont, "The Common Law Confessions Rule in the Charter Era: Current Law and Future Directions," *Supreme Court Law Review: Osgoode's Annual Constitutional Cases Conference* 40 (2008): 249–69; and Richard Jochelson and Kirsten Kramar, "Situating Exclusion of Evidence Analysis in Its Socio-legal Place: A Tale of Judicial Populism," *Crime, Law and Social Change* 61 (2014): 541–61.

31 Feminist agitation led the government to pass the *Criminal Law Amendment Act,* SC 1975, c 93, s 8, which prohibited questions over the complainant's sexual relationships unless the judge approved them in advance in camera. In 1982, *An Act to Amend the Criminal Code,* c 125, s 19, redefined rape as "sexual assault."

32 After a free vote, Parliament passed Bill C-84 in July 1976. On the 1950s as a turning point, see Carolyn Strange, "The Lottery of Death: Capital Punishment, 1867–1976," *Manitoba Law Journal* (1995): 599–600.

33 For general works, see Frank W. Anderson, *A Concise History of Capital Punishment in Canada* (Calgary: Frontier Publishing, 1973); David B. Chandler, *Capital Punishment in Canada: A Sociological Study of a Repressive Law* (Ottawa: Carleton University Institute of Canadian Studies, 1976); Kenneth Avio, "The Quality of Mercy: Exercise of the Royal Prerogative in Canada," *Canadian Public Policy / Analyse de Politiques* 13, 3 (1987): 366–79; and Strange, "The Lottery of Death." For studies of specific biases in capital justice, see F. Murray Greenwood and Beverley Boissery, *Uncertain Justice: Canadian Women and Capital Punishment,*

1754–1953 (Toronto: Dundurn Press / Osgoode Society for Canadian Legal History, 2000); Kimberley White, *Negotiating Responsibility: Law, Murder, and States of Mind* (Vancouver: UBC Press, 2007); Lesley Erickson, *Westward Bound: Sex, Violence, the Law, and the Making of a Settler Society* (Vancouver: UBC Press / Osgoode Society for Canadian Legal History, 2011); Barrington Walker, *Race on Trial: Black Defendants in Ontario's Criminal Courts, 1858–1958* (Toronto: University of Toronto Press, 2010); and Teresa Iacobelli, *Death or Deliverance: Canadian Courts Martial in the Great War* (Vancouver: UBC Press, 2013).

34 Canada, *Report of a Committee Appointed to Inquire into the Principles and Procedures Followed in the Remission Service of the Department of Justice of Canada* (Ottawa: Queen's Printer, 1956), 29–31.

35 Strange, "The Lottery of Death," 595.

36 George Roger Chadwick, *Bureaucratic Mercy: The Home Office and the Treatment of Capital Cases in Victorian England* (New York: Garland, 1992); and Carolyn Strange, "Mercy for Murderers? An Historical Perspective on the Royal Prerogative of Mercy," *Saskatchewan Law Review* 64, 2 (2001): 559–72.

37 A controversial exception to this custom occurred in 1895, when Lord and Lady Aberdeen actively intervened to ensure the commutation of Valentine Shortis's death sentence. See Martin Friedland, *The Case of Valentine Shortis: A True Story of Crime and Politics in Canada* (Toronto: University of Toronto Press, 1985).

38 Fitton capital case file, vol. 1. For the record series (over ninety metres of textual material, ranging from 1867–1976), see LAC, "Capital Punishment Case Files," https://recherche-collection-search.bac-lac.gc.ca/eng/home/record?app=fonandcol&IdNumber=133981.

39 The database was originally published in 1994. Some records, especially from the late nineteenth century and remote locations, are missing. However, it is the most comprehensive listing of cases publicly accessible. See Lorraine Gadoury and Antonio Lechasseur, "Persons Sentenced to Death in Canada, 1867–1976: An Inventory of Case Files in the Fonds of the Department of Justice," National Archives of Canada, 1994, https://data2.archives.ca/pdf/pdf001/p000001052.pdf.

40 Procedural rules for executive reviews of capital cases were formally set out in the *Criminal Procedure Act,* 1869, later codified in the *Criminal Code,* 1892, 55–56 Vict, c 29, s 937.

41 Coroner's inquest, November 21, 1956, in Fitton capital case file, vol. 2. The requirement was set out in "Rules and Regulations Made by His Excellency the Governor in Council, Pursuant to the Provisions of 32 and 33 Victoria, Chapter 20, Section 118," *Sessional Papers,* No. 48 (1870), 1.

42 Alexander Smirle Lawson (1887–1963) was the supervising coroner for the province as well as the city's chief coroner from 1937 to 1962. He was a captain

in the Canadian Army Medical Corp in the Great War and taught surgery at the University of Toronto. Toronto *Daily Star,* December 23, 1963.

43 Mary Lynn Young, "Crime Content and Media Economics: Gendered Practices and Sensational Stories, 1950–2000" (PhD diss., University of Toronto, 2005), 173–76.

44 Paul Rutherford, *When Television Was Young: Primetime Canada, 1952–1967* (Toronto: University of Toronto Press, 1990); and Paul Rutherford, *The Making of the Canadian Media* (Toronto: McGraw-Hill Ryerson, 1978). In 1956, televisions were advertised in Toronto for an average of two hundred dollars, or approximately 10 percent of the average annual income. Douglas Owram, *Born at the Right Time: A History of the Baby Boom Generation* (Toronto: University of Toronto Press, 1996), 88–89.

45 The *Globe and Mail* was more highbrow than the *Star* and the Toronto *Telegram,* which were "serious-popular press" archrivals in the 1950s. Young, "Crime Content and Media Economics, 181.

46 On the formulaic nature of such stories, see Carolyn Strange and Tina Loo, "The Moral of the Story: Gender and Murder in Canadian True Crime Magazines of the 1940s," in *Romancing the Tomes: Popular Culture, Law and Feminism,* ed. Margaret Thornton (London: Cavendish Publishing, 2002), 221–40; and Carolyn Strange and Tina Loo, *True Crime True North: The Golden Age of Canadian Pulp Magazines* (Vancouver: Raincoast Books, 2004).

47 "Toronto Enraged as 13-Year-Old Raped, Throttled," Windsor *Star,* January 19, 1956.

48 In Ontario, women were excluded from serving on juries until 1952; however, in the 1950s most opted for the sex-based exemption when summoned. Eileen Morris, "Why Canadian Women Shirk Jury Duty," Toronto *Star Weekly,* June 28, 1962.

49 Strange, *The Death Penalty,* 11.

50 For a comprehensive account, see "Federal/Provincial/Territorial Heads of Prosecutions Subcommittee on the Prevention of Wrongful Convictions," *Report of the Federal/Provincial/Territorial Heads of Prosecutions Subcommittee on the Prevention of Wrongful Convictions: Fall 2011* (Ottawa: Public Prosecution Service of Canada, 2011). For a critique of the problem of self-incrimination since the Charter, see Dale E. Ives and Christopher Sherrin, "R. v. Singh: A Meaningless Right to Silence with Dangerous Consequences," *Criminal Reports,* 6th series, 51 (2007): 250–61.

51 A 2023 poll by Research Canada revealed that most Canadians favoured the reinstatement of the death penalty. See Hayataullah Amanat, "Most Canadians Support Death Penalty for Murder," CTV News, March 18, 2023, https://www.ctvnews.ca/canada/most-canadians-support-death-penalty-for-murderers-poll-shows-1.6318835.

CHAPTER 1: THE PROBLEM OF SEX CRIME AND CRIMINALS

1 Toronto *Globe and Mail,* February 26, 1942. The declaration came from the president of the Canadian Legion.

2 Jordan Stanger-Ross, ed., *Landscapes of Injustice: A New Perspective on the Internment and Dispossession of Japanese Canadians* (Montreal/Kingston: McGill-Queen's University Press, 2020); Franca Iacovetta, Roberto Perin, and Angelo Principe, eds., *Enemies Within: Italian and Other Internees in Canada and Abroad* (Toronto: University of Toronto Press, 2000); and Nancy Christie and Michael Gavreau, eds., *Cultures of Citizenship in Post-war Canada, 1940–1955* (Montreal/Kingston: McGill-Queen's University Press, 2003).

3 Sydney Katz, "The Truth about Sex Criminals," *Maclean's Magazine,* July 1, 1947, 12, 46–48.

4 Hunter Crowther-Heyck, "Patrons of the Revolution: Ideals and Institutions in Postwar Behavioral Science," *Isis* 97, 3 (2006): 420–46.

5 A.J. MacLeod and J.C. Martin, "The Revision of the Criminal Code," *Canadian Bar Review* 33, 1 (1955): 3–19.

6 On the impact of US campaigns and legal reforms against sexual deviancy, see Elise Chenier, "The Criminal Sexual Psychopath in Canada: Sex, Psychiatry and the Law at Mid-century," *Canadian Bulletin of Medical History* 20, 3 (2003): 84.

7 Canada, *Report of the Royal Commission to Investigate the Penal System of Canada,* Joseph Archambault, Chairman (Ottawa: J.D. Patenaude, 1938). Although the report referred to "homosexual perverts," it did not refer to "sexual psychopaths." Carolyn Strange, *The Death Penalty and Sex Murder in Canadian History* (Toronto: University of Toronto Press / Osgoode Society for Canadian Legal History, 2020), 87.

8 Kathleen M. Jackson, "The Sex Offender," *Canadian Welfare* 23, 7 (1948): 15. Jackson was secretary of the CWA's Delinquency and Crime Division.

9 Matthieu Caron, "Taming the Jungle in the City: Uprooting Trees, Bushes, and Disorder from Mount Royal Park," *Urban History Review / Revue d'histoire urbaine* 47, 1–2 (2018): 39–54.

10 Strange, *The Death Penalty,* 111. In addition to the mainstream press, true crime magazines covered the Benson case. Carolyn Strange and Tina Loo, *True Crime True North: The Golden Age of Canadian Pulp Magazines* (Vancouver: Raincoast Books, 2004), 85.

11 Lawrence Conroy, "Mountain Slaying of Benson Boy Is Confessed by Refuge Inmate," Montreal *Gazette,* April 18, 1945.

12 Elise Chenier, *Strangers in Our Midst: Sexual Deviancy in Postwar Ontario* (Toronto: University of Toronto Press, 2008), 5–6.

13 *Justice Weekly,* May 31, 1947. The weekly paper, published by Phil Daniels in Toronto, specialized in brash muckraking and exposing sexual offences.

14 On segregated schooling and the stigmatization of children with disabilities, see Mona Gleason, "Navigating the Pedagogy of Failure: Medicine, Education and the Disabled Child in English Canada, 1900 to 1945," in *The End of Children? Changing Trends in Childbearing and Childhood,* ed. Graham Allan and Nathaniel Lauster (Vancouver: UBC Press, 2012), 140–60.

15 Marjorie Earl, "Might Never Have Happened, Dad Says, Had She Been Able to Get Schooling," Toronto *Daily Star,* November 7, 1947.

16 "Schools Banned Arlene, Broken-Hearted Parents Say," Toronto *Daily Star,* November 7, 1947. Pictures of the crime scene showed officers taking Anderson's body on a stretcher from the vacant lot.

17 "Crippled Girl's Murder Rouses Public Opinion," Toronto *Globe and Mail,* November 8, 1947.

18 The Kiwanis Club originated in the United States and expanded internationally in the early twentieth century. See Thomas A. Wikle, "The International Expansion of the American-Style Service Club," *Journal of American Culture,* 22, 2 (1999): 45–52.

19 "Sadism: Girl's Death Said Typical Sex Crime," Toronto *Globe and Mail,* November 7, 1947.

20 "Kiwanis Club Financing Research in Sex Crime," Toronto *Globe and Mail,* November 12, 1947.

21 Ken Johnstone, "We Can Do Something about Sex Crimes," Montreal *Daily Star,* January 10, 1948.

22 Chenier, *Strangers in Our Midst,* 28–29. These government inquiries were launched in 1947.

23 The event was held at the Bathurst Street United Church. Toronto *Daily Star,* May 5, 1948.

24 *House of Commons Debates,* 20th Parl, 4th Sess, No 5 (June 14, 1948), 1014–15.

25 *House of Commons Debates,* 20th Parl, 4th Sess, No 5 (June 14, 1948), 1021. The amended bill was reported and read a third time without holding a vote on division. The amendment was not, as Chenier states, endorsed unanimously through a vote. Chenier, *Strangers in our Midst,* 138.

26 Canada, *An Act to Amend the Criminal Code,* 1948, c 39. The amendment in full appeared in section 1054A of the revised code.

27 The Ontario Bar Association raised objections sufficient to provoke an amendment to the statute in the revised Criminal Code, which came into effect in 1955. It granted persons sentenced indefinitely as sexual psychopaths the right to appeal. "Sex Criminals Getting Right of Appeal," Ottawa *Citizen,* February 15, 1955.

28 *House of Commons Debates,* 20th Parl, 4th Sess, No 5 (June 14, 1948), 5199.

29 In 1950, Diefenbaker asked Ilsley's successor, Stuart Garson, how many sex offenders had been sentenced indefinitely as criminal sexual psychopaths. The

answer was "less than half a dozen." *House of Commons Debates,* 21st Parl, 2nd Sess, No 23 (May 29, 1950), 2978.

30 A.J. MacLeod and J.C. Martin, "Offences and Punishments under the New Criminal Code," *Canadian Bar Review* 33 (1955): 20–40. The amended code came into force in April 1955.

31 Carolyn Strange, "The Undercurrents of Penal Culture: Punishment of the Body in Mid-Twentieth-Century Canada," *Law and History Review* 19, 2 (2001): 353.

32 McRuer was also the country's most experienced expert in serving on royal commissions. J. Patrick Boyer, *A Passion for Justice: The Legacy of James Chalmers McRuer* (Toronto: Osgoode Society for Canadian Legal History, 1994), 280–82.

33 *House of Commons Debates,* 22nd Parl, 1st Sess, No 3 (March 11, 1954), 2895.

34 Frank Tumpane, "Casual Enforcement Apparent," Toronto *Globe and Mail,* March 16, 1954. Numerous Canadian papers published similar columns and editorials. "It appears obvious that there has been a failure to take advantage of the law ... [despite] scores of cases in which the offence seems to us to classify the offender as a criminal sexual psychopath": Kingston *Whig-Standard,* March 17, 1954.

35 Canada, *Report of the Royal Commission on the Criminal Law Relating to Criminal Sexual Psychopaths* (Ottawa: Queen's Printer, 1958), ix. The Order in Council was approved on March 25, 1954.

36 Toronto *Daily Star,* June 4, 1948.

37 Vancouver *Province,* April 11, 1947. Vancouver South MP, Howard Green, presented the association's resolutions in Parliament. *House of Commons Debates,* 20th Parl, 3rd Sess, No 6 (July 3, 1947), 5031.

38 "Edmonton Women Deserve Credit," Edmonton *Bulletin,* November 24, 1949. The article criticized the government's slow progress in implementing the revised Criminal Code.

39 Toronto *Telegram,* February 26, 1955.

40 Frank Tumpane, "The Judy Case," Toronto *Globe and Mail,* March 11, 1955. Tumpane noted that he had been contacted by several "mothers" about the case, possibly the PAL founders.

41 "The Problem of Sex Perverts," Toronto *Telegram,* March 17, 1955.

42 Evelyn Dorfman's husband was a manufacturing agent, Effie Hahn's husband owned a fur business, and Bertha Shvemar operated a pharmacy with her husband. Information culled from *Might's Greater Toronto City Directory,* 1955.

43 "No New Prisons until Committee Establishes Need," the Sault Ste. Marie *Star,* May 22, 1953. Chenier adds that the minister, John Foote, was undermined by the deputy minister, G. Hedley Basher, who refused to support any role for psychiatry in prison reform. Chenier, *Strangers in Our Midst,* 141–42.

44 "The Sex Psychopath," Toronto *Daily Star,* March 29, 1955. The editorial referred to the McRuer royal commission, the provincial select committee, and the CPA-CWA report of 1948 on the sex crime problem.

45 "Urge Law Changes to Halt Sex Crime," Toronto *Telegram,* March 21, 1955.

46 Elise Chenier, "Strangers in Our Midst: Male Sexual 'Deviancy' in Postwar Ontario" (PhD diss., Queen's University, 2002), 214. The journalist was Ron Kenyon.

47 Kenneth George Gray (1905–70) graduated in medicine at the University of Toronto in 1928 and was called to the Ontario bar in 1935. In 1945, he certified as a specialist in psychiatry. R. Edward Turner, "In Memoriam: Dr. Kenneth George Gray," *American Journal of Psychiatry* 127, 8 (1996): 1096–97.

48 "Study Recommended of 'Deviation' Law," Calgary *Herald,* April 1, 1953. In this capacity, Gray presented briefs to the federal government as it considered proposed changes to the criminal law respecting insanity.

49 Lotta Dempsey, "Person to Person," Toronto *Globe and Mail,* March 16, 1955.

50 The *Telegram* covered the discovery on its front page: "Fear Body in Creek is Missing Judy's," Toronto *Telegram,* April 9, 1955.

51 Ian Ball, "Scarf Knotted around Neck: Judy Strangled," Toronto *Daily Star,* April 11, 1955.

52 "Police Believe Tire Tracks Mark Spot Where Judy Slain," Toronto *Daily Star,* April 13, 1955.

53 "Parents Want Charter: Step Up Pervert Fight," Toronto *Telegram,* April 12, 1955.

54 "Parents Want Charter: Step Up Pervert Fight," Toronto *Telegram,* April 12, 1955.

55 "Judy Buried, Cry Justice," Toronto *Telegram,* April 12, 1955.

56 Chisholm was appointed chief constable in 1946. He served as the president of the Canadian Association of Chiefs of Police from 1950 to 1951 and became the first chief of the Metropolitan Toronto Police Force in 1957.

57 "Metro CIB Urged by Chief Chisholm," Toronto *Telegram,* April 25, 1955. The force did not amalgamate until 1957, when the Metropolitan Toronto Police Force was established. John Kiedrowski, Ronald-Frans Melchers, Michael Petrunik, and Rick Ruddell, *Amalgamation of Police Services* (Ottawa: Public Safety Canada, 2016), 3.

58 Special Joint Committee of the House of Commons and the Senate, "Final Report on Capital Punishment," *Debates of the Senate,* 22nd Parl, 3rd Sess, No 1 (June 27, 1956), 43. The committee held in-camera hearings in 1954 and 1955. See also Greg Marquis, *Policing Canada's Century: A History of the Canadian Association of Chiefs of Police* (Toronto: University of Toronto Press, 1983), 265–67.

59 "Police Chiefs Want to Retain Hangman," Vancouver *Sun,* March 31, 1955. Police consistently argued that abolishing the death penalty would expose

Canada to American "gangsters" and pose a greater danger to law enforcement when confronting "hardened" criminals. Strange, "The Undercurrents of Penal Culture," 364.

60 Canada, *Report of the Royal Commission on the Law of Insanity as a Defence in Criminal Cases* (Ottawa: Edmond Cloutier, 1956), 17.

61 Postwar national opinion polls indicated a substantial majority of Canadians (71 percent in 1953) supported the death penalty for murder. The first poll result from 1943 was only slightly higher at 73 percent. David B. Chandler, *Capital Punishment in Canada: A Sociological Study of a Repressive Law* (Ottawa: Carleton University Institute of Canadian Studies, 1976), 41.

62 Special Joint Committee, "Final Report," 16, 41; and Carolyn Strange, "Determining the Punishment of Sex Criminals in Confederation-Era Canada: A Matter of National Policy," *Canadian Historical Review* 99, 4 (2018): 541–62.

63 The Royal Commission found that as of 1956 just seven men convicted of rape or attempted rape had been sentenced to preventive detention, having been diagnosed as criminal sexual psychopaths. Canada, *Report of the Royal Commission on the Criminal Law Relating to Criminal Sexual Psychopaths,* 137–66.

64 Canada, *Report of the Royal Commission on the Criminal Law Relating to Criminal Sexual Psychopaths,* 19.

65 Canada, *Report of the Royal Commission on the Criminal Law Relating to Criminal Sexual Psychopaths,* 78.

66 Exhibit 54, in Canada, Royal Commission on the Criminal Law Relating to Criminal Sexual Psychopaths, "Report of Meetings Held in Toronto," February 9–13, 1956, LAC, R1064-0-9-E, RG33-131, 7:1609.

67 Canada, Royal Commission on the Criminal Law Relating to Criminal Sexual Psychopaths, "Report of Meetings Held in Toronto," 6:646.

68 Kenneth Gray, *Law and the Practice of Medicine* (Toronto: Ryerson Press, 1955), 121. This text was based on Gray's lectures at the University of Toronto, where he was then associate professor of psychiatry and a lecturer in medical jurisprudence.

69 Exhibit 65, in Canada, Royal Commission on the Criminal Law Relating to Criminal Sexual Psychopaths, 7:1667–68.

70 Exhibit 65, 7:1671.

71 Toronto *Daily Star,* April 22, 1955.

CHAPTER 2: PICKUP ON JANE STREET

1 In 1956, Might's directory listed 121 theatres in Toronto, population 1,304,363. All but a few were exclusively movie theatres. *Might's Greater Toronto City Directory* (Toronto: Might Directories, 1956), 109.

2 The plot of the film, written and directed by Hugo Haas, involved a man seduced by a femme fatale, who marries and plots to murder him. It was one of a series by Haas, and many other film noir writers, that featured hapless men seduced by attractive, designing women. Larry Langman, *Destination Hollywood: The Influence of Europeans on American Filmmaking* (Jefferson, NC: McFarland and Company 2000), 22–23.

3 Toronto *Globe and Mail*, January 19, 1956; and Toronto *Daily Star*, January 19, 1956.

4 Carolyn Strange, *The Death Penalty and Sex Murder in Canadian History* (Toronto: University of Toronto Press / Osgoode Society for Canadian Legal History, 2020), 141–42.

5 Toronto *Daily Star*, January 19, 1956.

6 "Scarf Knotted around Neck: Judy Found Strangled," Toronto *Globe and Mail*, April 11, 1955.

7 "Worst Rape-Murder the Coroner Has Known," Brantford *Expositor*, October 20, 1954.

8 Three of the most popular were *Deadline U.S.A.* (1952), *Headline Hunters* (1955), and *While the City Sleeps* (1956).

9 Mary Lynn Young, "Crime Content and Media Economics" (PhD diss., University of Toronto, 2005), 107–8.

10 The Brownies and Guides originated as an alternative to the Boy Scouts in Britain early in the twentieth century, and the movement quickly took hold in Canada. See Kristine Alexander, "The Girl Guide Movement and Imperial Internationalism during the 1920s and 1930s," *Journal of the History of Childhood and Youth* 2, 1 (2009): 37–63. On the 4-H Club, see John B. Lee, *Head, Heart, Hands, Health: A History of 4-H in Ontario* (Toronto: Ontario 4-H Council, 1995).

11 Phyllis Griffiths, "The Life Story of Linda Lampkin," Toronto *Telegram*, January 23, 1956. Griffiths was a pioneering female sports reporter and photo editor particularly interested in girls' and women's participation in sports. See Canadian Writing Research Collaboratory, "Phyllis Griffiths," https://cwrc.ca/islandora/object/ceww%3Afae9a054-4340-4f75-827a-6fc9dbb848d4.

12 These belongings were itemized in the list of exhibits. "The Queen v. Fitton," April 23, 1956, transcript, Library and Archives Canada (LAC), RG 13, Department of Justice, RG13-B-1, Capital Punishment Case Files, vol. 1755, "Fitton, Robert," vol. 3, pt. 1, iv. References to the trial transcript in this chapter cite fact matters uncontested by the defence or Crown at trial or on appeal.

13 Griffiths, "The Life Story of Linda Lampkin."

14 "The Queen v. Fitton," 195.

15 "The Queen v. Fitton," 563, 565.

16 "The Queen v. Fitton," 211–16, 221, 232.

17 Alexandrine Gibb, "Happy Eve Ends in Horror for Parents as Girl Found Dead," Toronto *Daily Star,* January 19, 1956. Like Griffiths, Gibb was a sportswoman and was the first woman the *Star* employed to write a regular column, "No Man's Land of Sport." See Canadian Writing Research Collaboratory, "Alexandrine Gibb," https://cwrc.ca/islandora/object/ceww%3A0b176327-7cdd-4f9d-b05e-57b45cfda0eb.

18 Gwyn Thomas, "Girl Died in Mail Truck Near Humber, Police Say," Toronto *Daily Star,* January 20, 1956. Gwyn "Jocko" Thomas (1913–2010) was the *Star*'s top reporter in its rivalry with the *Telegram* over crime news, which raged in the 1940s and 1950s. Sonia Miokovic, "Back When the Scoop Was King," *Review of Journalism,* Summer 2005, https://rrj.ca/back-when-the-scoop-was-king/. See also Jocko Thomas, *From Police Headquarters: True Tales from the Big City Crime Beat* (Toronto: Stoddart, 1990).

19 "The Queen v. Fitton," 57–59.

20 "The Queen v. Fitton," 334–40.

21 "Suspect," Toronto *Telegram,* January 19, 1956. The *Telegram* published the pathologist's autopsy results in detail.

22 Smirle Lawson testimony, "The Queen v. Fitton," 53–54.

23 "Girl, 13, Sex Killer's Victim," Toronto *Globe and Mail,* January 19, 1956.

24 "Warns Parents Keep Children Home at Night," Toronto *Daily Star,* January 19, 1956.

25 "Offer $7,000 Reward for Murder of Girl," Toronto *Daily Star,* January 19, 1956.

26 "Angry Citizens Offer Rewards for Arrest of Susan's Killer," Ottawa *Citizen,* January 9, 1956. Reports of the crime referred to the girl's "criminal assault." The autopsy indicated she died of exposure.

27 "Hold Till Cured Ontario's Plan," Toronto *Daily Star,* January 14, 1956.

28 Reports of suspects being questioned and released continued for months. In 1960, the Cadieux case was still featured as one of several unsolved murders of women and girls in southern Ontario. Gwyn Thomas, "Is Marian McDowell under Highway 401?," Toronto *Daily Star,* December 27, 1960. For recent attempts to use DNA evidence to solve Cadieux's murder, see Rebecca Zandbergen, "Local Sleuths Hope to Shed New Light on 1956 Death of 5-Year-Old Abducted in London, Ont.," CTV News, January 11, 2023, https://www.cbc.ca/news/canada/london/local-sleuths-hope-to-shed-new-light-on-1956-death-of-5-year-old-abducted-in-london-ont-1.6708712.

29 "Aroused Public Demands Sex Crime Prevention," Toronto *Daily Star,* January 19, 1956. Beland Honderich was editor-in-chief, and he presided over the paper's January 26 Forum.

30 "Quiz Father of Two 10 Hours in Slaying," Toronto *Telegram,* January 19, 1956.

31 "Unlikely to Pay Any of $7,000 Reward – Police," Toronto *Daily Star,* January 20, 1956.

32 "The Queen v. Fitton," 306.

33 "The Queen v. Fitton," 178–82.

34 Detective O'Driscoll testimony, "The Queen v. Fitton," 365.

35 Richard A. Leo, *Police Interrogation and American Justice* (Cambridge, MA: Harvard University Press, 2008), 41–77.

36 Canadian police and jurists routinely denied any use of "third-degree" tactics. William Banks, "Canada's Effective Criminal Law System," *Current History* 28, 3 (1928): 405–7; and William Renwick Riddell, "Administration of Criminal Law in Canada," *Journal of the American Judicature Society* 17 (1933): 141–44.

37 "Police Third-Degree Questioning of 'Slasher' Scored by Court of Appeal," Toronto *Globe and Mail,* November 19, 1946. For an extended analysis of the police questioning of Sears and its interpretation by the Court of Appeal, see Patrick Brode, *The Slasher Killings: A Canadian Sex-Crime Panic, 1945–1946* (Detroit: Wayne State University Press, 2009).

38 Detective O'Driscoll, *voir dire* testimony, "The Queen v. Fitton," 365.

39 Douglas Creighton, "Father of 2 Held," Toronto *Telegram,* January 20, 1956.

40 Detective Simmons testimony, "The Queen v. Fitton," 391–93.

41 "Girl Had Been in Truck but Wasn't Last Night Suspect Tells Police," Toronto *Daily Star,* January 19, 1956.

42 "Shocking Sex Crimes," Toronto *Telegram,* January 20, 1956.

43 "Arrest Ends Manhunt," Birmingham *Evening Mail* (England), January 20, 1956. The Canadian Press network, the United Press network, and the United Press alerted Canadian and international papers to the news.

44 "Linda 'Statement' Signed. Accused Taken to Scene. Shoe and Lipstick Found," Toronto *Telegram,* January 20, 1956.

45 "Young Father Charged with Murder of Linda Lampkin after 11 Hours of Questioning," Toronto *Daily Star,* January 20, 1956.

46 "Experts to Advise League of Parents," Toronto *Daily Star,* April 21, 1955. Although women did not speak as experts, PAL's campaign helped to publicize the forum.

47 In an interview toward the end of his life, Humphrey referred to the murder cases before Fitton's as "of no particular consequence." David Humphrey, interview, Osgoode Society for Canadian Legal History, Oral History Program, 2008 (hereafter Humphrey interview), 61.

48 John D. Honsberger, "The Ontario Legal Aid Plan," *McGill Law Journal* 15, 3 (1969): 436–51.

49 William B. Common, "The Administration of Criminal Justice in Canada," *Journal of Criminal Law and Criminology* 43, 1 (1952): 11.

50 Humphrey interview, 65.

51 Reporter Jack Gale covered both families' responses. Toronto *Daily Star,* January 20, 1956.

52 R.M. Harrison, "Now," Windsor *Star,* January 24, 1956.

53 "Fitton Hearing Feb. 3," Toronto *Telegram,* January 27, 1956.

54 Toronto *Telegram,* January 19, 1956. In this account, the *Telegram* used "Picked Up?" to describe the police theory of how Linda Lampkin ended up in Fitton's truck.

55 Griffiths, "The Life Story of Linda Lampkin," Toronto *Telegram,* January 23, 1956. The writer condemned these insults and criticized characterizations of the girl as fast and loose.

56 In 1951, a group of youths was found guilty of the indecent assault of girls, aged from twelve to fourteen, but the girls were also charged as delinquents. Mary Louise Adams, *The Trouble with Normal: Postwar Youth and the Making of Heterosexuality* (Toronto: University of Toronto Press, 1997), 59–62.

57 "Jails, Clinics Can't End Sex Deviation, Forum Told," Toronto *Telegram,* January 27, 1956.

58 Van Nostrand (1897–1975) served in both world wars. For his service as a consulting neuropsychiatrist in the Royal Canadian Army Medical Corp, he was appointed an Officer of the Order of the British Empire in 1945.

59 "All Sex Deviates Not Criminals, Must Use Caution – Doctor," Toronto *Daily Star,* January 27, 1956.

60 Canada, Royal Commission on the Criminal Law Relating to Criminal Sexual Psychopaths, "Report of Meetings Held at Toronto," February 9–13, 1956, LAC, R1064-0-9-E, RG33-131, 6:1190.

61 Jack Gale, "Could Happen to You, Too," Toronto *Daily Star,* January 21, 1956. A large image of the Lampkins glumly facing one another on their couch accompanied the story.

62 "City Has Learned to Shun Stranger since Judy Death," Toronto *Telegram,* April 18, 1955.

63 "2000 Hear Star Forum Experts on Sex Deviation," Toronto *Daily Star,* January 27, 1956.

64 Judges rarely imposed a life sentence for underage intercourse in the twentieth century. Sentences of five to ten years were most common. Constance Backhouse, *Carnal Crimes: Sexual Assault Law in Canada, 1900–1975* (Toronto: Irwin Books / Osgoode Society for Canadian Legal History, 2009), 281.

65 The book was publicized widely in the Canadian press, and it was cited at numerous points in hearings of the royal commission on psychopathy. Elise Chenier, *Strangers in Our Midst: Sexual Deviancy in Postwar Ontario* (Toronto: University of Toronto Press, 2008), 79–80.

66 House of Commons, *Special Committee on Bill No. 93 (Letter O of the Senate), Minutes and Proceedings and Evidence, 4, March 10, 1953* (Ottawa: Edmond

Cloutier, 1953), 155. Borins (1906–91) was called to the bar in 1930. Of Russian heritage, he changed his name from "Borinsky" and became the first Jewish Crown attorney in Ontario. Sophia Sperdakos, "'A Forum for Discussion' and a Place of Respite: Jewish Lawyers and Toronto's Reading Law Club," *Windsor Yearbook of Access to Justice* 30, 2 (2012): 176.

67 Under the revised Criminal Code of 1955, rape was subject to the maximum penalty of life in prison, and judges had the option to add a penalty of whipping for rape and attempted rape. A.J. MacLeod and J.C. Martin, "Offences and Punishments under the New Criminal Code," *Canadian Bar Review* 33 (1955): 22.

68 House of Commons, *Special Committee on Bill No. 93,* 55.

69 Chenier underscores the gender dimensions to this characterization, largely by men about women. See *Strangers in Our Midst,* 107.

70 "Cleric at Funeral Asks for Stronger Law," Toronto *Telegram,* January 23, 1956.

71 "Murder-Solving Payne Searches Sewers, Finds Wallet," Toronto *Daily Star,* January 23, 1956. Toronto's detective inspector Adolphus Payne was well known for his crime-solving skills, having solved several other murder cases.

72 The committee tabled its report in June 1956 and recommended minimal changes. Carolyn Strange, "The Lottery of Death: Capital Punishment, 1867–1976," *Manitoba Law Journal* 23, 3 (1995): 594–619.

73 Carolyn Strange, "The Undercurrents of Penal Culture: Punishing the Body in Mid-Twentieth-Century Canada," *Law and History Review* 19, 2 (2001): 371, 385.

74 Gwynn Thomas, "Fitton Nonchalant in Cell at Don Jail Cranks Call Family," Toronto *Telegram,* January 21, 1956.

75 This letter, published in the paper's regular Voice of the People section, appeared with several others that expressed a range of opinions on the problem of sex crime, including one that advocated the lash. "Sex Deviate Problem Alarms Readers," Toronto *Daily Star,* January 24, 1956.

76 Gallup polls of Canadians indicated that in 1950 70 percent favoured the retention of the death penalty. But support had declined to 53 percent by mid-1956, likely influenced by the Wilbert Coffin case. For poll figures, see Gallup, "Death Penalty," https://news.gallup.com/poll/1606/death-penalty.aspx. On the Coffin case and the death penalty, see Philip Girard, "St-Laurent, Judging, Justice, and the Death Penalty in the Shadow of the Cold War," in *The Unexpected Louis St-Laurent: Politics and Policies for a Modern Canada,* ed. Patrice A. Dutil (Vancouver: UBC Press, 2020), 349–51.

77 Carolyn Strange and Tina Loo, *True Crime, True North: The Golden Age of Canadian Pulp Magazines* (Vancouver: Raincoast Books, 2004), 99; and Mary Louise Adams, "Youth, Corruptibility and English-Canadian Postwar Campaigns against Indecency," *Journal of the History of Sexuality* 6, 1 (1995): 89–117.

78 In January 1956, a Canadian Institute of Public Opinion poll on movies revealed that one-third of Canadians believed them to be a bad influence on young people. Over half of that group thought they encouraged imitation and depicted too much crime and violence. Toronto *Daily Star*, January 21, 1956.

79 "Tearful Woman May Solve Child Murder Question 2 Deviates," Toronto *Daily Star*, January 10, 1956.

80 On prejudicial publicity, see Lawrence J. Freedman, "Fair Trial: Freedom of the Press," *Osgoode Hall Law Journal* 3, 1 (1964): 52–76. Freedman does not refer to prejudicial press coverage against the victim or her family.

CHAPTER 3: LET JUSTICE TAKE ITS COURSE

1 "Fitton Reads Comics in Jail," Toronto *Daily Star*, January 21, 1956. In 1949, the association between crime comics and juvenile delinquency was so strong that the Criminal Code was amended to make it an offence to print, publish, distribute, or sell "any magazine, periodical or book which exclusively or substantially comprises matter depicting pictorially the commission of crimes, real or fictitious." John Bell, *Invaders from the North: How Canada Conquered the Comic Book Universe* (Toronto: Dundurn, 2006), 94–95.

2 In Magistrates Courts in the 1950s, "many of the accused were not represented by lawyers," but in capital cases, courts ensured the accused was represented. Roy McMurtry, *Memoirs and Reflections* (Toronto: University of Toronto Press, 2013), 52.

3 Canada, *Criminal Code*, SC 1953–54, c 51, s 202 (hereafter Criminal Code, 1955). Subsections set out the acts that made culpable homicide murder. For a critique of the statute, see Graham Parker, "Criminal Law – Homicide – Constructive Murder – Canadian Criminal Code – Section 212(c) – Historical Origins of 'Unlawful Object,'" *Canadian Bar Review* 57, 1 (1979): 123.

4 Masculinist assumptions that "distorted definitions of 'consent'" prevailed in Canadian criminal prosecutions of male sexual offences against females in this period. Constance Backhouse, *Carnal Crimes: Sexual Assault Law in Canada, 1900–1975* (Toronto: Irwin Books / Osgoode Society for Canadian Legal History, 2009), 289.

5 Criminal Code, 1955, ss 413, 468.

6 Gullen (1882–1961) was called to the bar in 1913. "Former Toronto Magistrate," Toronto *Daily Star*, May 15, 1961. Yearbook accessed October 1, 2023, through Ancestry.ca.

7 "Welcomed to Court," *Toronto Star*, May 16, 1938. The attorney general officially appointed Gullen as a full-time magistrate on May 31, 1938.

8 *Durham Review*, January 11, 1940. Otto E. Klein was created a King's counsel in 1939 and appointed as a junior judge for the County of York a year later. His uncle was Judge Alphonse Basil Klein.

9 Arthur O. Klein, interview, Osgoode Society for Canadian Legal History, Oral History March 1996, 15, 34 (hereafter Klein interview).

10 Steven Suchan and Lennie Jackson were executed on December 16, 1952. Robert J. Horshowsky and Peter C. Newman, *The Last to Die: Ronald Turpin, Arthur Lucas, and the End of Capital Punishment in Canada* (Toronto: Dundurn Press, 2007), 21–22, 186.

11 In his eulogy for Justice Dubin, Justice Robert P. Armstrong noted that Dubin "never turned away a client because the client could not pay his fees. For him, the pursuit of justice had nothing to do with the bottom line." Court of Appeal for Ontario, "Eulogy for the Honourable Charles Leonard Dubin, October 29, 2008, https://www.ontariocourts.ca/coa/about-the-court/archives/charlesleonarddubin/.

12 The accused, Harvey Southerby, was charged with attacking a railroad steward on summer's night on the beachfront because the victim had made what he claimed was a sexual advance. "Kew Beach Murder Jury Out after Lengthy Charge," *Toronto Daily Star,* October 27, 1949.

13 David Humphrey, interview, Osgoode Society for Canadian Legal History, Oral History Program, 2008 (hereafter Humphrey interview).

14 W.O. Gibson, the senior Crown attorney who prosecuted the two Boyd gang members charged with murder, issued Humphrey the formal invitation to become an assistant Crown attorney. Humphrey interview, 38.

15 Humphrey interview, 36. The governor of the Don Jail kept the list.

16 "Boys Find Judy Body," Toronto *Daily Star,* April 11, 1955.

17 "Strangler Used Scarf," Windsor *Star,* March 16, 1956.

18 The transcript of the hearing was prepared for counsel at trial, but it has not survived. References to the hearing and direct passages from it subsequently appeared in the trial transcript. At trial, Humphrey referred to his objection in the hearing to McLean's testimony.

19 This comment appeared in numerous newspapers, transmitted through the Canadian Press network.

20 "Order Trial in Toronto Sex Slaying," Ottawa *Citizen,* March 20, 1956.

21 Ontario retained the tradition longer than England (which abolished the grand jury in 1937) despite the growing consensus that it was superfluous. Albert Lieck, "Abolition of the Grand Jury in England," *Journal of Criminal Law and Criminology* 29, 1 (1938): 3–22. In most other provinces, attorneys general or their agents preferred bills of indictment without presenting them to a grand jury. Criminal Code, 1955, ss 485–87, s 489.

22 William B. Common, "The Administration of Criminal Justice in Canada," *Journal of Criminal Law and Criminology* 43, 1 (1952): 8.

23 "Fitton," Toronto *Telegram,* April 23, 1956. The article does not refer to any potential jurors rejected by Klein.

24 Andrew L.-T. Choo and Jill Hunter, "Gender Discrimination and Juries in the 20th Century: Judging Women Judging Men," *International Journal of Evidence and Proof* 22, 3 (2018): 209. At the annual meeting of the Women's Law Association of Ontario in April 1951, the assembly toasted "women jurors" shortly after the provincial government amended the *Jury Act.* See Law Society of Ontario, "Programme from Women's Law Association of Ontario Annual Dinner, 14 April 1951," https://lso.ca/about-lso/osgoode-hall-and-ontario-legal-heritage/exhibitions-and-virtual-museum/exhibitions/scrapbooks-of-the-women-s-law-association/programme-from-women%E2%80%99s-law-association-of-onta-(1).

25 Fred Orpen owned the Dufferin Racetrack, which he sold for $4 million in 1955 to make way for the development of the Dufferin Mall. On Cole's employment by Orpen, see Toronto *Daily Star,* May 2, 1955.

26 Humphrey interview, 71–72.

27 Klein believed this since he learned, after the trial, about the defence's connection to the foreman. Klein interview, 120.

28 Treleaven served on the executive of the United Church and on Hamilton's school board.

29 Treleaven ran (unsuccessfully) as a Liberal in the 1929 provincial election. Russell E. Reinke represented Hamilton South from 1953 to 1957. He delivered his speech on Hamilton's sex crimes and issued a call for stronger laws the day after Fitton was arrested. Canada, *House of Commons Debates,* 22nd Parl, 3rd Sess, No 1 (January 20, 1956), 365–66.

30 "Fitton Fainted When He Saw Police – Crown," Toronto *Daily Star,* April 23, 1956; and "Fitton," Toronto *Telegram,* April 23, 1956.

31 McMurtry, *Memoirs and Reflections,* 87–88. After McMurtry began to practise, he considered Klein the prosecutor he most feared.

32 "The Queen v. Fitton," Library and Archives Canada, RG 13, Department of Justice, RG13-B-1, Capital Punishment Case Files, vol. 1755, "Fitton, Robert," vol. 3, pt. 1.

33 *Lizotte v R,* [1951] SCR 115, 116. The judgment overturned the Quebec Court of King's Bench, Appeal Side's confirmation of the conviction of Roger Lizotte, sentenced to death for murder. Justice Cartwright delivered the judgment that found numerous errors in the admission of evidence. Lizotte was retried and re-convicted of murder. On appeal to the Supreme Court, the conviction was set aside and a verdict of manslaughter entered.

34 "The Queen v. Fitton," 24.

35 "The Queen v. Fitton," 25, 27. Humphrey suggested that the police photographer use scissors to cut out "the other part" of the photo. "The Queen v. Fitton," 29.

36 The first appellate case to test the admissibility of morgue photographs concerned an earlier sex murder case in Toronto. In 1936, Harry O'Donnell was

convicted of the sexually motivated murder of Ruth Taylor. Justice Nicol Jeffreys allowed the admission of morgue photos, which the Ontario Court of Appeal upheld. *R v O'Donnell*, [1936] 2 DLR 517, 517–18.

37 "The Queen v. Fitton," 57–62.

38 "The Queen v. Fitton," 63.

39 "The Queen v. Fitton," 69.

40 "The Queen v. Fitton," 71, 74.

41 Preliminary hearing, transcript, quoted in "The Queen v. Fitton," 90.

42 Criminal Code, 1955, s 138.

43 "The Queen v. Fitton," 82–83. The book Humphrey cited was the 1952 edition of a text written by England's chief pathologist, Keith Simpson: *Forensic Medicine,* 2nd ed. (London: Arnold, 1952).

44 Criminal Code, 1955, s 202.

45 John Willis, "Criminal Law: Constructive Murder," *Canadian Bar Review* 29, 3 (1951): 793–94. On Willis's career, see Richard C.B. Risk, "In Memoriam: John Willis," *University of Toronto Law Journal* 47, 3 (1997): 302.

46 The term used by Mclean was "excoriated," which he defined as "haemorrhage and trauma in the tissues of the skin" plus a "superficial layer of skin torn off." "The Queen v. Fitton," 99.

47 "The Queen v. Fitton," 377, 382. In this voir dire testimony, Detective Bernard Simmonds said he took charge of obtaining the solicitation of the statement.

48 "The Queen v. Fitton," 441. Despite the overhaul of the Criminal Code in 1955, it provided little guidance on the admissibility of suspects' statements. Fred Kaufman, *The Admissibility of Confessions* (Toronto: Carswell, 1960), 2.

49 "The Queen v. Fitton," 435–36.

50 "The Queen v. Fitton," 395. Fitton never explained what happened to the change left from the five-dollar bill after the victim paid for her dance lesson.

51 "The Queen v. Fitton," 434. Robbery was another of the listed offences, the commission of which rendered culpable homicide murder under section 202.

52 "The Queen v. Fitton," 437. Willis argued that the doctrine of constructive murder was upheld primarily out of concern over robbery murders. Willis, "Criminal Law: Constructive Murder," 791.

53 "The Queen v. Fitton," 449–50.

54 "The Queen v. Fitton," 515–16.

55 "The Queen v. Fitton," 513, 516, 519.

56 "The Queen v. Fitton," 53. Humphrey used this line in his cross-examination of another police witness, Detective William McNeeley, who gathered evidence to test Fitton's first story and who took part in the interview that led to the statement.

57 "The Queen v. Fitton," 173, 176, 556, 558. The birth certificate was the final Crown exhibit.

58 S. Tupper Bigelow, *Legal Etiquette and Court-Room Decorum* (Toronto: Carswell, 1955). Bigelow was a Queen's counsel and magistrate for the Province of Ontario.

59 Dorothy Howarth, "Lampkins' Weary Wait," Toronto *Telegram,* March 17, 1956. The story included police commentary about the parents' dignity and their lack of vengeance toward Fitton.

60 "The Queen v. Fitton," 8.

CHAPTER 4: CONDEMNED TO DEATH

1 "Fitton to Die July 10 for Murdering Linda," Toronto *Globe and Mail,* April 28, 1953. According to this account, members of the public also attempted to bribe the sheriff to admit them to the courtroom.

2 Toronto *Daily Star,* April 27, 1956.

3 Canada, *Criminal Code,* SC 1953–54, c 51, s 202(c).

4 The difference between manslaughter and murder was debated in the lead up to the Criminal Code's revision. See Alfred Bull, "Murder or Manslaughter," *Canadian Bar Review* 24, 1 (1946): 16; and C.H. O'Halloran, "Criminal Law and the Supreme Court, 1923–1947," *Canadian Bar Review* 26, 1 (1948): 162–64.

5 "Guilty of Something Judge Tells Linda Jury," Toronto *Daily Star,* April 27, 1956. The transcript of Fitton's trial, which appears in his capital case file in Library and Archives of Canada (LAC), does not include closing statements: "The Queen v. Fitton," LAC, RG 13, Department of Justice, RG13-B-1, Capital Punishment Case Files, vol. 1755, "Fitton, Robert," vol. 3, pt. 1 (hereafter Fitton capital case file). The *Star* reported both counsels' closing statements in detail.

6 Toronto *Daily Star,* April 27, 1956; and "Jury in 4-Hour Debate Finds Fitton Slew Linda but Recommends Mercy," Toronto *Daily Star,* April 28, 1956.

7 The postwar trend toward funding the defence of criminal defendants who were impoverished found support in provincial law societies and governments, but the funding of appeals was generally not covered. On the rising number of appeals in sex murder cases in the postwar decade, see Carolyn Strange, *The Death Penalty and Sex Murder in Canadian History* (Toronto: University of Toronto Press / Osgoode Society for Canadian Legal History, 2020), 171, 18.

8 In 1956, Klein was forty-seven years old, Humphrey thirty.

9 Closing remarks reported in "Guilty of Something Judge Tells Linda Jury"; and "No Evidence Offered by Defence; Expect Fitton Case Verdict Today," Toronto *Globe and Mail,* April 27, 1956.

10 "Guilty of Something Judge Tells Linda Jury," Toronto *Daily Star,* April 27, 1956.

11 "Guilty of Something Judge Tells Linda Jury." The verb "to kibitz" is of German and Yiddish origin. According to the *Oxford English Dictionary Online,*

the colloquial term, originally associated with the underworld, had several meanings by the mid-twentieth century, including "meddling," "a desire to join in," or "to offer unwelcome advice."

12 Gray examined Fitton at Humphrey's request just after his arrest and reported, "I did not illicit [sic] any findings of sexual deviation in his case." Quoted in Humphrey and John O'Driscoll to Stuart Garson, November 12, 1956, Fitton capital case file, vol. 1, pt. 1.

13 Closing remarks quoted in "Guilty of Something Judge Tells Linda Jury."

14 "Guilty of Something Judge Tells Linda Jury."

15 "Guilty of Something Judge Tells Linda Jury."

16 "Guilty of Something Judge Tells Linda Jury."

17 "The Queen v. Fitton," 1004. The charge appears in full in the transcript, but it was reported by the press in less detail than the counsels' closing addresses.

18 "The Queen v. Fitton," 1018.

19 The judge referred to this verbatim passage from Humphrey's closing address, prepared by the court reporter. "The Queen v. Fitton," 1003.

20 "The Queen v. Fitton," 1005.

21 "The Queen v. Fitton," 1024–25.

22 "The Queen v. Fitton," 1015.

23 G.A. Children, "The Judge's Charge to the Jury in Criminal Cases," *Canadian Bar Review* 3, 4 (1925): 174. For a history of the charge, see Hyman Sokolov, "The Judge's Charge to the Jury in Criminal Cases," *Canadian Bar Review* 10, 4 (1932): 228–39.

24 "The Queen v. Fitton," 1022.

25 "The Queen v. Fitton," 1026, 1028, 1007.

26 "Club Hears Treleaven; Justice Explains System to Optimists," Windsor *Star,* May 9, 1952. The special joint committee appointed to consider the death penalty's possible abolition tested that claim. Canada, *Joint Committee on Capital and Corporal Punishment and Lotteries: Minutes of Proceedings and Evidence, No. 1* (Ottawa: Queen's Printer, 1954), 19 (hereafter *Minutes of Proceedings and Evidence*).

27 "Club Hears Treleaven; Justice Explains System to Optimists." The Optimist Club was formed in the United States and expanded into an international organization by the 1920s. For their history, see https://www.optimist.org/member/about5.cfm.

28 "The Queen v. Fitton," 1024–25.

29 Section 203 of the 1955 Criminal Code spelled out the grounds on which culpable homicide "that otherwise would be murder may be reduced to manslaughter."

30 The 1956 edition of A.E. Popple's criminal procedure manual stated that "the accused is at liberty to present evidence of good character," but that did not apply to evidence that could not be cross-examined by the Crown. Further, such

evidence "can have little (if any) effect on the verdict of the jury where the offence charged is clearly proved." A.E. Popple, *Criminal Procedure Manual: A Manual of Instruction for Constables, Justices of the Peace, Police Magistrates, Prosecutors and Lawyers, with Diagrams to Illustrate the Procedure in Criminal Cases* (Toronto: Carswell, 1954), 173.

31 "It is not the practice for judges to instruct [the jury] that this course is open to them": Canada, *Report of a Committee Appointed to Inquire into the Principles and Procedures Followed in the Remission Service of the Department of Justice of Canada* (Ottawa: Queen's Printer, 1956).

32 Judges were not obliged to inform juries they had the right to recommend mercy in capital trials until 1961, when the Criminal Code divided murder into capital and noncapital offences. *An Act to Amend the Criminal Code (Capital Murder),* SC 1961, c 44, s 15.

33 Arthur E. Maloney, the country's foremost abolitionist lawyer in the mid-1950s, opposed instructing juries about mercy recommendations before they delivered their verdict out of concern that it might deter them from findings of guilt for manslaughter. Canada, *Minutes of Proceedings and Evidence,* no. 4, March 16, 1954, 162.

34 "The Queen v. Fitton," 1030.

35 "The Queen v. Fitton," 1031.

36 "The Queen v. Fitton," 1034–35.

37 "The Queen v. Fitton," 1035–36.

38 "Jury in 4-Hour Debate," Toronto *Daily Star,* April 28, 1956.

39 "The Queen v. Fitton," 1038.

40 Don Goudy, "Can't Believe Verdict Wife Stumbles Screaming from Fitton Courtroom," Toronto *Daily Star,* April 28, 1956.

41 "Jury Plea Seen Likely to Save Fitton's Life," Toronto *Daily Star,* April 28, 1956.

42 "The Queen v. Fitton," 1040.

43 Justice Treleaven sent his report on May 7. Fitton capital case file, vol. 1, pt. 1. Section 643(1) of the Criminal Code required trial reports from judges in time sufficient for the governor general to consider if the sentence should be carried out.

44 "Jury Plea Seen Likely to Save Fitton."

45 "I'll Stick by Bobby to End, Wife Decides," Toronto *Telegram,* April 28, 1956. The article included references to letters Fitton wrote his wife while imprisoned, in which he claimed he was innocent.

46 "Save Fitton from Hanging Petition Aim," Toronto *Telegram,* May 1, 1956.

47 "Save Fitton from Hanging." It is possible that the Fittons contributed some funds. As Humphrey recollected, he "worked for free" to represent many of his clients, but "if the client could raise ten dollars," he accepted whatever they

could contribute. David Humphrey interview, Osgoode Society for Canadian Legal History, Oral History Program, 2008, 36–37.

48 "'Satisfied Justice Was Done' Linda's Father Not Bitter," Toronto *Telegram,* April 28, 1956.

49 Albert de Gasperis, thirty-eight, was charged with the February 1956 murder of Gina de Gasperis, the mother of their four children. Sault *Star,* May 19, 1956.

50 "Jury in 4-Hour Debate Finds Fitton Slew Linda but Recommends Mercy," Toronto *Daily Star,* April 28, 1956.

CHAPTER 5: CONTESTING THE CONFESSION

1 Section 743 of the Criminal Code referred to appeals being made "with leave" of courts of appeal. Convicted persons could appeal against conviction on any question of law alone or on any ground that concerned a "question of fact alone, or questions of mixed law and fact," "with leave of the court of appeal." Canada, *Criminal Code,* SC 1953–54, c 51 (hereafter Criminal Code, 1955).

2 William B. Common, interview, Osgoode Society for Canadian Legal History, Oral History Program, October 1979, 6–7 (hereafter Common interview). Common told the interviewer he was thrust into arguing appeals shortly after his appointment to the attorney general's department in 1926 when he was twenty-eight years old.

3 Fitton's conviction required his placement in the Don Jail's death cell. His shoelaces, tie, and belt were removed to reduce the likelihood of self-hanging. "Fitton," Toronto *Telegram,* April 28, 1956.

4 Goldwin Arthur Martin taught criminal law at Osgoode Hall Law School from 1942 to 1966. Humphrey studied under him and admired him as the "greatest criminal lawyer Canada has ever produced." David Humphrey, interview, Osgoode Society for Canadian Legal History, Oral History Program, 2008, 196 (hereafter Humphrey interview). John G.J. "Archie" O'Driscoll was called to the bar in 1955 and became a junior in Arthur Maloney's firm (Edmonds, Maloney, Neligan and Edmonds) after articling with him.

5 Criminal Code, 1955, s 598(1)(a) stated that the attorney general "may appeal to the Supreme Court of Canada on any question of law on which a judge of the court of appeal dissents."

6 On the rules regarding criminal appeals in the late 1940s, see Vincent del Buono, "Right to Appeal in Indictable Cases: A Legislative History," *Alberta Law Review* 16, 3 (1978): 464.

7 Canada, *Special Joint Committee of the Senate and the House of Commons on Capital and Corporal Punishment and Lotteries: Minutes of Proceedings and Evidence, No. 4* (Ottawa: Queen's Printer, 1954), 179. Maloney was also at that

point chairman of the Committee on Criminal Justice in the Canadian Bar Association's Ontario branch.

8 Christopher Moore, *The Court of Appeal for Ontario: Defining the Right of Appeal in Canada* (Toronto: University of Toronto Press, 2014), 82–83; and Richard Funston, "Criminal Appeals in Canada," *California Western International Law Journal* 2 (Winter 1971): 1–15. See also Peter D. Marshall, "A Comparative Analysis of the Right to Appeal," *Duke Journal of Comparative and International Law* 22, 1 (2011): 1–46.

9 The consideration of leave to appeal after a provincial court upheld a conviction was made by one justice of the Supreme Court, a restriction Maloney pointed out to the joint committee.

10 *Reference re R v Coffin,* [1956] SCR 191.

11 Philip Girard, "St-Laurent, Judging, Justice, and the Death Penalty in the Shadow of the Cold War," in *The Unexpected Louis St-Laurent: Politics and Policies for a Modern Canada,* ed. Patrice Dutil (Vancouver: UBC Press, 2020), 354–55. Coffin's original execution date was set for November 26, 1954. Stays of execution were granted seven times to allow for the consideration of appeals.

12 Maloney was a member of a prominent citizens' committee, formed in March 1956, which tried to prove Coffin had been wrongly executed. "Did We Hang an Innocent Man?," Montreal *Gazette,* February 27, 1956. Erle Stanley Gardner, founder of the "Court of Last Resort," which investigated possible wrongful convictions, lent his support. "Erle Stanley Gardner, Noted Writer of Crime Novels, Will Join Star Team Investigating Coffin Case," Toronto *Daily Star,* March 29, 1956.

13 Alan W. Mewett, "Criminal Law Revision in Canada," *Alberta Law Review* 7, 2 (1969): 277.

14 As late as 1961, 71 percent of appeals from conviction or acquittal on indictable offences were dismissed. Stuart Ryan, "The Adult Court," in *Crime and Its Treatment in Canada,* ed. W.T. McGrath (Toronto: Macmillan, 1965), 170.

15 These concerns led to the appointment of a royal commission on the sexual psychopath law in 1954. Elise Chenier, *Strangers in Our Midst: Sexual Deviancy in Postwar Ontario* (Toronto: University of Toronto Press, 2008), 80–81.

16 Justice John Andrew Hope, minutes of proceedings, no. 3, March 9, 1954, Canada, *Special Joint Committee,* 119. Hope was appointed to the High Court of Justice in 1933 and elevated to the Court of Appeal in 1945, where he served until 1954. He remained on the bench until his death on December 31, 1954, aged sixty-four.

17 Although there were several grounds in the appeal, the murder of Ellen Hedderwick in the summer of 1937 led the provincial police and Toronto detectives to interrogate the man who found the girl, John Comba, four times over several

days. Carolyn Strange, *The Death Penalty and Sex Murder in Canadian History* (Toronto: University of Toronto Press / Osgoode Society for Canadian Legal History, 2020), 81–83.

18 Common argued his first case in appeal in 1927.

19 Hope, Canada, *Special Joint Committee,* March 9, 1954, 119.

20 Criminal Code, 1955, s 592(1).

21 Hope, Canada, *Special Joint Committee,* March 9, 1954, 119.

22 This number was determined by searching for Treleaven's name in Lorraine Gadoury and Antonio Lechasseur, "Persons Sentenced to Death in Canada, 1867–1976: An Inventory of Case Files in the Fonds of the Department of Justice," National Archives of Canada, 1994, https://data2.archives.ca/pdf/pdf001/p000001052.pdf. This search was supplemented by newspaper searches of "Treleaven" paired with "murder."

23 William McAuliffe used a machine gun in his attempt to escape a citizen's arrest after he robbed a bank. He was executed on December 19, 1950. Library and Archives Canada (LAC), RG 13, Department of Justice, RG13-B-1, Capital Punishment Case Files, vol. 1691, "McAuliffe, William," 207.

24 Lloyd Robert Wyse was accused of stabbing to death a taxi driver in his home. He was executed on January 8, 1952.

25 LAC, RG13-B-1, vol. 1700, "Wyse, Lloyd Robert."

26 Police in Quebec arrested the pair in Rouyn, and they testified in the Sudbury trial. "Officer Says Boy Confessed Violent Crime," Sault *Star,* February 20, 1954.

27 "Sentence 2 to Die for Sudbury Murder," North Bay *Nugget,* February 25, 1954.

28 "Say Circumstances Warrant Verdict of Manslaughter," Owen Sound *Sun Times,* April 26, 1954.

29 "Crown Admits Judge Wrong in Murder Case," Toronto *Daily Star,* April 26, 1954; "2 Spared from Gallows, Get 8-Year Term Instead," North Bay *Nugget,* April 27, 1954.

30 "Montrealers' Murder Rap Is Reduced," Montreal *Gazette,* April 27, 1954. The clerk, R.N. Davies, was listed as the senior stenographer and reporter on the judges' staff as far back as 1933. Legislative Assembly of Ontario, *Public Accounts of the Province of Ontario, Sessional Paper No. 1* (Toronto: T.E. Bowman, 1935), D10.

31 Humphrey interview, 63.

32 William Common told the Joint Committee that "theoretically ... an application for leave to appeal" was required to appeal to the Court of Appeal. He added that in Ontario, "it is treated as an appeal as of right." Canada, *Special Joint Committee,* 88.

33 "The Queen v. Fitton," transcript, in LAC, RG 13, RG13-B-1, vol. 1755, "Fitton, Robert," vol. 3, pt. 1, 104–5 (hereafter Fitton capital case file).

34 Canada, *Special Joint Committee,* 114.

35 Moore, *The Court of Appeal,* 111. Three-judge panels were introduced in 1931, and Moore's sample of cases from the 1950s revealed that 84 percent of cases were heard by three judges.

36 Moore, *The Court of Appeal,* 105–6. Moore notes that Chief Justice Robert S. Robertson (who retired at eighty-three) was the last octogenarian to serve in the twentieth century.

37 Moore, *The Court of Appeal,* 119.

38 Canada, *Special Joint Committee,* March 9, 1954, 118.

39 "Hearing Begins for New Trial for Robert Fitton," Toronto *Daily Star,* June 19, 1956.

40 "Fitton Lawyer Opens Appeal for New Trial," Toronto *Globe and Mail,* June 19, 1956.

41 "Fitton Wins New Trial in Rape Slaying," Waterloo *Regional Record,* June 20, 1956.

42 "New Trial Ordered as Fitton Conviction Set Aside on Appeal," Toronto *Globe and Mail,* June 20, 1956.

43 "New Trial Ordered."

44 "New Trial Ordered."

45 Arthur Maloney supported the necessity of corroboration in a 1955 lecture. Maloney, "Corroboration," in *Law Society of Upper Canada: Special Lectures, 1955* (Toronto: Richard De Boo Ltd., 1955), 247. For a critique of the corroboration principle, see Marilyn G. Stanley, *The Experience of the Rape Victim with the Criminal Justice System Prior to Bill C-127* (Ottawa: Minister of Supply and Services, 1987), 49–75.

46 *R v Fitton,* [1956] OR 696, 702, 705 [*Fitton*].

47 *Fitton,* 709.

48 *Fitton,* 706, 709.

49 At trial, Boudreau was represented by a local lawyer, Charles Barbès. Lucien Gendron, one of the country's top criminal appeal barristers, represented Boudreau before the Supreme Court. For an account of his career, see "L'hon. Lucien Gendron célèbre juriste, décedé," *La Presse,* April 6, 1959.

50 Criminal Code, 1955, s 598(1)(a).

51 Quoted in *Fitton,* 713.

52 Quoted in *Boudreau v R,* [1949] SCR 262, 282 [*Boudreau*].

53 *Ibrahim v R,* [1914] AC 599 (PC), 609. On jurisprudential trends in the admissibility of confessions in this period, see T.D. Macdonald and A.H. Hart, "The Admissibility of Confessions in Criminal Cases," *Canadian Bar Review* 25, 8 (1947): 823–53.

54 *Boudreau,* 267.

55 *Boudreau,* 269–70.

56 *Fitton,* 713.

57 A.E. Popple, *Criminal Procedure Manual: A Manual of Instruction for Constables, Justices of the Peace, Police Magistrates, Prosecutors and Lawyers, with Diagrams to Illustrate the Procedure in Criminal Cases* (Toronto: Carswell, 1956), 179.

58 Aylesworth read law with his uncle, former minister of justice Allen B. Aylesworth, and was called to the bar in 1923. He was elevated to the Court of Appeal in 1946 directly from private practice, where he specialized in corporation law. Moore, *The Court of Appeal,* 124.

59 Roach was only the third Catholic appointee to the province's Protestant-dominated Court of Appeal. Moore, *The Court of Appeal,* 107.

60 These figures were determined by searching for cases in which Roach appeared as the trial judge as recorded in LAC, Capital Punishment Case Files.

61 John D. Arnup, ed., "Swearing Out: An Inside Look at the Court of Appeal for Ontario and Some of Its Judges," unpublished manuscript, c. 1998, Law Society Archives, 80. Roach was also remembered as "very modest and hard working." Moore, *The Court of Appeal,* 269.

62 *R v Sears* [1947] 5 CR 1.

63 This was an oral judgment that the *Globe* quoted at length. "Sears' Mother Weeps, Embraces Son at Jail as Conviction Quashed," Toronto *Globe and Mail,* November 21, 1946.

64 *R v Sears,* [1948] OR 9.

65 "'Unnecessary Violence Used' in University Stadium Case," Kingston *Whig Standard,* January 18, 1955.

66 *Fitton,* 723.

67 *Fitton,* 726.

68 "Follow Up the Roach Report," Toronto *Daily Star,* February 7, 1955. This editorial condemned the police commission for ignoring the report, given there were some sergeants on the force who believed suspects who did not answer questions when detained were guilty of obstructing the police.

69 *Fitton,* 729, 732.

70 *Fitton,* 735–36.

71 "Ex-Windsor Lawyers Feted by Society," Windsor *Star,* March 29, 1957.

72 *Fitton,* 737.

73 Common interview, 141.

74 "Hearing Begins for New Trial," Toronto *Daily Star,* June 19, 1956.

75 "Robert Fitton Granted New Trial for Slaying," Hamilton *Spectator,* June 20, 1956.

76 George Rolland to Minister of Justice, July 8, 1956, Fitton capital case file.

77 Moore, *The Court of Appeal,* 93. In Ontario, legal aid did not cover appeals until 1966. Moore, *The Court of Appeal,* 105.

78 J.G.J. O'Driscoll, "The Presentation of an Appeal to the Court of Appeal and to the Supreme Court of Canada in a Criminal Case," in *Law Society of Upper Canada, Special Lectures, 1969* (Toronto: Richard De Boo, 1969), 218.

79 Gwynn Thomas, "Appeal Fitton Ruling on Two Grounds," Toronto *Star,* June 28, 1957.

CHAPTER 6: AN UNCOMMON APPEAL

1 Canada, *Criminal Code,* SC 1953–54, c 51, s 598(1)(a) (hereafter Criminal Code, 1955). For a critique of this provision, see Graham Parker, "Jury Reversal and the Appellate Court View of Law and Fact," *Osgoode Hall Law Journal* 14, 2 (1976): 288–89.

2 Archibald Kelso Roberts, Conservative member of the provincial Parliament, was appointed attorney general of Ontario in August 1955. He was first elected in 1943. He was called to the bar in 1921 and created a King's counsel in 1944.

3 *R v Fitton,* [1956] SCR 958 [*Fitton*].

4 On Common's death in 1984, the Law Society of Upper Canada noted he had argued approximately five thousand appeals, many before the Supreme Court of Canada. "William B. Common Was Deputy to Ontario's Attorney General in the Ontario Legislature," Toronto *Daily Star,* April 5, 1984. The serving attorney general, Roy McMurtry, praised Common as "one of the leading crown prosecutors of this century." "Death of William Belmont Common," Ontario, Legislative Assembly, *House Documents,* 32 Parl, 4 Sess (April 5, 1984), https://www.ola.org/en/legislative-business/house-documents/parliament-32/session-4/1984-04-05/hansard#P13_2298.

5 G. Arthur Martin, "The Admissibility of Confessions and Statements," *Criminal Law Quarterly* 5, 1 (1962): 43.

6 E.K. Williams, "The Supreme Court of Canada Moves into Its 'New' Building," *American Bar Journal* 32, 2 (1946): 68–70.

7 As late as the 1960s, the federal government referred to the French and English as Canada's two "founding races." Malinda S. Smith, "Commissioning 'Founding Races' and Settler Colonial Narratives," *Canadian Ethnic Studies* 46, 2 (2014): 141–49.

8 James G. Snell and Frederick Vaughan, *The Supreme Court of Canada: History of the Institution* (Toronto: University of Toronto Press / Osgoode Society for Canadian Legal History, 1985), 197. Justice Thibaudeau Rinfret served on the Supreme Court from 1924 and was named chief justice in 1944.

9 Only 20 percent of the ten judges who joined the Supreme Court from 1935 to 1957 had prior judicial experience, indicating that appointments were

rewards for a "successful political career," compensation for "unsuccessful political activity," or recognition of a "life of public service." George Adams and Paul J. Cavalluzzo, "The Supreme Court of Canada: A Biographical Study," *Osgoode Hall Law Journal* 7, 1 (1969): 82–83.

10 Vincent C. MacDonald, "The Privy Council and the Canadian Constitution," *Canadian Bar Review* 29, 10 (1951): 1021–37. A Justice of the Supreme Court of Nova Scotia, MacDonald served as constitutional adviser to the Royal Commission on Dominion-Provincial Relations. The only formal change that impacted criminal matters was the expansion from a seven-judge tribunal to a nine-judge court in 1949.

11 Bora Laskin, "The Supreme Court of Canada: A Final Court of and for Canadians," *Canadian Bar Review* 29, 10 (1951): 1042.

12 Peter H. Russell, *The Judiciary in Canada* (Toronto: McGraw-Hill Ryerson, 1987), 112.

13 Laskin, "The Supreme Court of Canada," 1041. Laskin studied law at Harvard and lectured at the University of Toronto beginning in 1938. On his scholarly stature and progressive influence on the profession in the mid-twentieth century, see Philip Girard, *Bora Laskin: Bringing Law to Life* (Toronto: University of Toronto Press / Osgoode Society for Canadian Legal History, 2005).

14 For a later critique in this vein, see Paul Weiler, *The Last Resort: A Critical Study of the Supreme Court of Canada* (Carswell: Toronto, 1974), 16.

15 Snell and Vaughan, *The Supreme Court of Canada,* 155–56.

16 Stephen B. McKenna, *Grace and Wisdom: Patrick G. Kerwin, 1889–1963, Chief Justice of Canada* (Ottawa: Petra, 2018). The author, the judge's grandson, claims that the judge's daughter thought those executions anguished her father; however, Kerwin told his son, "I did not hang them, the law did." Book excerpt in *Canadian Law Library Review* 44, 2 (2019): 9–14, quote on page 12.

17 Biographical information on judges was derived from the Supreme Court of Canada's website.

18 The appointment of Abbott, an Anglican Anglo-Quebecer, was a snub to Quebec premier Maurice Duplessis. Displeasure over St-Laurent's move "did little to enhance respect for the Supreme Court." Snell and Vaughan, *The Supreme Court,* 200. See also Philip Girard, "St-Laurent, Judging, Justice, and the Death Penalty in the Shadow of the Cold War," in *The Unexpected Louis St-Laurent: Politics and Policies for a Modern Canada,* ed. Patrice Dutil (Vancouver: UBC Press, 2020), 336–55.

19 Laskin calculated that from 1944 to 1949 a total of 308 civil case appeals came before the Supreme Court, compared with just 37 criminal appeals. Laskin, "The Supreme Court of Canada," 1079.

20 Snell and Vaughan, *The Supreme Court,* 179. The court's final jurisdiction in criminal appeals was later incorporated in the Criminal Code, 1955, s 1025.

21 The chief justice complained that the decision conflicted with "recent recognition of [Canada's] status as a nation." "Address of the Right Honourable F.A. Anglin, P.C., Chief Justice of Canada, at the Twelfth Annual Meeting of the Canadian Bar Association," *Canadian Bar Review* 5, 8 (1927): 579–80.

22 Canada, *House of Commons Debates,* 17th Parl, 4th Sess, No 4 (March 28, 1933), 3459; and *Criminal Code Amendment Act,* SC 1932–33, c 53, s 17. On the reversal of the imperial policy in 1933 and its connections to Irish independence, see Jacqueline D. Krikorian, "British Imperial Politics and Judicial Independence: The Judicial Committee's Decision in the Canadian Case *Nadan v. The King,*" *Canadian Journal of Political Science / Revue canadienne de science politique* 33, 2 (2000): 291–332.

23 Snell and Vaughan, *The Supreme Court of Canada,* 185.

24 Bill 138, *An Act to Amend the Criminal Code,* received its first reading on May 14, 1930, and came into force on September 30, 1930. The federal election occurred on July 28, 1930, and the Liberals were defeated. Vincent M. Del Buono, "The Right to Appeal in Indictable Cases: A Legislative History," *Alberta Law Review* 16 (1978): 459.

25 Crown appeals against acquittals were rarely successful. Parker, "Jury Reversal," 288.

26 Robinette, already a respected member of the criminal bar, shot to national fame with the Dick case. George D. Finlayson, *John J. Robinette, Peerless Mentor: An Appreciation* (Toronto: Osgoode Society for Canadian Legal History, 2003), 48–72. The popular term for the murder arose from the fact the body was found headless and limbless.

27 *R v Dick,* [1947] SCR 211, 213.

28 "Dick Appeal Study in Contrasts," Hamilton *Spectator,* April 24, 1947.

29 "Refuse Appeal to High Court in Dick Case," Kingston *Whig-Standard,* February 12, 1947.

30 Brian Vallée, *The Torso Murder: The Untold Story of Evelyn Dick* (Toronto: Key Porter, 2001), 105–6, 221. Dick was subsequently convicted of the manslaughter of her infant in March 1948.

31 Carolyn Strange, *The Death Penalty and Sex Murder in Canadian History* (Toronto: University of Toronto Press / Osgoode Society for Canadian Legal History, 2020), 108–9. For an extended analysis of the Sears case, see Patrick Brode, *The Slasher Killings: A Canadian Sex-Crime Panic, 1945–1946* (Detroit: Wayne State University Press, 2009).

32 Canada, *House of Commons Debates,* 20th Parl, 3rd Sess, No 6 (July 3, 1947), 5029, 5028. Some Canadians advocated a national version of the American Uniform Rules of Evidence (1953). For an ambivalent account of the prospects, see John D. Martin, "Do We Need a Code of Evidence?," *Canadian Bar Review* 38 (1960): 35–46.

33 *Gach v R,* [1943] SCR 254.

34 *Boudreau v R,* [1949] SCR 270, 276 [*Boudreau*].

35 *Boudreau,* 238. On Rand's contributions to *Boudreau* and *Fitton,* see William Kaplan, *Canadian Maverick: The Life and Times of Ivan C. Rand* (Toronto: University of Toronto Press, 2009), 156–57.

36 Estey (1889–1956) was called to the bar of Saskatchewan in 1917 and created a King's counsel in 1928. He earned a master of arts and a bachelor of laws from Harvard University. From 1939 to 1944, the year of his appointment to the Supreme Court, he served as attorney general of Saskatchewan. "Obituaries," *Saskatchewan Bar Review and Law Society's Gazette* 21, 111 (1956): 3–4.

37 *Boudreau,* 238.

38 *Boudreau,* 269.

39 Estey's colleagues noted that he eschewed "fancy legal phraseology" and favoured a "common sense interpretation of the law." "Obituaries," 4.

40 Criminal Code, 1955, s 596(b). The reference directed the court to make a determination "as if it were an appeal by the convicted person."

41 *Reference re R v Coffin,* [1956] SCR 94, 191–252.

42 "The amendment as it affects criminal cases was undoubtedly a consequence of the 'Coffin Case'": Irving I. Finkelberg, "Statutes of Canada: Highlights of 1956," *McGill Law Journal* 3, 111 (1956): 71.

43 Canada, *House of Commons Debates,* 22nd Parl, 3rd Sess, No 7 (July 30, 1956), 6676. The Special Joint Committee recommended an automatic right of appeal after capital convictions at both the provincial level and the Supreme Court. *Reports of the Joint Committee of the Senate and House of Commons on Capital Punishment, Corporal Punishment and Lotteries* (Ottawa: Edmond Cloutier, 1956), 21.

44 For arguments on the abstraction of the distinction, see Ronald J. Allan and Michael S. Pardo, "The Myth of the Law: Fact Distinction," *Northwestern University Law Review* 97, 114 (2002–3): 1769–1808; and Stephen A. Simon, "Value Judgements in Judicial Reasoning, and the Instability of the Fact-Law Distinction," *University of Cincinnati Law Review* 92, 112 (2023): 455–84. For Canada, see Parker, "Jury Reversal."

45 Daved Muttart, *The Empirical Gap in Jurisprudence: A Comprehensive Study of the Supreme Court of Canada* (Toronto: University of Toronto Press, 2007), 41.

46 The right to appeal on a question of fact alone or mixed fact and law required leave of the Court of Appeal. Criminal Code, 1955, s 583a(ii).

47 Canada, *Joint Committee of the Senate and the House of Commons on Capital and Corporal Punishment and Lotteries: Minutes of Proceedings and Evidence, No. 4* (Ottawa: Queen's Printer, 1954), March 16, 1954, 155.

48 William B. Common, interview, Osgoode Society for Canadian Legal History, Oral History Program, October 1979, 6–7 (hereafter Common interview).

Common claimed he was conducting three hundred appeals annually by the 1940s, at the provincial and federal level.

49 "Inequalities of the Criminal Law," *Canadian Bar Review* 34, 113 (1956): 286–67. The forum was hosted by the Criminal Law Section of the Criminal Bar Association at its annual convention in Ottawa on August 30, 1955.

50 *An Act to Amend the Supreme Court Act and the Criminal Code,* SC 1956, c 48.

51 Rule 20(a) of the Criminal Appeal Rules for Ontario defined the factum as a "concise statement of the points of law and fact to be argued, which shall include with respect to each point references to the transcript and the authorities relied on." Rule 30 of the Rules of the Supreme Court set out its requirements. J.G.J. O'Driscoll, "The Presentation of an Appeal to the Court of Appeal and the Supreme Court of Canada in a Criminal Case," *Special Lectures of the Law Society of Upper Canada, 1969: Defending a Criminal Case* (Toronto: Richard De Boo, 1969), 204.

52 Factum of the Appellant, *R v Fitton* (September 15, 1956), *Records and Dossiers of the Supreme Court of Canada,* 6 (hereafter FOA).

53 FOA, 8.

54 M.F.E. Anthony and Arthur Moss, "The Status of Confessions in Our Modern Legal System," *Alberta Law Review* 1, 113 (1955): 146. Anthony was chief constable of Edmonton, and Moss was a former deputy assistant commissioner of the Ontario Provincial Police.

55 Criminal Code,1955, s 592(1)a(i).

56 FOA, 15. Common cited a further five Canadian and four British decisions.

57 "Crown Admits Judge Wrong in Murder Case," Toronto *Daily Star,* April 26, 1954.

58 FOA, 17.

59 F.J. Odgers, "Criminal Law – Murder or Manslaughter – Provocation," *Cambridge Law Journal* 12, 112 (1954): 165–68; and Graham E. Parker, "A Plea of Self-Defence Resulting in Manslaughter," *Alberta Law Review* 3 (1963): 16–49.

60 *R v Décary,* [1942] SCR 80.

61 *R v Howlett,* [1950] 2 DLR 143.

62 In an article published in 1960, Martin linked the Howlett case to Fitton's in a discussion of judicial discretion over the admissibility of statements. Martin, "The Admissibility of Confessions and Statements," 43–44.

63 Factum of the Respondent, *R v Fitton* (September 15, 1956), *Records and Dossiers of the Supreme Court of Canada* (hereafter FOR). The respondents' factum was forty pages in total, compared with Common's twenty-five.

64 FOR, 29, 38.

65 Snell and Vaughan, *The Supreme Court of Canada,* 208.

66 Common interview, 24.

67 Canada, *Report of a Committee Appointed to Inquire into the Principles and Procedures Followed in the Remission Service of the Department of Justice of Canada* (Ottawa: Edmond Cloutier, 1956). Although the committee recommended the establishment of a national parole board, it commended the Remission Service for its administration of death sentence reviews. Alan W. Mewett, "Criminal Law Revision in Canada," *Alberta Law Review* 7, 112 (1969): 275–76.

68 Common interview, 125, 126.

69 Dominique Clément, "The Royal Commission on Espionage and the Spy Trials of 1946–9: A Case Study in Parliamentary Supremacy," *Journal of the Canadian Historical Association* 11 (2000): 152. In 1949, Cartwright was backed by the Canadian Jewish Congress to fight racially restrictive covenant laws. See James St. James Walker, *"Race," Rights and the Law in the Supreme Court of Canada: Historical Case Studies* (Toronto: Osgoode Society for Canadian Legal History / Wilfrid Laurier University Press, 1997), 207–25.

70 Cartwright represented the Co-operative Committee on Japanese Canadians in "Reference to the Validity of Orders in Council in Relation to Persons of Japanese Race," *Supreme Court Reports* (1946): 248–327. Stephanie D. Bangarth, "The Co-operative Committee on Japanese Canadians and the American Civil Liberties Union: Engaging Debate, 1942–1946," *Princeton University Library Chronicle* 63, 113 (2002): 528–59.

71 Eric M. Adams, Jordan Stanger-Ross, and the Landscapes of Injustice Research Collective, "Constitutional Wrongs: The Wartime Constitution and Japanese Canadians, c 1942–6," in *Canadian State Trials,* vol. 5, *World War, Cold War, and Challenges to Sovereignty, 1939–1990,* ed. Barry Wright, Susan Binnie, and Eric Tucker (Toronto: University of Toronto Press, 2022), 67. William Kaplan provides a more complimentary appraisal of Rand in *Canadian Maverick,* 106–9.

72 Paul Weiler, "The Supreme Court of Canada and the Doctrines of Mens Rea," *Canadian Bar Review* 49, 112 (1971): 296.

73 *R v Fitton,* [1956] SCR 958, 982, 959 [*Fitton*]

74 "Common Argues against Granting Fitton New Trial," Toronto *Globe and Mail,* October 3, 1956.

75 O'Driscoll, "Presentation of an Appeal," 211.

76 "Fitton Case Decision Is Reserved," Kingston *Whig-Standard,* October 5, 1956. None of the press coverage of the hearing indicates that any questions were put to the Crown.

77 "Judgment Reserved on New Trial for Fitton," Windsor *Star,* October 5, 1956.

78 *Fitton,* 987–88, 962, 972, 975.

79 *Fitton,* 962, 963, 962.

80 *Fitton,* 963, 962, 963.

81 Kaplan, *Canadian Maverick,* 149–50. Kaplan claims Rand developed and refined "tests for determining whether a confession was voluntary" in *Boudreau* and *Fitton,* but see Martin, "The Admissibility of Statements," 43.

82 *Fitton,* 983, 964, 965.

83 Philip Girard comments that Rand provided "intellectual leadership" on the Supreme Court comparable to Bora Laskin's in the 1970s. Girard, *Bora Laskin,* 3, 196, 211.

84 Alan Mewett, "Criminal Law and Procedure in the Decisions of Ivan C. Rand," *University of Western Ontario Law Review* 18, 111 (1979): 51.

85 For an endorsement of Rand's use of judgments to criticize policy and legislation, see Ian Binnie, "Judging the Judges: May They 'Boldly Go Where Ivan Rand Went Before,'" *Canadian Journal of Law and Jurisprudence* 26, 111 (2013): 5–21.

86 *Cullen v R,* [1949] SCR 658, 665, 666, 668 [*Cullen*].

87 In *Cullen,* 658, the court held "there is no rule of law nor of practice that failure of counsel, whether, for an accused or for the Crown, to object to a charge to a jury on the grounds of misdirection is of necessity a bar to the right of appeal."

88 In 1957, the National Film Board's *The Suspects* (https://www.nfb.ca/film/suspects/) depicted harsh and manipulative interrogation techniques used by the police to interrogate two youths suspected of theft. The Canadian Association of Chiefs of Police pronounced it a travesty and devoted its 1956 annual meeting to police-media relations for the first time. Greg Marquis, *Policing Canada's Century: A History of the Canadian Association of Chiefs of Police* (Toronto: University of Toronto Press, 1993), 249–51.

89 Common interview, 144.

90 Tom Ford, "William Common: Gray Eminence of Ontario Law," Toronto *Daily Star,* November 21, 1964.

91 Common interview, 144.

92 Canada, *House of Commons Debates,* 20th Parl, 3rd Sess, No 6 (July 3, 1947), 5028.

93 Diefenbaker claimed, "No matter how well versed he may be in criminal law [no police officer] can state with certainty what the law is and what course he should follow before a statement which he secures will be admissible." Canada, *House of Commons Debates,* 20th Parl, 3rd Sess, No 6 (July 3, 1947), 5028.

94 On class, racial, and ethnic biases in the outcomes of capital cases, see Kenneth Avio, "Capital Punishment: Statistical Evidence and Constitutional Issues," *Canadian Journal of Criminology* 30, 113 (1988): 331–49; and Carolyn Strange,

"The Lottery of Death: Capital Punishment, 1867–1976," *Manitoba Law Journal* 23 (1995): 595–96.

95 Toronto *Telegram,* October 24, 1956.

96 When questioned about the lack of government action on sex crime in January 1956, the federal minister of justice referred to the stiff penalties for rape and attempted rape. Peter Dempson, "Angry MPs Ask Deviates Action," Toronto *Telegram,* January 25, 1956.

CHAPTER 7: REVERSAL OF FORTUNE

1 Carolyn Strange, "The Lottery of Death: Capital Punishment, 1867–1976," *Manitoba Law Journal* 23 (1995): 594–619.

2 Senator Asseltine to Minister of Justice, in Canada, *Joint Committee of the Senate and the House of Commons on Capital and Corporal Punishment and Lotteries: Minutes of Proceedings and Evidence, No. 1* (Ottawa: Queen's Printer, 1954), March 2, 1954, 31 (hereafter Joint Committee Minutes).

3 Jennifer Carter, "Capital Punishment: A Struggle to Satisfy Evolving Standards of Decency: Reviewing the Debate in the United States and Canada," *Southwestern Journal of International Law* 17, 112 (2011): 251.

4 One letter pleading for clemency was sent to the minister of justice and addressed to "Your Highness." It included a letter she claimed she had sent to Queen Elizabeth. Library and Archives Canada (LAC), RG 13, Department of Justice, RG13-B-1, Capital Punishment Case Files, vol. 1755, "Fitton, Robert," cc 821 (hereafter Fitton capital case file), vol. 5, November 17, 1956.

5 Strange, "The Lottery of Death," 598.

6 On the origins of this office, see Jonathan Swainger, *The Canadian Department of Justice and the Completion of Confederation, 1867–78* (Vancouver: UBC Press, 2000). The service's work was reviewed two years after the joint committee interrogated its operation. Canada, *Report of a Committee Appointed to Inquire into the Principles and Procedures Followed in the Remission Service of the Department of Justice of Canada* (Ottawa: Queen's Printer, 1956).

7 Judges' reports were also required to indicate the date set for the execution to allow ample time for the consideration of "royal mercy." Canada, *Criminal Code,* SC 1953–54, c 51, s 643(1)(a) (hereafter Criminal Code, 1955).

8 P.J. O'Hearn, "Criminal Law – Capital Punishment – Corporal Punishment – Lotteries – Joint Committee Reports," *Canadian Bar Review* 34, 117 (1956): 849.

9 *Special Joint Committee of the Senate and the House of Commons, Reports on Capital Punishment, Corporal Punishment and Lotteries* (Edmond Cloutier: 1956), 23 (hereafter Final Report). The committee did not recommend that women be exempt from the death penalty.

10 Roger Chadwick, *Bureaucratic Mercy: The Home Office and the Treatment of Capital Cases in Victorian England* (New York: Garland, 1992).

11 England, *Report of the Royal Commission on Capital Punishment, 1949–1953,* Sir Ernest Arthur Gowers, Chairman (London: Her Majesty's Stationery Office, 1953) (hereafter British Commission).

12 British Commission, 208. The report noted that judges informed the commission they did not want the responsibility to decide sentences in capital trials.

13 For critical reviews of the royal commission's proposals, see "A Symposium on the Report of the Royal Commission on Capital Punishment, 1949–1953," *British Journal of Delinquency* 4, 113 (1954): 157–98; and Melvin F. Wingersky, "Report of the Royal Commission on Capital Punishment (1949–1953): A Review," *Journal of Criminal Law, Criminology, and Police Science* 44, 116 (1954): 695–715.

14 Joint Committee Minutes, 504, March 2, 1954, 30.

15 Figures drawn from Lorraine Gadoury and Antonio Lechasseur, "Persons Sentenced to Death in Canada, 1867–1976: An Inventory of Case Files in the Fonds of the Department of Justice," National Archives of Canada, 1994. On the politics of capital punishment during Garson's tenure, see Philip Girard, "St-Laurent, Judging, Justice, and the Death Penalty in the Shadow of the Cold War," in *The Unexpected Louis St-Laurent: Politics and Policies for a Modern Canada*, ed. Patrice A. Dutil (Vancouver: UBC Press, 2020), 336–56, 54–55.

16 Joint Committee Minutes, March 2, 1954, 38.

17 Joint Committee Minutes, March 9, 1954, 122. Justice Hope described Cabinet decisions as "true exercises of the prerogative function and are not amenable to legal definition."

18 Joint Committee Minutes, March 9, 1954, 122. Harold Winch, the joint committee member most opposed to the death penalty, put the English royal commission's proposals to Justice Hope for comment.

19 Joint Committee Minutes, March 2, 1954, 39.

20 Joint Committee Minutes, March 9, 1954, 89.

21 Joint Committee Minutes, March 16, 1954, 156, 163, 156, 168.

22 The other was Harry Lee, an African Canadian man executed in Hamilton in February 1953 for shooting his paramour, a white woman. Maloney did not refer to racist prejudice against his client but cited it as another case in which a defendant's mental responsibility was questionable. Joint Committee Minutes, March 16, 1954, 156.

23 Joint Committee Minutes, March 16, 1954, 156.

24 Carolyn Strange, *The Death Penalty and Sex Murder in Canadian History* (Toronto: University of Toronto Press / Osgoode Society for Canadian Legal History, 2020), 144–47.

25 Joint Committee Minutes, March 16, 1954, 156.

26 Joint Committee Minutes, March 16, 1954, 168.

27 On October 10, Florence Fitton gave birth to a child she would have conceived shortly before the murder. "Third Child Born to Wife of Fitton," Toronto *Daily Star,* October 15, 1956.

28 Final Report, 23.

29 For the classic analysis of clemency requests as pardon tales, see Natalie Zemon Davis, *Fiction in the Archives: Pardon Tales and Their Tellers in Sixteenth-Century France* (Stanford, CA: Stanford University Press, 1987).

30 Humphrey and O'Driscoll to Minister of Justice, November 12, 1956, Fitton capital case file, vol. 1, pt. 3.

31 Humphrey and O'Driscoll to Minister of Justice, November 12, 1956, Fitton capital case file, vol. 1, pt. 3.

32 Humphrey and O'Driscoll to Minister of Justice, November 12, 1956, Fitton capital case file, vol. 1, pt. 3. Section 132 stated that when male persons were prosecuted under section 138(1) (intercourse with a female under the age of fourteen), consent was not a defence to the charge. The offence carried a maximum punishment of life and a whipping. Criminal Code, 1955.

33 Humphrey and O'Driscoll to Minister of Justice, November 12, 1956, Fitton capital case file, vol. 1, pt. 3.

34 David Humphrey, interview, Osgoode Society for Canadian Legal History, Oral History Program, 2008, 65 (hereafter Humphrey interview).

35 Humphrey and O'Driscoll to Minister of Justice, November 12, 1956, Fitton capital case file, vol. 1, pt. 3.

36 Humphrey and O'Driscoll to Minister of Justice, November 12, 1956, Fitton capital case file, vol. 1, pt. 3.

37 Humphrey and O'Driscoll to Minister of Justice, November 12, 1956, Fitton capital case file, vol. 1, pt. 3.

38 Pearl Fitton to Minister of Justice, November 12, 1956, Fitton capital case file, vol. 1, pt. 3.

39 Pearl Fitton to Minister of Justice, November 12, 1956. On November 14, 1956, A.J. MacLeod acknowledged this letter and the one she sent on November 8, 1956. Fitton capital case file, vol. 1, pt. 3.

40 The deaths led to an action under the *Fatal Accidents Act.* The plaintiff sought damages because of Fitton's and the other driver's negligence. The defence successfully claimed the accident had been unavoidable due to faulty steering. The decision was made on January 6, 1956, in *Drabik v Harris,* [1955] 2 DLR 384.

41 Pearl Fitton to Minister of Justice, November 8, 1956, Fitton capital case file, vol. 1, pt. 3.

42 Reverend Irwin G. Perkins to Allan MacLeod, November 19, 1956, Fitton capital case file. Perkins was the pastor at Donlands United Church, located a short walk from Fitton's home.

43 Reverend Malcolm P. Smith to Allan MacLeod, November 9, 1956, Fitton capital case file.

44 Allan J. MacLeod, memorandum for file, November 8, 1956, Fitton capital case file.

45 Allan J. MacLeod, memorandum for file, November 8, 1956.

46 The letter was posted on November 13, 1956, from the address of Parkdale Collegiate. Fitton capital case file.

47 Pearl Fitton to Minister of Justice, November 18, 1956, Fitton capital case file.

48 Mrs. Eileen MacIver to Prime Minister St-Laurent, November 20, 1956, Fitton capital case file. The writer's address was confirmed by consulting *Might's Greater Toronto Directory*.

CHAPTER 8: THE CLOSED CABINET

1 Stuart Garson, Canada, *Joint Committee of the Senate and the House of Commons on Capital and Corporal Punishment and Lotteries: Minutes of Proceedings and Evidence, No. 1* (Ottawa: Queen's Printer, 1954), May 11, 1954, 473 (hereafter Joint Committee Minutes).

2 Canada, *Reports of the Joint Committee of the Senate and the House of Commons on Capital Punishment, Corporate Punishment, and Lotteries* (Ottawa: Queen's Printer, 1956), 23 (hereafter Joint Committee Final Report).

3 Walter Skol, "See Jury's Clemency Plea Saving Fitton from Gallows," Toronto *Daily Star*, April 28, 1956.

4 The minister of justice set the terms of reference for the special joint commission and the review of the Remission Service, headed by Supreme Court Justice Gérard Fauteux, in December 1953. The Fauteux report was tabled on April 30, 1956, and the joint committee report on June 27, 1956. Canada, *Report of a Committee Appointed to Inquire into the Principles and Procedures Followed in the Remission Service of the Department of Justice of Canada* (Ottawa: Queen's Printer, 1956) (hereafter Fauteux Report).

5 Joint Committee Minutes, May 11, 1954, 478.

6 Fauteux Report, 28.

7 Carolyn Strange, "The Lottery of Death: Capital Punishment, 1867–1976," *Manitoba Law Journal* 23 (1995): 598–99.

8 J.R. Mallory, "Cabinet Government in Canada," *Political Studies* 2, 112 (1954): 153.

9 "British House Approves 'No Hanging' Bill in Close Vote; See Opposition by Lords," Ottawa *Citizen*, March 13, 1956. The Opposition leader, George Drew, was called to the bar in 1920. James William Coldwell was the Co-operative Commonwealth Federation's leader from 1942 to 1960.

10 Canada, *House of Commons Debates,* 22nd Parl, 1st Sess, No 3 (March 28, 1956), 2892–93, George Hugh Castleden and Stuart Garson.

11 The House of Lords voted down the bill to abolish the death penalty on July 10, 1956.

12 Canada, *Criminal Code,* SC 1953–54, c 51, s 658.

13 Joint Committee Final Report, 4.

14 Macdonald (1891–1976) was admitted to the bar of Ontario in 1919 and practised in Brantford with his brother until 1935. He was elected a Liberal MP, and in 1953 he was appointed to the Senate. As a senator, he also served as solicitor general from January 12, 1954, to June 20, 1957.

15 The minister of justice also retained the power to direct a new trial and to refer cases to courts of appeal. Joint Committee Minutes, March 2, 1954, 37.

16 Joint Committee Final Report, 4.

17 Joint Committee Final Report, 5.

18 Joint Committee Minutes, 489–90. Infanticide was subject to the death penalty until 1948. Kirsten Johnson Kramar, *Unwilling Mothers, Unwanted Babies: Infanticide in Canada* (Vancouver: UBC Press, 2005), 87–96. The committee's final report stated that murders by women were rare and committed "usually in circumstances which warrant the Royal Prerogative of Mercy," but it recommended against exempting women from the death penalty. Joint Committee Final Report, 18.

19 Joint Committee Final Report, 5.

20 "Table F, Recommendations as to Mercy (1920–1949)," Joint Committee Final Report, 31.

21 Joint Committee Final Report, 6.

22 Joint Committee Final Report, 5, 16, 17.

23 On the politics surrounding the English royal commission, see Victor Bailey, "The Shadow of the Gallows: The Death Penalty and the British Labour Government, 1945–51," *Law and History Review* 18, 112 (2000): 305–50. The Canadian joint committee closely followed the statistical analysis performed by the Home Office. Strange, "The Lottery of Death," 612–13.

24 Peter P. Lejins, "Thorsten Sellin: A Life Dedicated to Criminology," *Criminology* 25, 114 (1987): 980.

25 Sellin was an executive member of the American League to Abolish Capital Punishment. In 1959, he published a major compendium that incorporated his earlier work on the subject: *The Death Penalty: A Report for the Model Penal Code Project of the American Law Institute* (Los Angeles: American Law Institute, 1959).

26 The joint committee report noted that every attorney general (except Saskatchewan's) supported the death penalty's retention. The police believed it protected officers from professional criminals and deterred them from entering Canada. Joint Committee Final Report, 10.

27 Joint Committee Final Report, 10, 14.

28 "Table B, Proportion of Executions, 1920–1949," Joint Committee Final Report, 29. In the 1930s, 125 of 208 people sentenced to death were executed.

29 "Table H, Ages of Persons Convicted of Murder, 1920–1952," Joint Committee Final Report, 34.

30 Over more than eight hundred pages, the minutes of the joint committee hearings referred to rape only several times, mainly in reference to its definition in the Criminal Code. "Robbery" and "robbers" were mentioned eighty-eight times.

31 Joint Committee Final Report, 19.

32 Joint Committee Final Report, 7.

33 Treleaven to Minister of Justice, May 7, 1956, Library and Archives Canada (LAC), RG 13, Department of Justice, RG13-B-1, Capital Punishment Case Files, vol. 1755, "Fitton, Robert," vol. 1 pt. 1 (hereafter Fitton capital case file).

34 Inspector R.P. Hanson to Director of the Remission Service, June 11, 1956, Fitton capital case file, vol. 5.

35 Dr. W.H. Hills to Governor of the Don Jail, June 8, 1956, in Fitton capital case file, vol. 3.

36 Joint Committee Minutes, May 5, 1954, 454.

37 Alex M. Cathie to A.J. MacLeod, June 8, 1956, Fitton capital case file, vol. 5.

38 Biographical data on Cathie gleaned from Ancestry.com and newspapers.com.

39 "'Worst Rape-Murder' Coroner Has Known; Second within Month," Brantford *Expositor,* October 20, 1954. The coroner was Smirle Lawson. The victims were Mrs. Olga Zacharko and Mrs. Mary Lipoweckyj. Their bodies were stripped and mutilated. On the role of ethnopolitical suppositions and allegations of extramarital affairs in hampering the investigation, see Elise Chenier, *Strangers in Our Midst: Sexual Deviancy in Postwar Ontario* (Toronto: University of Toronto Press, 2008), 48–50.

40 Franca Iacovetta, "The Sexual Politics of Moral Citizenship and Containing 'Dangerous' Foreign Men in Cold War Canada, 1950s–1960s," *Histoire sociale / Social History* 33, 66 (2000): 478–82. Although the police closed the two cases, they attributed both murders to an Eastern European man, found in an asylum.

41 Alex M. Cathie to A.J. MacLeod, June 8, 1956, Fitton capital case file, vol. 5.

42 Alex M. Cathie to A.J. MacLeod, June 8, 1956.

43 Alex M. Cathie to A.J. MacLeod, June 8, 1956.

44 John Bird, "Cabinet's Toughest Tasks Are Death Sentence Reviews," Ottawa *Journal,* January 7, 1956. Bird was educated at Oxford and Harvard, served as editor of the Winnipeg *Tribune,* and headed Southam News Services. He became

a political columnist and was a life member of the Parliamentary Press Gallery. "John Bird Dies at 76," Ottawa *Journal,* August 18, 1978.

45 John Bird, "Cabinet's Toughest Tasks."

46 MacLeod (1918–90) studied law at Dalhousie University. He graduated in 1942 and was called to the bar in 1945 after military service. From 1947, he worked in the Department of Justice, and he entered the Remission Service in 1950. He became acting head in 1953 and took on the permanent role in 1954. "Staffing Changes," *Federal Corrections* 1, 111 (1961): 6.

47 John Bird, "Cabinet's Toughest Tasks."

48 Coffin was executed on February 10, 1956. The other executions occurred on May 22, June 15, July 17, October 26, and November 6, 1956.

49 The victim, Marie Anne Carrier, was left naked but not sexually assaulted in a ditch in October 1953. Justice McRuer, who headed the royal commission, was the judge who sentenced Balcombe to death. Balcombe was executed on May 25, 1954. Carolyn Strange, *The Death Penalty and Sex Murder in Canadian History* (Toronto: University of Toronto Press / Osgoode Society for Canadian Legal History, 2020), 315–16.

50 Tennant to Common, November 2, 1956, Fitton capital case file, vol. 5.

51 On the royal commission on criminal insanity and its work, see Kimberley White, *Negotiating Responsibility: Law, Murder and States of Mind* (Vancouver: UBC Press, 2008).

52 Joint Committee Minutes, May 11, 1954, 483–84.

53 Officers from the Remission Service were stationed in Ottawa and in branch offices in major centres from 1949. Prior to the establishment of a federal parole system (which the Fauteux report recommended), prisoners applied for "clemency" but had to satisfy officers of their "chances of rehabilitation." Fauteux Report, 3, 4.

54 Fauteux Report, 10, 9.

55 "Immigrant Charged with Murder," St. Catharines *Standard,* July 28, 1954.

56 *R v Tripodi,* [1955] 438. The judges in the Court of Appeal and the Supreme Court differed over the doctrine of sudden provocation as a defence to murder and its application to the circumstances. Fauteux, Taschereau, and Rand denied it applied to Tripodi's deliberate intention to "avenge his family honour" (439).

57 "Goes to Kingston for Life. Tripodi, Told of Reprieve, Cries," St. Catharines *Standard,* July 2, 1955.

58 Marginalia and text, Humphrey and O'Driscoll to Minister of Justice, November 12, 1956, Fitton capital case file, vol. 4.

59 Between 1920 and 1952, 40 percent of wife murderers had their sentences commuted versus 25 percent of robbery murderers and 11 percent of "sexual assault" killers. Joint Committee Final Report, 33, Table G.

60 Thompson's draft memorandum was completed on November 1, 1956, and final memoranda were generally completed no later than several days prior to the Cabinet meeting.

61 Joint Committee Minutes, March 2, 1954, 40.

62 A.D.P. Heeney, "Cabinet Government in Canada," *Canadian Journal of Economics and Political Science / Revue canadienne d'Economique et de Science politique* 12, 113 (1946): 283. Heeney was appointed the first secretary to the Cabinet in 1940.

63 Brian Heeney, ed., *The Things That Are Caesar's: Memoirs of a Canadian Public Servant – Arnold Heeney* (Toronto: University of Toronto Press, 1972), 78–80.

64 On the value of these records for exposing the exercise of the government's executive powers, see Michael Dufresne, "The Beginning of the Conclusions: Documenting the Exercise of Power," Library and Archives Canada blog, February 16, 2018, https://thediscoverblog.com/tag/cabinet-conclusions/.

65 LAC, RG 2, Privy Council Office, series A-5-a, vol. 5775, item 15434, November 19, 1956.

66 LAC, RG 2, Privy Council Office, series A-5-a, vol. 5775, item 15434, November 19, 1956.

67 "The Abolition of Capital Punishment," *Canadian Bar Review*, 32, 115 (1954): 518.

68 Joint Committee Minutes, May 11, 1954, 490.

69 Joint Committee Minutes, May 11, 1954, 493.

CHAPTER 9: A SECOND FATALITY

1 "Numbed by Hypodermic, Fitton Goes to Gallows," Toronto *Daily Star*, November 21, 1956. Other papers estimated a crowd of two hundred.

2 Section 648 of the *Criminal Code*, SC 1953–54, c 51 (hereafter Criminal Code, 1955) required the coroner to hold an inquest to determine "whether sentence of death was duly executed." Library and Archives Canada (LAC), RG 13, Department of Justice, RG13-B-1, Capital Punishment Case Files, vol. 1755, "Fitton, Robert," cc 821 (hereafter Fitton capital case file).

3 "The Abolition of Capital Punishment," *Canadian Bar Review* 32, 115 (1954): 486. The article recorded a forum held on February 5, 1954, and hosted by Edson Haines Queen's counsel, the vice-president of the Ontario branch of the Canadian Bar Association.

4 In 1953, Gallup polls recorded that support for the death penalty stood at 71 percent. David B. Chandler, *Capital Punishment in Canada: A Sociological Study of a Repressive Law* (Toronto: McClelland and Stewart, 1976), 41.

5 The recommendation of the Joint Committee of the Senate and the House of Commons to switch the method of execution received greater coverage than their final report's other recommendations. "Ban Noose, Use Gas," was the banner headline in the Toronto *Telegram,* June 20, 1956.

6 W. Ross Macdonald to John E. Saul, November 23, 1956, Fitton capital case file, vol. 5. This phrase reappeared in numerous communications with writers who objected to Fitton's execution. It was the standard response drafted by the Remission Service for the minister's signature.

7 In 1868, the British parliament passed a bill that provided for hangings to be conducted behind walls. Canada followed suit in 1869. Canada, *An Act respecting Procedure in Criminal Cases, and other matters relating to Criminal Law,* SC 1869, c 29.

8 Philip Girard, "St-Laurent, Judging, Justice, and the Death Penalty in the Shadow of the Cold War," in *The Unexpected Louis St-Laurent: Politics and Policies for a Modern Canada,* ed. Patrice A. Dutil (Vancouver: UBC Press, 2020), 338–39.

9 In Lee Mellor's book, the chapter on the case is titled "The Fort Rouge Sex Maniac." Mellor, *Cold North Killers: Canadian Serial Murder* (Toronto: Dundurn, 2012). The Manitoba Police Museum refers to Vescio's crime as "The Pervert Murders." See Patrol Sergeant Mark Hodgson's article by the same name, https://winnipegpolicemuseum.ca/wp-content/uploads/2021/03/the-pervert-murders.pdf.

10 Garson was premier of Manitoba, representing the Liberal-Progressive Party from 1943 to 1948. He accepted the ministerial post prior to his election in a federal by-election in December 1948. He also served as solicitor general from 1950 to 1952. Ralph Campney held that post between 1952 and Ross Macdonald's appointment in 1954.

11 The appeal was against the judgment of the Manitoba Court of Appeal, which had affirmed Vescio's conviction, with two of five judges in dissent. The final decision to dismiss the appeal was delivered on November 2, 1948. *Vescio v R,* [1949] SCR 139.

12 Statistics culled from Lorraine Gadoury and Antonio Lechasseur, "Persons Sentenced to Death in Canada, 1867–1976: An Inventory of Case Files in the Fonds of the Department of Justice," National Archives of Canada, 1994. One woman, Margarite Pitre, was executed in 1953 for her involvement in the bombing of a plane. No other woman was executed after Pitre.

13 Statistics Canada's historical statistics of Canada, section Z (Justice), series Z66-172 (Statistics on Court Proceedings), provides a crude indication of an increase in criminal appeals: https://www150.statcan.gc.ca/n1/pub/11-516-x/pdf/5220025-eng.pdf. In 1945, 557 appeals were filed in provincial courts, with 80

convictions quashed and 26 new trials ordered. In 1956, 1,093 appeals were filed. The proportion of verdicts quashed declined (8 percent), but the proportion of new trials ordered, including Fitton's, remained about the same (5 percent). See https://www150.statcan.gc.ca/n1/pub/11-516-x/sectionz/Z168_172-eng.csv.

14 Statistics culled from Gadoury and Lechasseur, "Persons Sentenced to Death."

15 Canada, *Joint Committee of the Senate and the House of Commons on Capital and Corporal Punishment and Lotteries: Minutes of Proceedings and Evidence* (Ottawa: Queen's Printer, 1954), March 16, 1954, 155 (hereafter Joint Committee Minutes).

16 Justice W.J. Major to Secretary of State, March 2, 1950, in LAC, RG 13, vol. 1687, vol. 1.

17 Justice W.J. Major to Secretary of State, March 2, 1950.

18 Sherbrooke *Daily Record,* January 21, 1956.

19 Philpott (1896–1964) was "devoted to human progress and human understanding." He was a member of the Co-operative Commonwealth Federation in the 1930s and worked mainly as a journalist. He was elected as the member for Vancouver South in 1953. "Writer, Soldier, MP Elmore Philpott Dies," Montreal *Gazette,* December 11, 1964.

20 Elmore Philpott, "To Check Sex Crimes," Vancouver *Sun,* January 24, 1956. Philpott praised the impact of Reinke's speech in Parliament.

21 Robert Taylor, "2 Killers Die Tonight Clemency Is Denied. No Word from Queen," Toronto *Daily Star,* December 15, 1956.

22 Stuart Garson, Joint Committee Minutes, May 11, 1954, 507.

23 Sex murderers were denied clemency in 64 percent of cases from 1867 to 1967, and persons accused of robbery-murder were hanged at a rate of 54 percent. Carolyn Strange, *The Death Penalty and Sex Murder in Canadian History* (Toronto: University of Toronto Press / Osgoode Society for Canadian Legal History, 2020), 5.

24 For an extended analysis of the O'Donnell case, see Strange, *The Death Penalty,* 83–87.

25 On Teolis's botched execution and its connection to debates on hanging, see Donald Fyson, "The Execution of Tommasina Teolis: Capital Punishment, Gender and Ethnicity in Quebec in the First Half of the Twentieth Century," in *Women's History and the Law: Past, Present, Future,* ed. Lori Chambers and Joan Sangster (Toronto: University of Toronto Press / Osgoode Society for Canadian Legal History, 2023), 173–212.

26 Canada, *Special Committee on the Criminal Code (Death Penalty): Minutes of Proceedings and Evidence* (Ottawa: King's Printer, 1937), 67 (hereafter Death Committee).

27 The chairman acknowledged the "grave errors" that had created a "revulsion of public feeling." Death Committee, 69.

28 Ontario and New Brunswick had not established centralized sites for execution by the time the joint committee conducted its inquiries. Joint Committee Minutes, May 11, 1955, 570.

29 Ontario's deputy minister of reform institutions told the joint committee that no accidents had occurred at any of the province's forty-two jails, but he could not supply information about the time between hanging and the pronouncement of death. Joint Committee Minutes, March 24, 1954, 252–53.

30 Malcolm S. MacLean, testimony, Joint Committee Minutes, May 27, 1954, 646. MacLean served as jail surgeon from 1935 to 1952.

31 The first interior execution in the Don Jail occurred on January 8, 1908. "Boyd Hanged in the Jail Building," Toronto *Daily Star,* January 8, 1908.

32 "Boyd Hanged." Sheriff Frederick Mowat, first appointed in 1887, added that it was "much easier for all concerned."

33 Criminal Code, 1955, ss 644, 645.

34 Death Committee, 54.

35 Death Committee, 55–56.

36 Conover was appointed sheriff in 1945. Death Committee, 450.

37 Death Committee, 450. Conover also referred to two cases that were traversed and did not discuss verdicts quashed.

38 Prison doctors were required to sign the death certificate "as soon as possible after a sentence of death has been executed." Criminal Code, 1955, s 646(1).

39 Joint Committee Minutes, May 5, 1954, 454.

40 Joint Committee Minutes, May 5, 1954, 456.

41 Joint Committee Minutes, May 5, 1954, 454.

42 Joint Committee Minutes, May 5, 1954, 458.

43 Carolyn Strange, "The Undercurrents of Penal Culture: Punishment of the Body in Mid-Twentieth-Century Canada," *Law and History Review* 19, 112 (2001): 348.

44 Joint Committee Minutes, May 5, 1954, 454, 460.

45 Joint Committee Minutes, May 5, 1954, 454. On the botched execution of a man hanged twice in 1922, after the first attempt left his heart still beating, see Michael Boudreau, "'The Disgust of the Community against Hanging': The Execution of Bennie Swim and the Debate over Capital Punishment in New Brunswick," *Acadiensis* 51, 111 (2022): 66–89.

46 Joint Committee Minutes, May 5, 1954, 457.

47 Stuart Garson opened his presentation on May 11, 1954, on execution procedures by saying, "Contrary to popular belief, there is no official hangman or executioner for the dominion." Joint Committee Minutes, May 11, 1954, 476.

48 Death Committee, 15.

49 Joint Committee Minutes, May 5, 1954, 468. Phenobarbital is a barbiturate that was primarily used in the mid-twentieth century to treat epilepsy, but it was

also used to relieve anxiety. Francisco López-Muñoz, Ronaldo Ucha-Udabe, and Cecilio Alamo, "The History of Barbiturates a Century after Their Clinical Introduction," *Neuropsychiatric Disease and Treatment* 1, 114 (2005): 329–43.

50 Joint Committee Minutes, May 13, 1954, 529–30.

51 Joint Committee Minutes, May 13, 1954, 528. The minutes indicate that a subcommittee considered the prospect on May 5, 1954, and that Quebec's official hangman sent a telegram six days later, requesting an in-camera appearance. However, the testimony was reported *in extensio.* Joint Committee Minutes, 1955, Appendix D, 835.

52 Joint Committee Minutes, May 11, 1955, 569, 572–73.

53 Cameron – a lawyer, not a doctor – was quoting from testimony by J.K.W. Ferguson, head of the Department of Pharmacology, University of Toronto, and an anonymous neurologist, who confirmed that loss of consciousness did not rule out death by asphyxiation. Joint Committee Minutes, May 10, 1955, 547.

54 Joint Committee Minutes, May 11, 1955, 576–78. The press focused on Branchaud's allegations of drunkenness. "Executioner Tells Parliament Probe: 'Officials Incapably Drunk at Hangings,'" Vancouver *Province,* May 25, 1955.

55 Joint Committee Minutes, May 10, 1955, 530.

56 Joint Committee Minutes, March 17, 1954, 250–51. Branchaud was on salary as the official hangman of Quebec and carried out executions elsewhere, including British Columbia and the Northwest Territories. Kenneth B. Leyton-Brown, *The Practice of Execution in Canada* (Vancouver: UBC Press, 2010), 72–75.

57 "Hopes Son Will Die First Cheat Rope," Toronto *Telegram,* November 20, 1956.

58 Osgoode Society, oral history, David Humphrey, interview, Osgoode Society for Canadian Legal History, Oral History Program, 2008, 67 (hereafter Humphrey interview).

59 Humphrey interview, 68. David Humphrey's son, David M. Humphrey, said his father's religious faith declined after the 1950s, but he does not attribute that to the outcome of the Fitton case. Interview with author, January 6, 2023.

60 The *Daily Star* reported that Pearl Fitton had moved from the Anglican Church to the Pentecostal Church and that her pastor, Earl McDowell, had visited her son during his incarceration. Reverend W.P. Smith was employed by the Toronto Police Court and ministered at the Don Jail.

61 "'Now I Can Only Pray' Says Mother of Fitton," Toronto *Daily Star,* November 20, 1956. The article covered the responses of both women.

62 "Fitton Given Morphine before Going to Gallows," Toronto *Telegram,* November 21, 1956.

63 Death Committee, 55–56.

64 Death Committee, 56. John Power Howden earned his medical degree from the University of Manitoba in 1904. He entered politics in 1914 as mayor of Boniface, and he was elected a Liberal MP in 1925. See Manitoba Historical Society Archives, "Memorable Manitobans: John Power Hayden (1879–1959), https://www.mhs.mb.ca/docs/people/howden_jp.shtml.

65 MacLean, who administered drugs in executions in the 1940s and 1950s, used half a grain; Deputy Sheriff Wills said in 1937 that doctors used three-quarters of a grain.

66 Joint Committee Minutes, May 25, 1954, 647–48. A cover was put over the scaffold to prevent the public from seeing the execution.

67 Joint Committee Minutes, May 4, 1954, 459.

68 Canada, *Reports of the Joint Committee of the Senate and the House of Commons on Capital Punishment, Corporate Punishment, and Lotteries* (Ottawa: Queen's Printer, 1956), 21.

69 Smith to MacLeod, November 8, 1956, Fitton capital case file, vol. 1, pt. 3.

70 Joint Committee Minutes, May 5, 1954, 457.

71 "Numbed by Hypodermic Fitton Goes to Gallows," Toronto *Daily Star,* November 21, 1956.

72 "Numbed by Morphine Fitton Is Executed. 300 Wait in Rain," Toronto *Daily Star,* November 21, 1956. Other papers on the Canadian Press wire service reported nineteen minutes.

73 "'Now I Can Only Pray' Says Mother of Fitton," Toronto *Daily Star,* November 20, 1956.

74 William Lusanko's family did not claim his body, and he was buried in the Headingley Jail cemetery. See Manitoba Historical Society Archives, "Historic Sites of Manitoba: Headingley Gaol Cemetery (RM of St. Francois Xavier)," https://www.mhs.mb.ca/docs/sites/gaolcemetery.shtml. The redevelopment of the Don Jail uncovered the burial of fifteen men on the grounds, the last of whom was executed in 1930. Jeff Gray, "The Forgotten 15," Toronto *Globe and Mail,* 2017.

75 Final Report, 14.

76 Frank M. Deakin to Prime Minister, November 20, 1956, Fitton capital case file, vol. 3. *Might's Greater Toronto Directory* does not list the writer's occupation.

77 Irwin G. Perkins to Allan MacLeod, November 19, 1956, Fitton capital case file, vol. 3. Perkins was the minister at Donlands United Church in Toronto.

78 This was the last line in numerous letters sent under the signature of the solicitor general, W. Ross Macdonald. Fitton capital case file, vol. 5, November 20, 1956.

79 Saul to Minister of Justice, November 21, 1956, Fitton capital case file, vol. 5.

80 Macdonald to Saul, November 23, 1956, Fitton capital case file, vol. 5.

81 On the principles, see "Atkinson Principles," *Toronto Star,* https://www.thestar.com/site/atkinson/atkinson-principles.html.

82 "An Eye for an Eye," Toronto *Daily Star,* November 21, 1956.

83 Circulation figures published on editorial page, December 28, 1956.

84 Toronto *Daily Star,* November 21, 1956. Hindmarsh, a close associate of the prime minister, died in office one month later. "H.C. Hindmarsh Towering Figure, Leaders Say," Toronto *Daily Star,* December 21, 1956.

85 "No Mercy Shown," Toronto *Daily Star,* November 23, 1956. The *Daily Star* published several letters critical of the execution under the title "All Canadians Guilty of Fitton's Death."

86 In 1956, almost 60 percent of men and 52 percent of women were in favour of the death penalty for murder. Ezzat Fatah, "The Canadian Public and the Death Penalty: A Study of a Social Attitude," Criminology Department, Simon Fraser University, 1976, 20, https://www.publicsafety.gc.ca/lbrr/archives/hv%208699.c2%20f3c%201976-eng.pdf.

87 Humphrey interview, 72.

88 Humphrey interview, 72. Humphrey referred to Cole only by his first name in the interview.

89 Joint Committee Minutes, March 24, 1954, 252.

90 "Numbed by Hypodermic Fitton Goes to Gallows," Toronto *Daily Star,* November 21, 1956.

UNFINISHED BUSINESS

1 For citations to Fitton that criticize irresolution over the questioning of suspects and the admissibility of confessions, see Stanley M. Beck, "The Investigation of Offences and Police Powers," *Canadian Journal of Corrections* 12, 113 (1970): 209–20; and Ed Ratushny, "Is There a Right against Self-Incrimination in Canada?" *McGill Law Journal* 19, 111 (1973): 1–77.

2 Andrew S. Thompson, "Uneasy Abolitionists: Canada, the Death Penalty, and the Importance of International Norms, 1962–2005," *Journal of Canadian Studies* 42, 113 (2008): 172–92; Amy Helen Bell, "Cop-Killers, Emotion, and Capital Punishment in Moncton, New Brunswick: The Ambrose and Hutchison Case, 1974–75," *Canadian Historical Review* 101, 113 (2020): 346–69; and Margaret Dudson, "The Death Penalty Debate in Canada: Ethnicity, Abolition and the Current Debate," in *Capital Punishment: New Perspectives,* ed. Peter Hodgkinson (London: Routledge, 2013), 275–96.

3 Constance B. Backhouse, "A Feminist Remedy for Sexual Assault: A Quest for Answers," in *Sexual Assault in Canada: Law, Legal Practice, and Women's Activism,* ed. Elizabeth Sheehy (Ottawa: University of Ottawa Press, 2012), 725–39.

4 Bernard Schissel, "Law Reform and Social Change: A Time-Series Analysis of Sexual Assault in Canada," *Journal of Criminal Justice* 24, 112 (1996): 123–38; Liat Levanon, "Sexual History Evidence in Cases of Sexual Assault: A Critical Re-evaluation," *University of Toronto Law Journal* 62, 114 (2012): 609–51; and Lise Gotell, "Canadian Sexual Assault Law: Neoliberalism and the Erosion of Feminist-Inspired Law Reforms," in *Rethinking Rape Law: International and Comparative Perspectives,* ed. Clare Mcglynn and Vanessa Munro (London: Routledge, 2010), 225–39.

5 *Canadian Charter of Rights and Freedoms,* Part I of the *Constitution Act, 1982,* being Schedule B to the *Canada Act 1982* (UK), 1982, c 11.

6 Fred E. Inbau, "Law and Police Practice: Restrictions in the Law of Interrogation and Confession," *Northwestern University Law Review* 52, 111 (1957): 85. Inbau was a professor at Northwestern University and the coauthor (with John E. Reid) of *Lie Detection and Criminal Interrogation,* 3rd ed. (Baltimore: Williams and Wilkins, 1953).

7 The phrase "handcuffing the police" was used frequently in criticism of court restraint on police interrogations. See, for instance, Edward L. Barrett Jr., "Police Practices and the Law: From Arrest to Release or Charge," *California Law Review* 50, 111 (1962): 11–55.

8 G. Arthur Martin, "Police Interrogation Privileges and Limitations under Foreign Law," *Journal of Criminal Law and Criminology* 52, 111 (1961): 49. Martin was invited to present his interpretation of Canadian law for the journal's symposium, titled "Police Interrogation Privileges and Limitations: An International Symposium."

9 "Developments in the Law: Confessions," *Harvard Law Review* 79, 115 (1966): 1106.

10 Beverley M. McLachlin and Andrea M. Miller, "*Rothman*: Police Trickery – Is the Game Worth the Candle. Case Comment," *University of British Columbia Law Review* 16, 111 (1982): 127. The authors identified *Rothman* as further evidence of the court's acceptance of police trickery. See also Donald G. Casswell, "The Law Reform Commission of Canada, the Proposed Canada Evidence Act and Statements by an Accused," *Canadian Bar Review* 63, 112 (1985): 322–57; and Law Reform Commission of Canada, Working Paper 32, "Questioning Suspects," Minister of Supply and Services, 1984.

11 Brian Dickson, "The Canadian Charter of Rights and Freedoms: Dawn of a New Era?" *Review of Constitutional Studies* 2, 111 (1995): 1, 17.

12 *R v Oickle,* 2000 SCC 38, [2000] 2 SCR 3, 6, 5.

13 *R v Spencer,* [2007], 1 SCR 500, 501. The majority in *Singh* also cited *Fitton* and *Boudreau* in affirming what the common law rule and the Charter considered paramount in determining the voluntariness of confessions: "The usual police caution given to a suspect." *R v Singh,* [2007] 3 SCR 405, 422.

14 Hamish Stewart, "The Confessions Rule and the Charter," *McGill Law Journal* 54, 113 (2009): 529. On the significance of psychological coercion, see Jeffrey Kaplan, Brian L. Cutler, Amy-May Leach, Joseph Eastwood, and Stephanie Marion, "Evaluating Coercion in Suspect Interviews and Interrogations," *Advances in Psychology and Law* 4 (2019): 1–40.

15 Lisa Dufraimont, "The Common Law Confessions Rule in the Charter Era: Current Law and Future Directions," *Supreme Court Law Review* 40 (2008): 249. See also Kimberly M. Campbell, *Miscarriages of Justice in Canada: Causes, Responses, Remedies* (Toronto: University of Toronto Press, 2017), 89.

16 Steven Penney, "What's Wrong with Self-Incrimination: The Wayward Path of Self-Incrimination Law in the Post-Charter Era – Part II: Self-Incrimination in Police Investigations," *Criminal Law Quarterly* 48, 113 (2004): 287. See also, "Spencer: Has the Confessions Rule Changed ... Again?," Court.ca, April 19, 2007, https://canliiconnects.org/fr/commentaires/35425.

17 John Willis, "Case and Comment," *Canadian Bar Review* 29, 117 (1951): 793.

18 Graham Hughes, "The English Homicide Act of 1957: The Capital Punishment Issue, and Various Reforms in the Law of Murder and Manslaughter," *Journal of Criminal Law, Criminology and Police Science* 49, 116 (1958–59): 523.

19 John Ll. J. Edwards, "Constructive Murder in Canadian and English Law," *University of Malaya Law Review* 1, 111 (1959): 25, 38; and Isabel Grant and A. Wayne MacKay, "Constructive Murder and the Charter: In Search of Principle," *Alberta Law Review* 25, 112 (1987): 129–59.

20 Kent Roach, "Common Law Bills of Rights as Dialogue between Courts and Legislatures," in "Administrative Law Today: Culture, Ideas, Institutions, Processes, Values," special issue, *University of Toronto Law Journal* 55, 113 (2005): 761, 762. See also Isabel Grant, "Rethinking the Sentencing Regime for Murder," *Osgoode Hall Law Journal* 39 (2001): 655–701.

21 Alan W. Mewett, "The Canadian Criminal Code, 1892–1992," *Canadian Bar Review* 72 (1993): 11, 27.

22 *R v Martineau,* [1990] 2 SCR 633, 634 [*Martineau*]. For this ruling in the context of Dickson's views on democratic rights, see Robert J. Sharpe and Kent Roach, *Brian Dickson: A Judge's Journey* (Toronto: University of Toronto Press, 2003), 344–46.

23 *Martineau,* 636, 679.

24 Kent Roach, "The Problematic Revival of Murder under Section 229(c) of the *Criminal Code,*" *Alberta Law Review* 47 (2010): 681–82. See also Kent Roach, *Criminal Law,* 8th ed. (Toronto: Irwin, 2022), 456; Law Reform Commission of Canada, "Homicide," Working Paper 33, Minister of Supply and

Services Canada, 1984, 53; and Terry Skolnik, "Causation, Fault and Fairness in the Criminal Law," *McGill Law Journal* 65, 111 (2019): 1–28.

25 S. Ferguson of Toronto, letter to the editor, Toronto *Daily Star,* November 23, 1956.

26 Toronto *Daily Star,* October 4, 1958.

27 The amendment defined as "capital" any killing, even if not premeditated, of a public official, serving police officer, constable sheriff or delegate, warden, jail instructor, or keeper or guards. *An Act to Amend the Criminal Code (Capital Murder),* SC 1961, c 44, s 1.

28 Correctional Service Canada defines the death penalty's abolition as a direct result of the triumph of human rights, starting in the late 1950s. See "Corrections in Canada: A Historical Timeline," Correctional Service Canada, https://www.canada.ca/en/correctional-service/corporate/history-csc/timeline/1960-1979.html. The Canadian Institute of Public Opinion's polls showed that support for capital punishment dropped from 71 percent in 1953 to 52 percent in 1958.

29 C.H.S. Jayewardene and H. Jayewardene, "The Public Opinion Argument in the Death Penalty Debate," *Canadian Journal of Criminology* 22, 114 (1980): 404–11.

30 "Open Mind Needed. Capital Punishment Supported," Toronto *Globe and Mail,* October 22, 1956. Marie Ann Shipley, Liberal MP for Temiskaming (1953–57) made this statement to the Annual Conference of Business and Professional Women. She was one of only four women in Parliament in the session that opened in January 1956.

31 Section 202(a) of Canada, *Criminal Code,* SC 1953–54, c 51 (hereafter Criminal Code, 1955) defined capital murder as "planned or deliberate" homicide committed during certain crimes of violence or the murder of a police or corrections officer who was on duty. Until the abolition of the death penalty, all persons convicted of capital murder were sentenced to the mandatory penalty of death.

32 In the mid-1970s, polls showed support for the death penalty as varying anywhere from 48 percent to 79 percent, largely depending on the questions asked. In 1977, a news release from the Canadian Institute of Public Opinion calculated retentionism at 68 to 75 percent. Joel Kropf, "'A Matter of Deep Personal Conscience': The Canadian Death-Penalty Debate, 1957–1976" (master's thesis, Carleton University, 2007), 231–32. See also C.H.S. Jayewardene, "The Canadian Movement against the Death Penalty," *Canadian Journal of Criminology and Corrections* 14, 114 (1972): 366–90.

33 Carolyn Strange, "The Lottery of Death: Capital Punishment, 1867–1976," *Manitoba Law Journal* 23, 113 (1995): 618; and Joel Kropf, "Pursuing Human Techniques of Progressive Justice: The Ethical Assumptions of Early-to-mid-Twentieth-Century English-Canadian Penal Reformers" (PhD diss., Carleton

University, 2014), 233–34. Diefenbaker championed the Bill of Rights and supported the introduction of noncapital murder, but he did not support abolition in Parliament until the Liberals were in power. Denis Smith, *Rogue Tory: The Life and Legend of John G. Diefenbaker* (Toronto: Walter and Ross MacFarlane, 1997), 415.

34 Ministry of the Solicitor General of Canada, *Questions and Answers Relating to the Capital Punishment Issue* (Ottawa: Research and Statistics Development Branch, 1976).

35 In 1963, Montreal journalist Jacques Hébert published *J'accuse les assassins de Coffin,* and in 1966 Isobel le Bourdais published *The Trial of Steven Truscott,* which became a bestseller.

36 Roy McMurtry, *Memoirs and Reflections* (Toronto: University of Toronto Press, 2013), 112. McMurtry's opposition to the death penalty began through his association with Maloney's defence of Leonard Jackson (110–11).

37 McMurtry, *Memoirs,* 524. McMurtry became the president of the Toronto chapter of the Canadian Society for the Abolition of the Death Penalty, which he'd cofounded in 1964. McMurtry, *Memoirs,* 111.

38 The vote was 131 in favour of abolition and 124 against. C.H.S. Jayewardene, *After Abolition of the Death Penalty* (Ottawa: Crimcare, 1989), 46.

39 Ezzat Fattah, *The Canadian Public and the Death Penalty: A Study of a Social Attitude* (Ottawa: Solicitor General of Canada, 1976), 105. Support was highest for killings of serving law enforcement agents.

40 Greg Marquis, *Policing Canada's Century: A History of the Canadian Association of Chiefs of Police* (Toronto: University of Toronto Press / Osgoode Society for Canadian Legal History, 1993), 286–89.

41 On abolition as a victory, see Ezzat Fattah, "Canada's Successful Experience with the Abolition of the Death Penalty," *Canadian Journal of Criminology* 25, 114 (1983): 421–31.

42 Thompson, "Uneasy Abolitionists," 178.

43 Julian V. Roberts, "The Evolution of Penal Policy in Canada," *Social Policy and Administration* 32, 114 (1998): 420–37. On recent evidence of pro-death penalty sentiment, see Kevin Jiang, "Majority of Canadians Are in Favour of Bringing Back the Death Penalty, New Poll Suggests," Toronto *Star,* March 17, 2023. The survey, by Research Co., found that 54 percent of respondents favoured reinstatement of the death penalty for murder, but that proportion rose to 70 percent for Conservative voters.

44 Prior to 1976, defence counsel were permitted to question complainants about their sexual history. Constance Backhouse, *Carnal Crimes: Sexual Assault Law in Canada, 1900–1975* (Toronto: Irwin / Osgoode Society for Canadian Legal History, 2008), 151.

45 The Criminal Code, 1955, substituted "sexual intercourse" for "carnal knowledge," but it retained the offence of male intercourse with a female between the ages of fourteen and sixteen, which applied only if the female was of "previously chaste character." Backhouse, *Carnal Crimes,* 317–18.

46 Backhouse, *Carnal Crimes,* 294.

47 The joint committee reviewed evidence from the Department of Justice that showed that thirty-eight men in Canada were convicted of carnal knowledge from 1950 to 1952, and of that number, three had a whipping added to their prison sentences. Canada, *Special Joint Committee of the Senate and the House of Commons on Capital and Corporal Punishment and Lotteries: Minutes of Proceedings and Evidence* (Ottawa: Queen's Printer, 1954), Table 4, 797. The committee recommended abolishing whipping as a judicial punishment, but the government did not act on its advice.

48 Renee Goldsmith Kasinki, "The Rise and Institutionalization of the Anti-rape Movement in Canada," in *Violence in Canada,* ed. Mary Alice Beyer Gammon (Toronto: Methuen, 1978), 151–67.

49 Law Reform Commission of Canada, *Criminal Law: Sexual Offences,* Working Paper 22 (Ottawa: Law Reform Commission of Canada, 1978). This report was one of a series of working papers in response to the Liberal government's invitation for submissions to inform legislative change. The publication of American Susan Brownmiller's *Against Our Will: Men, Women and Rape* (New York: Simon and Schuster, 1975) increased public and political support for law reform in Canada.

50 June A. Osborne, "Rape Law Reform: The New Cosmetic for Canadian Women," in *Criminal Justice Politics and Women: The Aftermath of Legally Mandated Change,* ed. Claudine Schweber and Clarice Feinman (New York: Taylor and Francis, 1985): 49; and Backhouse, *Carnal Crimes,* 98.

51 Minister of Justice and Attorney General of Canada, *Sexual Assault Legislation in Canada: An Evaluation – Overview, Report Number 5* (Ottawa: Department of Justice, 1991), 9.

52 Prior to 1976, judges were required to instruct juries in unlawful sexual intercourse trials that it was "not safe to find the accused guilty" without corroboration of the complainant's sworn testimony, if that was the only evidence that implicated the accused. Criminal Code, 1955, s 134.

53 Lorenne Clark and Debra Lewis, *Rape: The Price of Coercive Sexuality* (Toronto: Women's Press, 1977). See also Marilyn G. Stanley, *The Experience of the Rape Victim with the Criminal Justice System prior to Bill C-127, Report No. 1* (Ottawa: Minister of Supply and Services Canada, 1987).

54 Thomas J. Lewis, "Recent Proposals in the Criminal Law of Rape: Significant Reform or Semantic Change," *Osgoode Hall Law Journal* 17, 112 (1979): 451; and

Lucinda Vandervort, "Mistake of Law and Sexual Assault: Consent and Mens Rea," *Canadian Journal of Women and the Law* 2 (1987–88): 233–309.

55 Sharon L. Barnes, "Take Back the Night," in *Public Feminisms: From Academy to Community,* ed. Carrie N. Baker and Aviva Dove-Vieban (Ann Arbor: University of Michigan Press, 2022), 129–55; and Finn Mackay, "From Brussels to Leeds, San Francisco, Delhi: The Global March of Reclaim the Night," in Mackay, *Radical Feminisms: Feminist Activism in Movement* (Basingstoke, UK: Palgrave Macmillan, 2015), 71–102.

56 Andrea Quinlan, *The Technoscientific Witness of Rape: Contentious Histories of Law, Feminism, and Forensic Science* (Toronto: University of Toronto Press, 2017), 174.

57 The term arose in the 2010s. See, for instance, Nicola Henry and Anastasia Powell, eds., *Preventing Sexual Violence: Interdisciplinary Approaches to Overcoming a Rape Culture* (London: Palgrave Macmillan, 2014); Pivi Honkatukia, Anna-Karina Henriksen, Hannah King, and Marja Peltola, "Editorial: Pleasures, Practices and Troubles – Young People's Gendered Sexualities in the 21st Century," *YOUNG* 31, 115 (2003): 407–12.

58 For critiques of carceral feminism, see Holly Johnson, "Limits of a Criminal Justice Response: Trends in Police and Court Processing of Sexual Assault," in Sheehy, *Sexual Assault in Canada,* 613–34; and Lorna N. Bracewell, "Sex Wars, Slutwalks, and Carceral Feminism," *Contemporary Political Theory* 19, 111 (2020): 61–82.

59 The literature in this field is extensive. See, for instance, Madeline Schneider and Jennifer S. Hirsch, "Comprehensive Sexuality Education as a Primary Prevention Strategy for Sexual Violence Perpetration," *Trauma, Violence, and Abuse* 21, 113 (2020): 439–55. On building resistance to sexual assault, see Jason A. Laker and Erica M. Boas, *Advancing Sexual Consent and Agential Practices in Higher Education: Toward a New Community of Practice* (Abingdon, UK: Routledge, 2024). On antifeminism and ongoing challenges, see Carrie Rentschler, "Rape Culture: Anti-Feminist Backlash against a Feminist Concept," *Canadian Journal of Communication* 47, 114 (2022): 649–75; and Rebecca M. Hayes, *Defining Rape Culture: Gender, Race and the Move toward International Social Change* (Leeds, UK: Emerald Studies in Criminology, Feminism and Social Change, 2023).

Index of Cases

Index

Note: "(i)" after a page number indicates an illustration; "(t)," a table

Printed and bound in Canada

Set in Garamond by Artegraphica Design Co. Ltd.

Copyeditor: Lesley Erickson

Proofreader: Helen Godolphin

Cover designer: Will Brown

Cover image: iStock, keiichihiki

Authorized Representative:
Easy Access System Europe –
Mustamäe tee 50, 10621 Tallinn, Estonia,
gpsr.requests@easproject.com